FAMILY PLANNING PRACTICE AND THE LAW

Titles in the series

A Patient's Right to Know: Information, Disclosure, the Doctor and the Law
Sheila A. M. McLean, University of Glasgow

New Reproductive Techniques: A Legal Perspective
Douglas J. Cusine, University of Aberdeen

Medico-Legal Aspects of Reproduction and Parenthood
J. K. Mason, University of Edinburgh

Law Reform and Human Reproduction
Edited by *Sheila A. M. McLean*, University of Glasgow

Legal and Ethical Issues in the Management of the Dementing Elderly
Mary Gilhooly, University of Glasgow

Legal Issues in Human Reproduction
Edited by *Sheila A. M. McLean*, University of Glasgow

Mental Illness: Prejudice, Discrimination and the Law
Tom Campbell, Australian National University, Canberra and *Chris Heginbotham*, King's Fund College

Pharmaceuticals in the European Community
Ken Collins, Member of the European Parliament and *Sheila A. M. McLean*, University of Glasgow

Pregnancy at Work
Noreen Burrows, University of Glasgow

Changing People: The Law and Ethics of Behaviour Modification
Alexander McCall Smith, University of Edinburgh

The Law and Economics of Health Care Allocation
R. Lee, University of Lancaster

Surrogacy and the Moral Economy
Derek Morgan, University College, Swansea

Reproductive Rights and Artificial Reproduction
Athena Liu, University of Hong Kong

Mental Health Law in Context: Doctors' Orders?
Michael Cavadino, University of Sheffield

The Changing Nature of Medical Autonomy
Leanna Darvall, La Trobe University

Abortion Regimes
Kerry Petersen, La Trobe University

FAMILY PLANNING PRACTICE AND THE LAW

KENNETH McK. NORRIE
University of Strathclyde

Dartmouth
Aldershot · Brookfield USA · Hong Kong · Singapore · Sydney

Published by
Dartmouth Publishing Company Limited
Gower House
Croft Road
Aldershot
Hants GU11 3HR
England

Dartmouth Publishing Company
Old Post Road
Brookfield
Vermont 05036
USA

British Library Cataloguing in Publication Data
Norrie, Kenneth McK.
Family planning practice and the law. – (Medico-legal series).
1. Family planning. Legal aspects
I. Title II. Series
342.448

Library of Congress Cataloging-in-Publication Data
Norrie, Kenneth McK. (Kenneth McKenzie), 1959–
Family planning practice and the law / Kenneth McK. Norrie
p. cm.
1. Human reproduction—Law and legislation. 2. Birth control—Law and legislation. 3. Abortion—Law and legislation. I. Title.
K2000.N67 1991
344′.048—dc20
[342.448] 90–46053
CIP

ISBN 1 85521 035 5

Printed in Great Britain by
Billing & Sons Ltd, Worcester

To
my Parents

Contents

Table of Cases

Accident Compensation Commission v. Auckland Hospital Board [1980] 2 *NZLR* 748
Akron v Akron Centre for Reproductive Health Inc. 426 *US* 416, 76 *L. Ed*. 2d 687 (1979)
A.L. v. G.R.H. 325 *NE* 2d 501, 74 *ALR* 3d 1220 (1975)
Associated Picture Houses Ltd. v. Wednesbury Corp. [1948] *KB* 223
Attorney General of Queensland ex rel. Kerr v. T. (1983) 46 *ALR* 275

B. (A Minor), Re [1981] 1 *WLR* 1412
B. (A Minor) (Sterilisation) [1987] 2 *WLR* 1213
Baird v. Bellotti 393 *F. Supp*. 847 (1975)
Battersby v. Tottman (1985) 37 *SASR* 524
Baxter v. Baxter [1947] 2 *All ER* 886
Bell v. McCurdie 1981 *SLT* 159
Bellotti v. Baird 443 *US* 662, 61 *L. Ed*. 2d 797 (1979)
Benarr v. Kettering Health Authority (1988) 138 *NLJ* 179
Bennan v. Parsonnet 83 *NJLR* 20 (1912)
Blyth v. Bloomsbury Health Authority, The Times, 11 February 1987
Bolam v. Friern Hospital Management Committee [1957] 2 *All ER* 118
Borowski v. Attorney General for Canada (1987) 39 *DLR* (4th) 731 (Sas. CA); (1989) 57 *DLR* (4th) 231 (SCC)
Bradlaugh & Besant v. The Queen (1877) *LR* 3 *QBD* 607
Bravery v. Bravery [1954] 3 *All ER* 59
Brown v. Harvey 1907 *SC* 588
Brushett v. Cowan (1987) 40 *DLR* (4th) 488
Buck v. Bell 274 *US* 200, 71 *L. Ed*. 1000 (1927)
Buchan v. Ortho Pharmaceutical (Canada) Ltd. (1984) 8 *DLR* (4th) 373, aff. (1986) 54 *OR* (2d) 92

C. v. S. [1987] 2 *WLR* 1108
C. v. Wren (1986) 35 *DLR* (4th) 419
Canterbury v. Spence 464 *F*. 2d 772 (1972)
Carey v. Population Services International 431 *US* 678, 52 *L. Ed*. 2d 675 (1977)
Casey v. Grossman (1949) 51 *WALR* 77
Cataford v. Moreau (1978) 114 *DLR* (3d) 585

Grey v. Webster (1984) 14 *DLR* (4th) 706
Griswold v. Connecticut 381 *US* 479, 14 *L. Ed.* 2d 510 (1965)
G-U, Re [1984] *FLR* 811

H.L. v. Matheson 450 *US* 398, 67 *L. Ed.* 2d 388 (1981)
Halushka v. University of Saskatchewan (1965) 53 *DLR* (2d) 436
Hart v. Brown 29 *Conn. Supp.* 368, 289 *A.* 2d 386 (1972)
Harvey v. Harvey (1860) 22 *D.* 1198
Hedley Byrne & Co Ltd. v. Hellar & Partners Ltd. [1964] *AC* 465
Hewer v. Bryant [1969] 3 *All ER* 578
Hickman v. Group Health Plan Inc. 396 *NW* 2d 10 (1986)
Hills v. Potter [1983] 3 *All ER* 716
Hollis v. Commonwealth 652 *SW* 2d 61 (1983)
Hopp v. Lepp (1980) 112 *DLR* (3d) 67
Hunter v. Hanley 1955 *SC* 200
HM Adv. v. Anderson 1928 *JC* 1
HM Adv. v. McCallum (1858) 3 *Irv.* 187
HM Adv. v. Scott (1892) 3 *White* 240
HM Adv. v. Semple 1937 *JC* 41
HM Adv. v. Smart 1975 *SLT* 65

Ingram v. Ritchie, 28 July 1989, Court of Session (Outer House)

Jefferson v. Griffin Spalding County Hospital 274 *SE* 2d 457 (1981)
Johnston v. Wellesley Hospital (1970) 17 *DLR* (3d) 139
Jones v. Berkshire Area Health Authority 2 July 1986
Jones v. Jones [1985] *QB* 704
Jones v. Lanarkshire Health Board 1990 *SLT* 19
Jones v. Smith 278 *SO* 339 (1973)
Joyce v. Yeomans [1981] 1 *WLR* 549

K. v. Minister for Youth and Community Services [1982] 1 *NSWLR* 311
K. & Public Trustee, Re (1985) 19 *DLR* (4th) 255
Kelly v. Hazlett (1976) 75 *DLR* (3d) 536
Kenny v. Lockwood (1932) 1 *DLR* 507
Klink v. G. D. Searle & Co 26 *Wash. App.* 951, 9 *ALR* 4th 364 (1980)
Knott v. Knott [1955] 2 *All ER* 305

MacCormick v. Lord Advocate 1953 *SLT* 255
McKay v. Essex Area Health Authority [1982] *QB* 1166
MacLeod v. MacAskill 1920 *SC* 72
McLoughlin v. O'Brien [1983] 1 *AC* 410
Marshall v. Curry [1933] 3 *DLR* 260
Maynard v. West Midlands Regional Health Authority [1984] 1 *WLR* 634

Medhurst v. Medhurst (1984) 9 *DLR* (4th) 252
Medhurst, Re (1984) 7 *DLR* (4th) 335
Minister of Justice for Canada v. Borowski (1981) 130 *DLR* (3d) 588
Mohamed v. Knott [1968] 2 *All ER* 563
Morgentaler, Smoling & Scott v. The Queen (1988) 44 *DLR* (4th) 385
Morris, Petitioner 1987 *SLT* (News) 69
Murray v. Fraser 1916 *SC* 623
Murray v. McMurchy (1949) 2 *DLR* 442
Murray v. Merschall (1555) *M.* 16226

O'Reilly v. Mackman [1983] 2 *AC* 237

P (A Minor), Re (1981) 80 *LGR* 301
Park v. Chessin 400 *NYS* (2d) 110 (1977)
Parry v. Cleaver [1970] *AC* 1
Paton v. Trustees of the British Pregnancy Advisory Service [1978] 2 *All ER* 987
Pattison v. Hobbes, 5 November 1985
Planned Parenthood of Central Missouri v. Danforth 428 *US* 52, 49 *L. Ed.* 2d 788 (1976)
Priestley, Re. Decision No. 14/84 [1984] *NZACR* 787
Pritchard v. J. H. Cobden Ltd. [1987] 2 *WLR* 627
Procanik v. Cillo 478 *A.* 2d 755 (1984)

Quinlan, Re 70 NJ 10, 355 *A.* 2d 647 (1976)

R. v. Bourne [1939] 1 *KB* 687
R. v. Case (1850) 4 *Cox. CC* 220
R. v. Central Birmingham Health Authority, ex p. Collier, 6 January 1988 (CA)
R. v. Donovan [1934] 2 *KB* 498
R. v. Ethical Committee of St Mary's Hospital ex p. Harriott [1988] *Fam. Law* 165
R. v. Howard [1965] 3 *All ER* 684
R. v. Newton & Stungo [1958] *Crim. LR* 469
R. v. Price [1968] 2 *All ER* 282
R. v. Salford Health Authority ex p. Janaway [1988] 2 *WLR* 442
R. v. Secretary of State for Social Services, ex p. Walker, The Times 26 November 1987
R. v. Smith [1974] 1 *All ER* 376
R. v. Virgo [1988] *Crim. LR* 199
R. v. West (1848) 2 *Cox. CC* 500
Rance v. Mid-Downs Health Authority & Anor, 5 February 1990
Reibl v. Hughes (1980) 114 *DLR* (3d) 1
Rieck v. Medical Protective Co. 219 *NW* 2d 242 (1974)

Robertson v. Robertson 1981 *SLT* (Notes) 7
Roe v. Wade 410 *US* 113, 35 *L. Ed.* 2d 147 (1973)
Royal College of Nursing v. DHSS [1981] *AC* 800

S., Margaret v. Edwards 794 *F.* 2d 994 (1986)
S., Margaret v. Treen 597 *F. Supp.* 636 (1984)
Scheinberg v. Smith 659 *F.* 2d 476 (1981)
Sciuriaga v. Powell (1979) 123 *SJ* 406, aff. 24 July 1980
Shaheen v. Knight 11 *Pa. D. & C.* 2d 41 (1957)
Sherlock v. Stillwater Clinic 260 *NW* 2d 169 (1977)
Sidaway v. Bethlem Royal Hospital [1984] *QB* 493 (CA) [1985] *AC* 871 (HL)
Simms & H., Re (1979) 106 *DLR* (3d) 435
Smith v. Auckland Hospital Board [1964] *NZLR* 241, Sup. Ct.; [1965] *NZLR* 191, Ct. App.
State v. Burke 368 *NW* 2d 182 (1985)
Stephens v. Avery [1988] 2 *All ER* 477
Stopes v. Sutherland (1924) 39 *TLR* 677 (CA), (1924) 41 *TLR* 106 (HL)
Strunk v. Strunk 445 *SW* 2d 145, 35 *ALR* 3d 683 (1969)
Stump v. Sparkman 435 *US* 349, 55 *L. Ed.* 2d 331 (1976)

T. v. T. & Another [1988] 2 *WLR* 189
Terrell v. Garcia 496 *SW* 2d 124 (1973)
Thake v. Maurice [1985] 2 *WLR* 215 (QBD), [1986] QB 644 (CA)
Tremblay v. Daigle (1989) 59 *DLR* (4th) 609 (Quebec CA); (1990) 62 *DLR* (4th) 634 (SCC)
Tresemer v. Barke 86 *Cal. App.* 3d 656, 12 *ALR* 4th 27 (1975)
Troppi v. Scarf 187 *NW* (2d) 511 (1971)
Tulley, Re 146 *Cal. Rptr.* 266 (1978)
Turpin v. Sortini 31 *Cal.* 3d 220, 182 *Cal. Rptr.* 337 (1982)

US v. One Package 86 *F.* 2d 737 (1936)
Udale v. Bloomsbury Area Health Authority [1983] 1 *WLR* 1098

Venner v. North East Essex Health Authority The Times, 21 February 1987

Wall v. Livingstone [1982] 1 *NZLR* 734
Weatherley v. Weatherley [1946] 2 *All ER* 1
Webster v. Reproductive Health Services 109 *Sup. Ct.* 3040, 106 *L. Ed.* 2d 410 (1989)
Wells v. Surrey Area Health Authority, The Times 29 July 1978
Wentzel v. Montgomery General Hospital, 459 *US* 1147, 74 *L. Ed.* 2d 995 (1982)

White v. Turner (1981) 120 *DLR* (3d) 269 (Ont. HC), (1985) 12 *DLR* (4th) 319 (Ont. CA)
Whitehouse v. Jordan [1981] 1 *WLR* 246
Williams v. New York 223 *NE* 2d 849 (1963)

X. v. United Kingdom (1980) 3 *EHRR* 408, *ECHR* 19 BR. 244
X. v. Y. [1988] 2 *All ER* 648

Zepeda v. Zepeda 41 *Ill. App.* 2d 240 (1963).

List of Abbreviations

AC	*Appeal Cases* (England)
ALDU	Association of Lawyers for the Defence of the Unborn
All ER	*All England Law Reports*
ALR	*Australian Law Reports*
ALR (3d)	*Annotated Law Reports* (USA)
Am. JL Med.	*American Journal of Law and Medicine*
Am. J. Comp. L.	*American Journal of Comparative Law*
Am. J. Pub. Health	*American Journal of Public Health*
BJ Fam. Plan.	*British Journal of Family Planning*
BMA	British Medical Association
BMJ	*British Medical Journal*
Cal. Rptr.	*Californian Reporter*
Can. J. Fam. Law	*Canadian Journal of Family Law*
Cinc. LR	*Cincinatti Law Review*
CLJ	*Cambridge Law Journal*
Columb. LR	*Columbia Law Review*
Cox CC	*Cox's Criminal Law Cases*
Crim. LR	*Criminal Law Review*
DLR	*Dominion Law Reports*
ECHR	*European Convention on Human Rights*
EHRR	*European Human Rights Reports*
Fam. Law	*Family Law*
Fam. Plan. Persp.	*Family Planning Perspectives*
FLR	*Family Law Reports*
Harv. Women's LJ	*Harvard Women's Law Journal*
hCG	human chorionic gonadotrophin
ICLQ	*International and Comparative Law Quarterly*
Int. J. Gyn. Obs.	*International Journal of Gynaecology and Obstetrics*
IPPF Medical Bulletin	*International Planned Parenthood Federation Medical Bulletin*
Irv.	*Irvine's Reports* (Scotland)
IUD	intra-uterine device
JC	*Justiciary Cases* (Scotland)
J. Med. Ethics	*Journal of Medical Ethics*

JR	*Juridical Review*
KB	*King's Bench Reports* (England)
LQR	*Law Quarterly Review*
Law Soc. Gaz.	*Law Society Gazette*
Leg. Stud.	*Legal Studies*
LGR	*Local Government Reports*
M.	*Morison's Dictionary* (Scotland)
Med. Sci. Law	*Medicine, Science and the Law*
Mod. LR	*Modern Law Review*
NAFPD	*National Association of Family Planning Doctors*
Neb. LR	*Nebraska Law Review*
New Eng. J. Med.	*New England Journal of Medicine*
New LJ	*New Law Journal*
NSWLR	*New South Wales Law Reports*
NW	*North Western Reporter* (USA)
NZACR	*New Zealand Accident Compensation Reports*
NZLR	*New Zealand Law Reports*
QB	*Queen's Bench Reports* (England)
Os. HLJ	*Osgood Hall Law Journal*
RDUS	*Revue de droit Université Sherbrooke*
SALR	*South African Law Reports*
SASR	*South Australian State Reports*
SC	*Session Cases* (Scotland)
SJ	*Solicitors' Journal*
SLT	*Scots Law Times*
SW	*South Western Reporter* (USA)
UNFPA	United Nations Population Fund
U. Tor. LJ	University of Toronto Law Journal
WALR	Western Australian Law Reports
Wash. LR	Washington Law Review
Wash. ULQ	Washington University Law Quarterly
WHO	World Health Organization
WLR	*Weekly Law Reports* (England)

Acknowledgements

There are a number of people whom I should like to thank for their help during the writing of this book. In particular I am very grateful to those who took the time and trouble to read various portions of it before the manuscript was sent to the publishers. I received extremely helpful comments that put me right on a number of fundamental points from the following: Mr D. P. Lessels, Mr C. T. Reid, and Dr A. I. L. Campbell, all of the University of Aberdeen; Dr Rebecca Cook, the University of Toronto; Professor Peter Howie, the University of Dundee; and Professor J. M. Thomson, the University of Strathclyde. Mr Amish Amin provided editorial and other assistance, and I am grateful to him.

I should also like to thank my word processing machine, Dougal, without whose help and companionship, and quirky sense of humour, this book would not have appeared in quite the form it has today.

Finally, for her encouragement in writing this book, and her ready acceptance of my suggestion that the subject was worth writing about, I should like to thank Dr Sheila A. M. McLean, the general editor of this Medico-Legal series of textbooks.

I have attempted to state the law up to the end of May 1990.

Kenneth McK. Norrie
The University of Strathclyde
Scotland

1 Introduction

In 1965 the late Sir Dugald Baird, then Regius Professor of Obstetrics and Gynaecology at the University of Aberdeen, Scotland, brought attention to Roosevelt's vision of a world founded upon four essential freedoms: freedom of speech, freedom to worship, freedom from want, and freedom from fear; and to that vision Baird added a 'Fifth Freedom', namely, 'freedom from the tyranny of excessive fertility'.[1] Baird regarded the problem of excessive fertility not only as one which, through excessive population, brought hunger and want to many parts of the world, but also as one which affected the freedom of choice of individuals to plan their own lives in the way they desired. His purpose was to encourage society to accept certain family planning procedures, such as therapeutic abortion and sterilization, that would enhance individual freedom of choice; and he placed much hope on the benefits that the recently introduced oral contraceptive pill would bring.

Because individuals have always wanted to enjoy sexual relations without necessarily incurring the great disruption in their lives that parenthood inevitably brings, efforts to limit fertility have been made throughout history; but until very recently such efforts were frowned upon by the church and state, and indeed by society as a whole. In countries that followed the Christian tradition, sex used to be seen solely in terms of reproduction. The sexual act itself was regarded as a sin, the pleasures of which had to be atoned for by the pains of childbirth (although it was only the female partner that did the atoning while the male partner generally received at least as much of the pleasure). This curious religious view was found convenient to the rulers of society that had vested interests in the status quo. Sex and marriage were considered to be inextricably bound in with property rights, legitimate succession, and the stable structure of established society itself. There was a fear that to allow sex outwith marriage would destroy the very basis upon which society rested; and to sanction sex without the risk of reproduction would, of course, allow illicit sexual relations to remain hidden.

This was a harsh morality, and it caused much suffering throughout history. The human sex drive is one of our strongest instincts. It is an impulse over which we have little control, and it can overbear the will of even the most powerful. Efforts were of course made by individual couples to inhibit reproduction, both from fear of discovery of the very existence of their sexual relationships, and also from fear of the consequences to their life and health that pregnancy and childbirth could bring. However, so long as sex and reproduction were seen as *necessarily and morally* linked, these efforts remained hidden and disapproved of.

But Western society has changed. This century has seen an increasing recognition that the sexual act can be something which is good in itself, and that it can be justified and should be experienced for the physical and emotional pleasure that it can bring. The loving and emotional aspects of sexual intercourse are now recognized as having as much importance to the human condition as its potential reproductive aspects. It is recognized that sex has more justification than simply the continuation of the race. Family planning in its fundament is aimed at allowing people to experience heterosexual sexual relations for these other, non-reproductive, reasons, and one of the great changes in society this century has been the acceptance of this aim as legitimate.

The medical profession too has changed, and, after initial hostility, it has to a large extent acquired a dominant role in family planning. The most reliable forms of family planning are now firmly within the control of the medical profession. But while this medicalization of family planning has given power to the medical profession it has also imposed upon practitioners a number of ethical and legal duties, which previously did not exist, and which must now be taken into account in providing this form of medical treatment.

Like society and the medical profession, the law itself has altered its view on sex and reproduction, and there is no doubt that the law today does not regard the two as being necessarily conjoined. This is so in many legal systems, but clear indication of the change in attitude was given in Britain in 1967, for that year saw three very different pieces of legislation that were all based on a recognition that individuals could legitimately indulge in sexual activity without running the risk of reproduction. The National Health Service (Family Planning) Act 1967 (which was wholly unopposed in Parliament) allowed local health authorities in England and Wales to provide contraceptive advice and treatment within the National Health Service. The Abortion Act 1967 provided a number of defences to the crime of abortion in both Scots law and English law, and the Sexual Offences Act 1967 legalized some homosexual acts in England and Wales, so recognizing that people could indulge in a form of sexual activity that could not ever have reproductive consequences. Reproduction may now be seen as little more than a risk attached to heterosexual sexual activity, rather like disease, which people can accept or avoid as they like, by means other than abstinence.

Family planning is aimed at the deliberate interruption of the process of human reproduction. That process is long and complex and there are many different points at which it can be interrupted. Sterilization is designed to remove a person's fertility completely and permanently, often long before a particular act of sexual intercourse. Traditional methods of contraception are designed to take effect shortly before or during sexual intercourse, by preventing, in some way, a man's sperm from fertilizing a woman's egg. So the cap and the condom prevent the two joining, as do the so-called natural methods, like the rhythm method and coitus interruptus (and, incidentally, abstinence). Other methods, such as hormonal contraceptive pills, are designed to inhibit ovulation and so effectively make the woman's egg unavailable for fertilization. There are other methods that are designed to take effect at a later stage in the reproduction process. So the intra-uterine device (IUD) aims to prevent the fertilized egg from implanting into the womb, as do certain forms of hormonal treatment. Abortion is designed to interrupt the process after pregnancy has commenced, but before that process has been completed by the birth of a living child.

None of these methods is completely satisfactory. Sterilization and abortion are generally serious surgical operations, which will inevitably carry risks. Some contraceptive methods are not reliable, while others have potentially serious side-effects. Consequently the search has gone on for new and better ways of interrupting the process of human reproduction: indeed that search has gathered momentum the more respectable family planning practice has become.

But efforts to limit fertility create personal, medical and legal problems. Each new method that is developed has given rise to new problems for the law, and the problems with the established methods have not all been solved. In recent years the law's attention has been diverted somewhat to the seemingly intractable difficulties that are caused by the new reproductive technologies, such as *in vitro* fertilization, embryo transfer, among others.[2] However, the vast literature that has grown up in the legal, medical and ethical press concerning these issues must not cloud the fact that individuals who suffer from unwanted or inconvenient fertility vastly outnumber those who suffer from an unwanted lack of fertility. The legal and medical problems are of course very different for these two groups of individuals, but the legal problems for the fertile are just as complex as those for the infertile, and, from a numerical point of view, are far more significant.

This book is written with primary reference to Scots and English law, but in family planning as in other areas of medicine, these legal systems are better understood within the context of comparative study. Consequently, the position in various other jurisdictions will be examined and described, this not only for illustrative purposes but also because an understanding of how different legal systems solve problems contribute to an understanding of how any single system does or should tackle the same problems. For practical purposes the legal systems examined are restricted to those that accept the principle of self-determination as the predominant ethic in health care.

But it must be remembered that the availability and acceptability of family planning are fundamentally dependent on the political (which often means religious) structures of the societies in which it is provided. Birth control can be, and in many parts of the world is, used as an instrument of policy to achieve political goals. So in countries like China and India where population growth is seen as a threat to society as a whole, all forms of family planning are officially sanctioned and encouraged, and their (sometimes enforced) acceptance by individuals often carries benefits from the state, of a financial or political nature.[3] Other countries, where falling birth rates threaten the viable existence of the state, strongly discourage family planning, and even punish those who practise it. So, for example, the use of contraceptives and abortion were criminal offences in pre–1989 Romania and remain so today in Mongolia. Again, the population balance can be manipulated by the carefully targeted state provision of family planning in countries that are made up of different racial and cultural groupings. In Nazi Germany Jews were allowed to have abortions while this was illegal for 'Aryan' women; today, countries like Israel and Sri Lanka have different groups of citizens with very different rates of reproduction, which, if unchecked, will significantly alter the population balance.

The policies and philosophies behind such attitudes, although of great interest, are too diverse to be usefully studied in a book like this; and for that reason the discussion will be limited to those jurisdictions where attitudes towards family planning is governed by the principle of autonomy, or freedom of individual choice.

The aim of this book is primarily to attempt to identify precisely what family planners can, and cannot, do for their patients within the law, and to discuss the legal consequences of their actions. In so doing, it is hoped that this will contribute to the ethical debate surrounding many of the issues discussed. It is important to know what the law says on any ethical matter, for, within a democracy as understood in the Western world, the law must remain the ultimate arbiter even of ethical problems. The issues to be examined are restricted to those that directly affect practitioners – that is, health care professionals involved in the advice and treatment of patients wishing, with medical help, to restrict their fertility. Many other issues, such as product liability and drug licensing, could have been covered in a larger book; but the legal principles governing these issues are not significantly different in the area of family planning than in any other field. This book will look only at the areas where family planning practice creates special, sometimes unique, problems for the health care professional.

The legal problems arising from family planning practice have recently given rise to many actions before the courts, as well as campaigns for legislative reform. Highly significant cases with consequences far beyond the limited parameters of family planning practice have in recent years been decided by the supreme courts of a number of countries. In 1989 alone the English House of Lords considered the legality of non-consensual sterilization of mentally disabled adults;[4] the Supreme Court of Canada was faced with a claim by a putative father to prevent a pregnant woman aborting their child;[5] and the Supreme Court of the United States handed down a ruling that seemed to signal a retrenchment from the position on abortion that the Court had previously adopted.[6] Legislatures too have become involved with the issues: so for example in April 1990 the British Parliament debated and approved the Human Fertilisation and Embryology Bill, which affected the law of abortion in Great Britain, as well as embryo research. All these issues, and many others, will be examined in the following pages.

Family planning is out in the open. It is a respectable, indeed responsible, act, and is practised by millions. The law is presently being faced with the difficult legal problems that arise from this now common activity. The solution that the law gives to these problems will fundamentally affect whether or not individuals within society will ever truly be able to enjoy Baird's 'Fifth Freedom'.

Notes

1 Baird, 'A Fifth Freedom?' 2 *BMJ* 1141, 1965.
2 The legal issues are examined by Cusine in *New Reproductive Techniques: A Legal Perspective* Dartmouth, Aldershot 1989.
3 See, for example, the incentives for women from low-income groups to be sterilized given by the government of Singapore: *Annual Review of Population Law*, UNFPA, Cambridge MA, 1988 at p. 25.
4 *F. v. West Berkshire Health Authority* [1989] 2 *All ER* 545.
5 *Tremblay v. Daigle* (1990) 62 *DLR* (4th) 634.
6 *Webster v. Reproductive Health Services* 109 *Sup. Ct* 3040; 106 *L. Ed.* 2d 410 (1989).

2 The Legality of Contraception and Sterilization

Introduction

Contraception and sterilization for birth control purposes are procedures intimately connected with – indeed find rational justification only in relation to – heterosexual sexual activity. This may seem axiomatic but it must be borne in mind when examining the law's attitude towards family planning, for the way any society and its laws regard family planning is invariably and fundamentally influenced by its attitudes towards sex itself. Cultures with open and liberal attitudes towards sex tend to have liberal laws dealing with contraception and sterilization; and societies that attempt to suppress open discussion about sex, as well as the sexual act itself (often reacting to the influence of a predominant religion)[1] frequently attempt to further that suppression with laws prohibiting the use of or restricting access to contraceptive or sterilization treatment.

In Western societies, particularly since the end of the Second World War, the principle of autonomy of the individual has emerged as the predominant ethic, and the tyranny of unwanted fertility has been recognized as a real and significant challenge to that ethic. However, the strength of this principle, allied with the recognition that women's health is significantly improved with less pregnancies and sensible spacing of births, has effectively overturned the previous domination of that cold-hearted morality that regarded sex as a sin to be atoned for (by women) through the pains of childbirth. The law today in most Western countries purports to protect autonomy and individual choice in relation to reproduction, and, as a consequence, in the matter of contraception and sterilization.

However, autonomy may be compromised when other strong societal interests are recognized and protected by the law. So the availability of abortion is controlled in every legal system more or less strictly because the life of the foetus is regarded as a significant interest that is worthy of protection. On the other hand, only if the state's interest in furthering sexual abstinence or chastity is considered to be stronger than the principle of autonomy will the law restrict the availability of contraception or sterilization. In countries like Scotland and England, where the law has traditionally been rather cautious in regulating sexual morality, there is not, and never has been, any provision rendering these methods of family planning unlawful.[2] Some other countries have had no qualms about legislating to enforce perceived morality, and there are many examples of legislation criminalizing the use or promotion or supply of contraception or the performance of sterilization operations. For almost a century until 1965 many jurisdictions in the United States contained legislation based on the so-called 'Comstock Act' of 1873,[3] which had made the provision or use of contraceptives in New York State a criminal offence. France too had a similar provision, which was only abolished there in 1967, but which survived much longer as a colonial hangover in many countries that were previously part of the French colonial empire.[4] Other countries have legislation which, while not prohibiting the use of contraception, has in various ways limited its availability – for example, by prohibiting the manufacture or import of, or advertizing about, contraceptives.

In common law jurisdictions it is assumed that that which is not legally forbidden is legally permitted, and the absence of prohibitions on contraceptive or sterilization treatment in such countries might suggest that these family planning methods are legally innocuous. However, the use or provision of contraception or sterilization can be influenced by other legal rules that indirectly affect the availability of these methods. This chapter will examine indirect barriers, such as are found in Scots and English law, and then the more direct legal prohibitions that were previously to be found in many American jurisdictions.

Indirect Barriers to Contraception and Sterilization

Although neither Scots nor English law has ever expressly prohibited the provision of contraceptive or sterilization treatment, its availability to all those who want such treatment was, in the past, limited by the influence of a number of different areas of law.

The Obscenity Laws

Obscenity is a criminal offence defined as the publication of any material that is intended to deprave or corrupt public morals.[5] Because it may be considered to be the promotion of sexual activity, the promotion of the use of contraceptives might also be regarded as the corruption of public morals because the purpose of contraceptives is to allow the pleasures of sexual intercourse without the 'atonement' of childbirth. Certainly last century it was (publicly) assumed that sex could be justified only for its legitimate procreative ends, and to suggest otherwise was deemed immoral. So in 1877 Charles Bradlaugh, the freethinking MP and founder of the Malthusian League, and the women's rights campaigner Annie Besant, were convicted and imprisoned for a breach of the (English) Obscene Publications Act 1857, for having published an American book which contained advice on birth control. The conviction was quashed, not because the book was not considered obscene, but because the indictment had failed to specify in what way it was obscene.[6] Paradoxically, however, the main social effect of that case was to generate much public support for the embryonic birth control movement in Britain.

The level of public support is of fundamental importance to the legal concept of obscenity, because the definition thereof depends upon the nature of 'public morality', and this is an ever-changing concept: something that is against public morals in one decade may not be so in the following decade because of altered public perception. This was recognized by Scrutton L.J. in an action for libel brought by the great pioneer of birth control in Britain, Dr Marie Stopes, against an author who had accused her of 'exposing the Poor to experiment' and of obscenity for her work in her birth control clinic, which she had opened in 1921.[7] In the Court of Appeal, which found in her favour, Scrutton L.J. pointed out that 'the standard of what is considered [obscene] varies enormously from time to time'. He pointed out that while a few decades previously venereal disease could not be discussed openly, nowadays it could be, and he went on,

> The merits and methods of artificial birth prevention seem to me to stand in a similar position. In 1877 it would have been impossible to discuss them publicly; in 1923 there is probably a great change in public opinion as to the necessity for discussion, coupled with great difference of opinion about the advisability of such methods.[8]

Although Stopes lost her case in the House of Lords (on the ground that she had failed to prove that the comments were unfair), the fact that Scrutton L.J. recognized family planning as a proper subject for public discussion indicates that the courts did not regard talking about it to be obscene *per se*. A few years later the House of Lords in its parliamentary capacity concluded in its very first discussion of the matter[9] that the provision of birth control was an acceptable, indeed desirable, thing. A motion had been proposed by Lord Buckmaster calling on the British government to change its policy whereby it withheld grants from maternity and child welfare clinics if they gave advice on birth control. Notwithstanding strong opposition from the clerics, and from some temporal peers who feared an attack on 'moral and natural law',[10] the motion was passed by the House of Lords, and the government changed its policy in 1930.[11] This was the first governmental sanction of contraception in Britain, and it buried any possibility of the obscenity laws being used against its provision. Again, the House of Lords in its judicial capacity considered contraception in the case of *Baxter v. Baxter*[12] in which it decided that the use of condoms did not prevent a marriage from being consummated. Lord Chancellor Jowitt pointed out that

> . . . long before the passing of the Matrimonial Causes Act 1937 it was a matter of common knowledge that *reputable* clinics had come into existence for the purpose of advising spouses on what is popularly called birth control.[13]

His use of the word 'reputable' shows that by 1947 the highest court in Britain did not consider that such clinics were indulging in anything that the law would punish as obscenity.

The time has therefore passed when the promotion or supply of contraceptives can be considered to be obscene. Of course, it would be possible to advertise contraceptives in a way that was designed more for sexual stimulation than for the purpose of giving information about birth control, and in that sort of case a prosecution for obscenity is certainly still possible. However, that would be because of the nature of the advertisement rather than the nature of what was being advertised, and a professional health care worker is hardly likely to be involved in such circumstances.

Matrimonial law

The use of any family planning method by a married person may potentially have some effect on the matrimonial relationship (as will be seen in more detail in Chapter 5). Previously, cruelty was a ground of divorce in both Scots and English law; now in both jurisdictions divorce can be granted if either party behaves in such a way that it would not be reasonable to expect the other to continue cohabiting[14] (shortly, but inaccurately, referred to as 'unreasonable behaviour').

Sex, and more particularly procreative sex, was for many centuries seen as being at the heart of the marriage relationship and its absence could have destructive effects. Even as late as 1946 the Court of Appeal in England could be found saying, in a case in which it was alleged that the refusal to have sex amounted to desertion, 'this appeal raises a question of extreme importance to the well-being of the nation, as it goes to the very root of the marriage relationship'.[15] A year earlier the same court had held that a marriage could not be considered consummated when the husband practised coitus interruptus or used a condom.[16] (This particular rule was overturned by the House of Lords in *Baxter v. Baxter*.)[17]

Nevertheless, the practice of coitus interruptus could amount to cruelty justifying a divorce,[18] as could the insistence upon the use of contraceptives.[19] But it should be noted that the cruelty (and now the unreasonableness) lies not in the use of these methods themselves, but in the overbearing of the wishes of the other spouse. If both spouses agree to adopt any such family planning measure, then such a measure would be legally innocuous, for the purposes of the law of divorce.

The same principles apply to sterilization operations. For one spouse to undergo such an operation against the wishes of the other, and in the face of that other's known desire to have children or more children, could potentially amount to cruelty,[20] and today might well amount to unreasonable behaviour. But it is to be emphasized that spouses have no legal right to veto any medical procedure upon the other, and the only effect of disagreement is the possibility of divorce: it does not render the treatment itself unlawful.

Public Policy

Depending upon the court's perception of public morality, the availability of contraceptive or sterilization treatment may be characterized as being unlawful because it is contrary to public policy. The most famous exposition of this view is found in the judgement of Denning L.J. (as he then was) in the case of *Bravery v. Bravery*.[21] The continual quotation of Denning L.J.'s remarks gives them a significance they do not deserve,[22] and they will simply be paraphrase here. Denning L.J. had tried to argue that a sterilization operation was illegal in itself, apparently as being against public morals, and accordingly that the patient's consent thereto was invalid, rather in the way that consent to sexual flagellation[23] or consent to a street brawl[24] is of no effect for public policy reasons. Those reasons were mainly to the effect that sterilization would encourage licentiousness and would allow irresponsible sexual pleasure with no resultant responsibilities. Yet the very point of family planning is to allow people sexual pleasure without the immense responsibilities that parenthood brings. The other judges in *Bravery* expressly disassociated themselves from Denning L.J.'s remarks and therefore his minority judgement, though frequently quoted, cannot be taken to reflect English law, even as it stood in 1954. To liken a surgical operation to either sexual flagellation or a street brawl is clearly ludicrous.[25]

The question of whether voluntary sterilization is contrary to public policy was expressly raised in the Canadian decision of *Cataford v. Moreau*.[26] There, the Quebec Superior Court was faced with a claim for damages against a surgeon who was allegedly negligent in the performance of a sterilization operation (on which issue, see Chapter 8). Deschenes C.J. said of sterilization:

> Everyone is aware of the increasing popularity of this type of operation. Even if it is not for the Court to bear judgment upon the value of this development, it is, nevertheless, unable to ignore it.[27]

After examining the views of the medical profession and of the Government of Quebec, as expressed in the report of a Royal Commission,[28] he concluded:

> If there has been a time in which voluntary sterilization could have offended public order and good morals, this time, for better or worse, is over.[29]

The question has never arisen in Scotland and, although the Scottish High Court of Justiciary has the power to declare new crimes (or at least to extend the scope of existing crimes), it is extremely unlikely that it would characterize this consensual surgical operation as being criminal – evil intent (*dolus*) is of the essence of liability in Scots criminal law, and that element would clearly be missing.[30]

In England, the matter was put beyond all doubt, in relation to contraception, in 1967 when for the first time statute provided for contraceptive services to be available within the National Health Service. A procedure with statutory sanction cannot be considered to be contrary to public policy, because parliament is the ultimate arbiter of policy. The National Health Service (Family Planning) Act 1967 was passed with *no* votes against it, and in the following year s. 15 of the Health Services and Public Health Act 1968 made the same provision for Scotland. The present legislation is now s. 5 of the National Health Act 1977 (England and Wales) and s. 41 of the National Health Service (Scotland) Act 1978, which impose duties on the respective Secretaries of State to make arrangements, to such extent as they consider necessary,

> . . . for the giving of advice on contraception, the medical examination of persons seeking advice on contraception, the treatment of such persons and the supply of contraceptive substances and appliances.

As for sterilization, this has become an increasingly popular method of birth control; and the fact that damages are being awarded for the birth of children when sterilization operations fail,[31] together with the fact that the courts are sanctioning the non-consensual sterilization of the mentally disabled when it is in their best interests,[32] leaves no room for doubt that sterilization is not an operation that is unlawful as being contrary to public policy. The recognition of autonomy carries with it a right to practise birth control,[33] and that right ought not to be denied because of outmoded concepts of morality. One should always bear in mind the words of Sir Nicholas Browne-Wilkinson, V-C, who said (in a very different context):

> The court's function is to apply the law, not personal prejudice. Only in a case where there is still a generally accepted moral code can the court refuse to enforce rights in such a way as to offend that generally accepted code.[34]

It certainly cannot be said today that contraception and sterilization offend a 'generally accepted moral code'.

Direct Prohibitions to Contraception and Sterilization

Although direct legislative prohibitions never existed in Scots or English law, such legislation can be found in many US jurisdictions. Legislation based on the Comstock Act, which expressly defined contraceptive information and material as obscene, was passed in many states in the 1870s. This legislation was used against Margaret Sanger, the American birth control pioneer who opened the first birth control clinic in the United States in 1916.[35] Other legislation prohibited the performance of contraceptive sterilizations (ironically often at the same time as requiring *compulsory* sterilization of the mentally disabled),[36] but this was much less common and no example survives today.

Other statutes prohibited the importation of contraceptives and the use of the mails to deliver contraceptives. However, American courts have proved themselves a good deal less opposed to contraceptive practices than have American legislatures. In 1936 the US Circuit Court of Appeals decided in the case of *US v. One Package*[37] that the US Tariff Act 1930 did not forbid the importation of contraceptives for use by physicians for therapeutic purposes. This was the first judicial recognition in the USA of physicians' clinical freedom in prescribing contraceptives to patients. And in 1944 the US Court of Appeals held in *Consumers' Union v. Walker*[38] that an organization could send through the post details about contraceptives to persons who had requested them.

In some states there were direct prohibitions on the actual use of contraceptives, rendering liable to criminal penalty any person who had sexual intercourse while using an artificial contraceptive method. However, these direct prohibitions were substantially undermined by the Supreme Court in 1965. In *Griswold v. Connecticut*[39] the Planned Parenthood League of Connecticut challenged that state's statute that made the use of contraceptives, even by married couples, a criminal offence. The Supreme Court held that the statute was an unconstitutional invasion of the right of privacy of married persons. It rejected the state's argument that such a provision was necessary to prevent indulgence by some in extramarital relations – an argument which, to many eyes today, must seem quaintly naive (or 'purely fanciful' as Justice White described it).[40] Justice Douglas, giving the opinion of the court, pointed out that forbidding the *use* of contraceptives rather than the regulation of their manufacture or sale was designed to have the maximum destructive impact on the marriage relationship: as a method of discouraging fornication and illicit sex it was therefore constitutionally overbroad. The Court was horrified at the prospect of the police being called upon to 'search the sacred precincts of marital bedrooms for telltale signs of the use of contraceptives'.[41] Justice Goldberg, joined by two others, said this:

> While it may shock some of my Brethren that the Court today holds that the Constitution protects the right of marital privacy, in my view it is far more shocking to believe that the personal liberty guaranteed by the Constitution does not include protection against such totalitarian limitation of family size, which is at complete variance with our constitutional concepts.[42]

Although *Griswold* was clearly based on the sacred nature of the marriage relationship, in its fundament it involved – some would say created[43] – the right of privacy (and thus, incidentally, laid the foundations for the later and even more significant case of *Roe v. Wade*).[44] Privacy is an attribute attaching to individuals, not to a relationship between two individuals, and therefore it was not long before the constitutional protection granted in *Griswold* was extended to the unmarried also. In *Eisenstadt v. Baird*,[45] a Massachusetts statute forbidding the distribution of contraceptives except by physicians to married persons was struck down on the ground that the distinction drawn between the married and the unmarried violated the equal protection clause of the 14th Amendment. Justice Brennan, delivering the opinion of the court, pointed out that *Griswold* could not logically be restricted to married couples:

> If the right of privacy means anything, it is the right of the *individual*, married or single, to be free from unwarranted governmental intrusion into matters so fundamentally affecting a person as the decision whether to bear or beget a child.[46]

The question of the legality of contraception is therefore settled in the United States, and its use and supply are regarded as constitutionally protected rights based on the concept of privacy. Although sterilization has been discussed a good deal less frequently in the Supreme Court, the same principles should apply to that procedure as apply to contraception. In the 1980s the greatest challenge to the availability of family planning in the United States has again come from legislators rather than the courts, and there have been attempts to block funds to family planning organizations. Legislators in the USA refuse to be inhibited from attempting to enforce their own ideas of morality through statute. However, although the Supreme Court may now be backtracking from its most liberal position on abortion,[47] there seems little likelihood that it will change its views on contraception. The principle of autonomy of the individual is now too ingrained into American jurisprudence, and the availability of contraceptive or sterilization treatment is too essential to that concept, for the legality of these methods of family planning to be open to serious challenge.

Provision of Family Planning Services to Children

One situation in which the legality of contraceptive or sterilization treatment is more vulnerable to challenge is in their provision to children. The legal capacity of children to consent to family planning treatment will be examined in depth in Chapter 6, but it is convenient here to examine whether the provision of such treatment can ever amount to a criminal offence on the part of the provider.

All Western legal systems contain provisions rendering criminal sexual intercourse with persons below a certain age. In England and Wales it is an offence under s. 5 of the Sexual Offences Act 1956 for a man (that is, a male over the age of 14) to have unlawful[48] sexual intercourse with a girl under 13; and under s. 6 it is a (less serious) offence for a man to have unlawful sexual intercourse with a girl between 13 and 16. In Scotland it is the common law crime of rape for a man (that is, a male over the age of 8) to have sexual intercourse with a girl under 12; it is an offence under s. 3(1) of the Sexual Offences (Sc) Act 1976 for a man to have unlawful sexual intercourse with a girl under 13; and under s. 4(1) it is a (less serious) offence for a man to have unlawful sexual intercourse with a girl between 13 and 16. The girl's consent is an irrelevance in these crimes, for lack of consent would make them all rape: the existence of these crimes cannot therefore affect or indicate the capacity of the girl to consent.[49] S. 28(1) of the English Act makes it an offence to 'cause or encourage' the commission of unlawful sexual intercourse, and in Scotland a person who does so would be guilty art and part (that is, as an accessory) to the main crime.

The existence of offences such as these clearly shows the law's disapproval of under-age sex, and it might be thought to follow from this that the principle would be seriously undermined by doctors prescribing contraception to children under the statutory age. Some countries avoid this problem by legislatively allowing for the provision of family planning to children, subject to certain safeguards. For example in New Zealand, the Contraception, Sterilisation and Abortion Act 1977 provides that contraception can be given to persons under the age of 16 years, but only by specified persons (including registered medical practitioners) whom the state considers capable of doing so responsibly.[50] The Act makes it a crime for any other person to supply contraceptives to a child under 16.

Some other jurisdictions ban contraceptive provision for children completely, or make it subject to parental consent.[51] In the USA, a number of states (though a minority) have legislative controls of contraceptive provision for children, but an absolute ban has been held by the Supreme Court to be unconstitutional. In *Carey v. Population Services International*[52] the Supreme Court struck down a New York statute that had made it a crime for anyone other than a physician exercising clinical judgement to sell or distribute contraceptives to anyone under the age of 16. The Court held that the constitutional right of privacy concerning procreative decisions (discussed above) extended to minors as well as to adults, and that the state's interest in protecting children was not of sufficient significance to supersede children's rights of privacy. The Court followed its earlier decision in *Planned Parenthood of Central Missouri v. Danforth*[53] which had held that states could not constitutionally forbid a minor from terminating her pregnancy without parental consent, and concluded:

> . . . since the State may not impose a blanket prohibition, or even a blanket requirement of parental consent, on the choice of a minor to terminate her pregnancy, the constitutionality of a blanket prohibition of the distribution of contraceptives is a fortiori foreclosed.[54]

Allowing a physician to decide to give a child contraceptives could not save the constitutionality of the statute, because the physician's discretion might be used arbitrarily, and therefore in effect the statute gave a veto power to a third party, in contravention of the *Danforth* rule. Nor was the statute saved by the fact that the state could legitimately have a policy of discouraging sexual activity in the young. The Court pointed out that the same argument had been rejected in relation to the suggestion that abortion and contraception ought not to be available to the unmarried. Quoting *Eisenstadt v. Baird*,[55] the Court said:

> 'It would be plainly unreasonable to assume that [the State] has prescribed pregnancy and the birth of an unwanted child (or the physical or psychological dangers of an abortion) as punishment for fornication' . . . We remain reluctant to attribute any such 'scheme of values' to the State.[56]

It was as if, said Justice Stevens, a statute prohibited the use of safety helmets in order to enhance the state's policy of discouraging the use of motor cycles.[57]

As pointed out above, neither Scots nor English law contains any statute prohibiting the provision of contraceptives. Nor is there statutory regulation of the provision of contraceptives to children. Consequently, it has been left to the courts to resolve the apparent conflict between the provision of contraceptives and the criminal law. The best known, and most reverberative, challenge to the legality of doctors prescribing family planning treatment for children came in the English case of *Gillick v. West Norfolk & Wisbech Area Health Authority*.[58] Here it was argued by the plaintiff that for a doctor to provide contraception or abortion advice or treatment to a girl below the age of 16 without the consent of the child's parents amounted to causing or encouraging unlawful sexual intercourse and was therefore a breach of s. 28(1) of the Sexual Offences Act 1956. Woolf J. at first instance rejected this argument on the ground that the crime of causing or encouraging unlawful sexual intercourse was a crime of intent, and that the doctor's intention will generally not be to cause or encourage unlawful sexual intercourse, but rather to provide a palliative against the consequences thereof.[59] None of the judges in the Court of Appeal (who otherwise found in favour of the plaintiff on other grounds) disagreed with this approach, and in the House of Lords four of the five judges held that the mere provision of contraceptive treatment to children would not in itself amount to a breach of the criminal law. They held, rather, that the legality of the provision depended upon the mental maturity of the child. Only Lord Brandon held that to provide contraception to an under 16 year-old girl 'necessarily' amounted to promoting, encouraging or facilitating unlawful sexual intercourse, because it removed one of the major inhibitions to sex (that is, the risk of pregnancy). He held that the civil law must be consistent with the criminal law, and that given the criminal law prohibition on sex with girls under 16 it would be against public policy to allow doctors to subvert these criminal prohibitions. Although this may sound less unreasonable, this 'inhibition to sex' argument is in fact identical to the one that regards pregnancy as the just punishment for sex. Lord Bridge gave the best answer to Lord Brandon. He said:

> It seems to me that the policy consideration underlying the criminal sanction imposed by statute upon men who have intercourse with girls under 16 is the protection of young girls from the untoward consequences of intercourse. Foremost among these must surely be the risk of pregnancy leading either to abortion or the birth of a child to an immature and irresponsible mother. In circumstances where it is apparent that the criminal sanction will not, or is unlikely to, afford the necessary protection it cannot, in my opinion, be contrary to public policy to prescribe contraception as the only effective means of avoiding a wholly undesirable pregnancy.[60]

However, it should be remembered that the majority in the House of Lords made it quite clear that a doctor *could* be charged if she or he failed to assess the child's maturity properly, or if she or he did indeed act with the express intention of encouraging unlawful sexual intercourse. A doctor who automatically prescribes contraceptives to all children who ask for them will therefore be at risk of prosecution. The matters to be considered by family planners when dealing with children are examined in Chapter 6.

In holding that the risk of pregnancy cannot be used by the state as a deterrent to the crime of under-age sex, the English approach is to this extent consistent with that of the US Supreme Court. To use the risk of pregnancy as punishment for such an act would be harsh indeed, considering that the risk attaches to the girl, while the crime is committed, at least in Britain, by her paramour.

But the differences between the approach of the Supreme Court and of the House of Lords are greater than the similarities. The decisions in *Carey* and *Gillick* illustrate a sharp contrast between American and English judicial attitudes towards the provision of contraception. In the USA the use of, and access to, contraceptives are seen as constitutional rights, with the decision to exercise them being a moral issue which doctors are no more capable of assessing than anyone else, whether the patient is an adult or a child. In England, on the other hand, the decision to provide contraceptives to children is regarded as primarily a medical decision, and therefore one almost solely for the medical profession to make. Although the Court of Appeal in *Gillick* was strongly of the view that the matter was not one for the doctor's clinical judgement, the majority in the House of Lords were equally strongly of the view that it was. Lord Fraser went so far as to say that the duty of deciding whether a child in any particular case should receive family planning treatment was one which '[doctors] alone are in a position to discharge satisfactorily'.[61]

There is no authority in Scots law one way or the other, and the House of Lords is not a court of appeal on matters of Scots criminal law. However, it may safely be predicted that any Scottish decision will be consistent with the position reached in England. In both jurisdictions, as will be seen later in this book, the law reposes trust in the doctors in many ways. For a doctor to be guilty of an offence in Scotland it would have to be shown, as in England, that she or he intended, by providing contraceptives, to encourage the child to embark on or continue a sexual relationship. As in England, this is certainly possible, but it is highly unlikely. A doctor in both jurisdictions acting responsibly and for what she or he believes to be for the benefit of the patient has little to fear from the criminal law.

Notes

1 For a brief examination of the Roman Catholic Church's views on contraception, see Mason, *Medico-Legal Aspects of Reproduction and Parenthood*, Dartmouth, Aldershot, 1989 at pp. 39/40.

2 Although there was, in 1909, an unsuccessful attempt in the House of Lords – supported by the BMA – to outlaw the sale of contraceptives: see Potts and Diggory, *Textbook of Contraceptive Practice*, 2nd edn, Cambridge University Press, Cambridge, 1983 at p. 5.

3 (1873) 17 Stat. 598 (NY).

4 See Stepan and Kellogg, 'The World's Laws on Contraceptives', 22, *Am. J. Comp. L.* 615, 1974 at pp. 629–630.
5 Gordon, *Criminal Law of Scotland* 2nd edn, Green, Edinburgh, 1978 at p. 991, Smith and Hogan, *Criminal Law* 6th edn, Butterworths, London, 1988 at pp. 719–720. See also s. 1(1) Obscene Publications Act 1959 (England).
6 *Bradlaugh & Besant, v. The Queen* (1877) *LR* 3 *QBD* 607.
7 *Stopes v. Sutherland* (1924) 39 *TLR* 677 (CA), (1924) 41 *TLR* 106 (HL).
8 (1924) 39 *TLR* at p. 680.
9 26 April 1926, *H L Deb.* Vol 63, Cols. 996–1058.
10 In the words of Viscount Fitzalan at Col. 1032.
11 Ministry of Health Memorandum 153 MCW (1930).
12 [1947] 2 *All ER* 886.
13 Ibid. at p. 892.
14 Matrimonial Causes Act 1973, s. 1(2)(b) (England); Divorce (Scotland) Act 1976, s. 1 (2)(b).
15 *Weatherley v. Weatherley* [1946] 2 *All ER* 1.
16 *Cowan v. Cowan* [1945] 2 *All ER* 197.
17 [1947] 2 *All ER* 886. Although opinions were in fact reserved on the question of coitus interruptus, it would be illogical to make any distinction between that and the use of condoms.
18 *Knott v. Knott* [1955] 2 *All ER* 305.
19 *Forbes v. Forbes* [1955] 2 *All ER* 311.
20 *Bravery v. Bravery* [1954] 3 *All ER* 59.
21 Ibid.
22 A fact pointed out by Dickens, 'Reproduction Law and Medical Consent' 35 *U. Tor. LJ* 255, 1985 at p. 266.
23 *R. v. Donovan* [1934] 2 *KB* 498.
24 *H.M. Adv. v. Smart* 1975 *SLT* 65.
25 Denning L. J.'s reasoning is very effectively demolished by Kouri 'The Legality of Purely Contraceptive Sterilization' 7 *RDUS* 1, 1976.
26 (1978) 114 *DLR* (3d) 585.
27 Ibid. at p. 591.
28 *Royal Commission of Inquiry into the Status of Women in Canada* (The Bird Commission) 1970.
29 (1978) 114 *DLR* (3d) at p. 593.
30 See Gordon, op. cit. at p. 829. See also McLean and Maher, *Medicine, Morals and the Law*, Gower, Aldershot 1983 at pp. 129–130. In *Re Conciani* (1987) the Italian Supreme Court overruled the Florence Court of Appeal which had held a doctor guilty of a breach of the penal code in performing consensual vasectomies: see (1988) *Annual Review of Population Law* UNFPA, Cambridge MA, at p. 24.
31 See Chapter 8.
32 See Chapter 7.
33 A sheriff in Scotland was even prepared to postulate a positive *duty* to use contraceptives (though for other reasons he was overruled): see *Bell v. McCurdie* 1981 *SLT* 159.
34 *Stephens v. Avery* [1988] 2 *All ER* 477 at p. 481.
35 See *70 Years of Family Planning in America*, Planned Parenthood Federation of America, New York, 1988.
36 See Kouri, op. cit. at pp. 18–31.
37 86 *F.* 2d 737 (1936).
38 145 *F.* 2d 33 (1944).
39 381 *US* 479, 14 *L. Ed.* 2d 510 (1965).
40 381 *US* at p. 506, 14 *L. Ed.* 2d at p. 528.

41 381 *US* at pp. 485/486, 14 *L. Ed.* 2d at p. 516.
42 381 *US* at p. 497, 14 *L. Ed* 2d at p. 522.
43 See for example the dissenting Justices Stewart and Black, 381 *US* at p. 530, 14 *L. Ed.* 2d at p. 542.
44 410 *US* 113, 35 *L. Ed.* 2d 147 (1973).
45 405 *US* 438, 31 *L. Ed.* 2d 349 (1972).
46 405 *US* at p. 453, 31 *L. Ed.* 2d at p. 362 (original emphasis).
47 See Chapter 3.
48 That is, outwith marriage: *Mohamed v. Knott* [1968] 2 *All ER* 563. And see the discussion of the significance of this word in Mason, *Medico-Legal Aspects of Reproduction and Parenthood*, op. cit., note 1 above at pp. 14–16.
49 See *R. v. Howard* [1965] 3 *All ER* 684. Another crime that is perpetrated even when the child consents is tattooing of minors: see Tattooing of Minors Act 1969.
50 These provisions apply only to contraception, and not the other forms of family planning dealt with by the Act.
51 See Cook and Dickens, *Issues in Reproductive Health Law in the Commonwealth*, The Commonwealth Secretariat, London, 1986 at pp. 65–66 for a discussion of such provisions in Commonwealth countries.
52 431 *US* 678, 52 *L. Ed.* 2d 675 (1977).
53 428 *US* 52, 49 *L. Ed.* 2d 788 (1976).
54 431 *US* at p. 694, 52 *L. Ed.* 2d at p. 690.
55 405 *US* 438, 31 *L. Ed.* 2d 349 (1972).
56 431 *US* at p. 695, 52 *L. Ed.* 2d at p. 691.
57 431 *US* at p. 715, 52 *L. Ed.* 2d at p. 704.
58 [1983] 3 *WLR* 859 (QBD); [1985] 2 *WLR* 413 (CA); [1985] 3 *WLR* 830 (HL).
59 Cf. the Australian case of *Casey v. Grossman* (1949) 51 *WALR* 77 in which a shopkeeper was charged with 'causing or contributing' to a child becoming a 'neglected child' within the meaning of the Child Welfare Act 1947, by selling contraceptives to a 14 year-old boy. His conviction was overturned on appeal on the ground that in this case there was insufficient evidence linking the defendant's actions with the child's unsatisfactory living conditions.
60 [1985] 3 *WLR* at p. 863.
61 Ibid. at p. 845. See also Lord Scarman at p. 860.

3 The Legality of Abortion

Introduction

Unlike contraception and sterilization, induced termination of pregnancy as a method of family planning has always been subject to strict control in most of the world's legal systems. Abortion is a subject that generates widespread discussion in the legal and medical literature, for it raises very many more issues of legal, ethical and medical import than any other form of family planning. Most of the ethical and medical issues have been explored in depth by Mason,[1] and it would be prolix to go into the same detail here. However, the subject of abortion causes many more legal problems than the other forms of family planning dealt with in this book, and some time must therefore be spent examining these problems, although this will be done from a strictly legalistic point of view.

This chapter will deal with three main issues. First, the very nature of abortion itself will be examined. This is important because the word 'abortion' is surprisingly ambiguous and, since it means different things to people of differing ethical and legal standpoints, we must be aware of what the law understands by the word. Secondly, the criteria for the legality of abortion will be examined, but for practical reasons the discussion will be limited to Scots and English law. Each legal system in the world has vastly differing criteria for the legality of abortion, and a more comprehensive examination would require a whole book in itself. Thirdly, the contentious issue of time limits in abortion will be examined, this from the point of view of the law in both Great Britain and abroad. This is an issue that has proved particularly troublesome for the courts.

The Nature of Abortion

The question of what actions will amount to abortion in law is surprisingly difficult to answer. Although most of the world's legal systems contain laws regulating when abortion will actually be allowed (if at all), few attempt to define with precision what will amount to abortion. The reason for this is probably the fact that most abortion laws were drafted many years ago, long before our understanding of reproductive biology had developed to today's levels. Newer laws, of which the British Abortion Act 1967 is a good example, have tended to restrict themselves to providing defences to the previously existing prohibitions, and such statutes therefore give no indication at all about what it is that was forbidden. Indeed, often the laws creating the prohibitions themselves do not specify with precision what acts are illegal. So, for example, the English Offences Against the Person Act 1861 provides that it is an offence for any person to administer any noxious thing or use any instrument with the intent to procure a miscarriage, but there is no interpretation section which explains what 'procuring a miscarriage' means. Similarly in Scotland it is a common law crime to 'procure abortion', but there is no authoritative judicial pronouncement defining exactly what acts will amount to the procuring of abortion. In the absence of statutory or express judicial guidance, an attempt must be made to discover what the law understands by abortion by an analysis of how the courts have dealt with charges of unlawful abortion. Unfortunately, however, there are very few cases from which to draw such an analysis, and most of those that do exist were decided long before medicine achieved the sophisticated understanding of reproduction and pregnancy that it has today. The following discussion therefore, at the end of the day, reflects no more than a personal opinion.

It is submitted that, while abortion as understood by the law requires the termination of a pregnancy, many other factors must be present besides. There is a tendency, particularly amongst medical practitioners (in an effort, one suspects, to make the phrase more 'user-friendly') to use the phrase 'termination of pregnancy' as if it were synonymous with abortion. But it is not. The safe delivery of a living child at term is the termination of the pregnancy, but it is not abortion. Induction of labour and Caesarian section are medically induced terminations of pregnancy, but are not abortion. Rather, to constitute that which the law understands by abortion there must be a congruence of a number of elements, of which termination of pregnancy is only one. The necessary elements are as follows.

Intent

Medically speaking, the word 'abortion' is used to cover any untimely expulsion of the conceptus from the womb, whether deliberately induced or not. Keown has shown how the terms 'abortion' and 'miscarriage' are often used interchangeably in both medicine and the law;[2] but to the lay mind these two concepts are very different. 'Miscarriage' is associated with an unintended unwanted event, which will normally cause grief, whereas 'abortion' is seen as a deliberately induced event which is desired.[3] Although the English Offences Against the Person Act 1861 refers to 'miscarriage', English law understands by that what the layman understands by the term 'abortion' – that is, a deliberate act, done intentionally.

Abortion is a deliberate act of interference with the reproductive process, with the intent of preventing the birth of a living child. In both Scots and English law it is a crime of very particular intent: the crime is 'procuring' abortion, which requires acting with the deliberate aim of achieving a desired end result. Recklessness cannot be a substitute for knowledge in crimes of particular intent: consequently, the crime of abortion cannot be committed recklessly[4].

English law adopts this position particularly strongly, for in that jurisdiction, and in legal systems that have followed the English legislation, the crime does not require the desired end result to be achieved, or even to be capable of achievement. The crime is simply the doing of an act with a particular intent.[5] Indeed it is, somewhat illogically, possible to be convicted under s. 58 of the Offences Against the Person Act 1861 even when the woman who is the subject of the act is not pregnant: this seems to confuse the crime of abortion with the crime of attempted abortion.[6]

Scots law also demands intent but, unlike English law, it also requires the existence of pregnancy. Before a charge of abortion can be brought in Scotland, the prosecutor must be able to prove that the woman was pregnant at the time of the wrongful act. So in *HM Adv. v. Semple*, Lord Justice-Clerk Aitchison said,

> Now, in this case the Crown has not libelled pregnancy, only a belief in the mind of the panel[7] that the woman was pregnant, and it is said that what was done was done in that belief and with the intent to cause an abortion. In my judgment, that does not disclose a crime as the law of Scotland at present stand.[8]

This is the position in many other jurisdictions, such as those that follow the Indian Penal Code of 1860.[9] But the crime in these jurisdictions, as in England, remains one that requires an intent to bring about the wrongful end result. The only difference is that, in these jurisdictions, the additional element of pregnancy in fact must also be proved.[10]

Destruction

The desired end result of an abortion is the destruction of potential human life. This indeed is primarily why the act is prohibited, as is expressly recognized in a number of legal systems, though the desire to protect women's health is also a consideration. A Scottish judge once said:

> Abortion in the sense of the criminal law is held to be criminal because its successful accomplishment results in the destruction of potential human life. That is its main consideration.[11]

A number of statutory provisions also recognize this. For example, in the New Zealand Contraception, Abortion and Sterilisation Act 1977 the crime of 'abortion' is defined as a procedure carried out for the purpose of procuring 'the destruction or death' of an embryo. So too does the South African Abortion and Sterilisation Act 1975 define the crime as 'the abortion of a live foetus of a woman with the intent to kill such foetus'.

It is necessary that a 'potential human life' be destroyed, and it follows that, if a product of conception is destroyed but that product had no potential to become human life, then such destruction would not be abortion. Certain medical procedures are designed to evacuate the uterus of a conception that, because of its nature, could not develop into a living foetus, and will inevitably be expelled naturally. This eventuality may occur when that part of the conceptus designed to become the future placenta develops, but that part that should have become the foetus does not: in medical practice such a product of conception is described as a 'blighted ovum', or an 'anembryonic pregnancy'. Such products could not be described as 'potential human life' for in reality they lack that very potential, and their removal would not therefore need to satisfy the criteria for legality in the abortion laws.

The English legislation tends to cloud the fact that destruction is essential for abortion by the use of the term 'miscarriage', for that word may suggest that mere expulsion of the foetus, rather than its destruction, is the essence of the crime. But if this were so, then abortion could be committed by the expulsion of a living child. It has been argued by Somerville[12] that the purpose of abortion is the evacuation of the uterus, and that this should be done, where possible, in such a way as to preserve the life of the foetus. Although attractive, this line of reasoning is not persuasive. The argument that doctors may have a duty to preserve the life of a foetus even when aborting it is based on an analysis of the particular Canadian statutory provisions[13] and is not necessarily appropriate in other jurisdictions. And, in any case (as Somerville herself later concedes), in common parlance an abortion presupposes destruction. A woman who seeks an abortion wants not to be a mother, even if the child is subsequently adopted: she wants the child not to exist. That the law also takes the view that abortion presupposes destruction can be seen by examining how it regards cases both of expulsion without destruction, and of destruction without expulsion.

If a foetus is untimeously expelled from the womb, but it happens to survive, it is difficult to see how this could be characterized as abortion. At most it would be attempted abortion, and the attempt would have failed because the desired end result (a dead foetus) has not come about (and if the living abortus – that is, the living child – were then deliberately killed the crime would probably be murder).[14] It is just possible that non-destructive but untimely expulsion may be sufficient to constitute the crime of inducing miscarriage under the peculiarly worded English legislation, which, as pointed out above, does not prohibit abortion, but acts intended to procure abortion. But unless the law also requires destruction before a crime is committed it is difficult to avoid the conclusion that *all* premature inductions of labour come within the terms of the prohibition of abortion. This is obviously nonsense, and it is difficult to imagine a prosecution ever being successful, even in England, if the result of the allegedly wrongful act is a living child rather than a dead foetus. In *State v. Burke*[15] the Iowa Supreme Court upheld a conviction for 'unlawful termination of pregnancy' when the act resulted in a living child. But the crime in that jurisdiction was unlawful termination of pregnancy, which does not in itself require destruction, rather than abortion, which does.

On the other hand, if a foetus were deliberately destroyed but not expelled, then it would be difficult to characterize that as anything other than abortion. It happens that the destruction of very early embryos can result in their being naturally absorbed into the woman's body by the process of phagocystosis, rather than their being expelled: if that destruction were carried out intentionally, this would be as much abortion as, say, dilatation and curettage. It follows that the expulsion of the foetus is, in Price's words, 'a consequence of the abortion rather than the abortion itself . . . Whether an expulsion occurs may merely depend on the method of termination of pregnancy adopted'.[16]

Other acts may be done deliberately with the intent to destroy the foetus even though it is not expelled from the womb. If a pregnant woman is physically attacked, the intent of the assailant being to cause the death of the foetus, and the foetus is indeed killed but for some reason not expelled from the womb, then this should be characterized as abortion, for the necessary intent, the wrongful act and the desired end result are all present: such an act was considered to be abortion by the majority in the Kentucky Supreme Court in the case of *Hollis v. Commonwealth of Kentucky*.[17] Conversely, if a pregnant woman is attacked with no intent to cause her to abort, but just through wickedness directed towards the woman, this would be a very serious crime but probably not the crime of 'procuring' abortion, as the act is not motivated by the necessary intent. In *R. v. Virgo*[18] a man assaulted his pregnant girlfriend, causing the death of the foetus she was carrying. Because the child was so advanced as to be 'capable of being born alive' within the meaning of the Infant Life (Preservation) Act 1929 (see below), he was convicted of the crime of child destruction created by that English Act; but, unlike abortion, that crime is one that can be committed recklessly. For the purposes of the crime of abortion reckless destruction is insufficient: it must be intentional destruction.

But nor is it enough that the destruction be intentional. Contrary to what many moralists claim (or desire), the law does not prohibit the intentional destruction of potential human life – the law prohibits abortion, of which destruction is only one element. A woman's egg has the potential to become human life, but only after it has gone through numerous processes; so too does each of a man's sperm. Yet society does not mourn the monthly loss of most of a woman's eggs during her fertile lifetime,[19] nor does it punish the wilful destruction of millions of sperm every time a man masturbates or has intercourse wearing a condom.[20] Mere potentiality is not enough for the law. As Glanville Williams has pointed out,

> One could speak of an acorn as a 'quercine being' along with the oak tree; but that would not hoodwink anyone into thinking that an acorn is an oak. By 'human being' in common speech, we refer to a human organism of a certain stage of development.[21]

So another necessary element of abortion is that the potential human life that is destroyed has reached a certain stage of development. That stage is referable to the commencement of pregnancy – for the third element of abortion is termination of pregnancy.

Termination of Pregnancy

Fundamentally, abortion is a form of termination of pregnancy – that is, the bringing of a pregnancy to an end.[22] Termination becomes abortion when it is combined with the elements discussed above. Termination requires the pregnancy to have commenced, and so the question of when a pregnancy commences becomes the significant one.

Because of its insistence on the protection of human life from the moment of conception (which it takes to mean the moment of fertilization), the Roman Catholic Church's traditional view is that pregnancy begins at that very moment. However, the law clearly does not take this view, at least not in Scotland or England, or in systems based on English law. In the reproduction process an egg and sperm must go through a number of stages (with ill-defined boundaries) before a pregnancy is constituted.[23] They must first join together (fertilization). At this stage, the entity thus created is often called a pre-embryo, but the precise terminology used has no effect in law. Then it must make its way down the fallopian tube to the womb (which normally takes between seven and ten days). After that, the process of implantation must be successfully completed. The successful completion of implantation requires more than the attaching of placental tissue to the wall of the uterus for, as pointed out above, an anembryonic conceptus can occur with a placenta successfully developing, but a foetus not. A successful implantation would be one in which the placenta *and* the embryo begin to develop – that is, at the moment of differentiation (which occurs when the primitive streak is formed). This normally occurs a few days after the placenta begins to attach to the wall and is usually completed by 14 days after initial fertilization. In medical terms, pregnancy begins at that moment[24] and, although there is no express legal acceptance of this, the law is likely to follow the definition of pregnancy accepted by medical practice. The law in most common law jurisdictions is happy to accept the medical definition of such concepts as death, mental competence, maturity and many other things besides; and so in the absence of express legal provision defining pregnancy, we may assume that the law will accept the medical definition here also.

Now, some legal systems contain statutory definitions of when human life itself begins. In *Webster v. Reproductive Health Services*[25] the US Supreme Court refused to hold unconstitutional a statute's preamble which declared that human life begins on conception (although that refusal was based on technical grounds). However, the question of when human life begins as a matter of morality or biology is not the same as the question of when pregnancy begins for the purposes of the law, and so far as the law of abortion is concerned, it is only the latter question that is relevant. A number of legal systems do contain statutory definitions of the commencement of pregnancy rather than human life, and many define it to commence on the completion of implantation. So, for example, New Zealand's Contraception, Sterilisation and Abortion Act 1977 defines abortion as the destruction of 'an embryo or fetus *after implantation*'. Similar statutory provisions are found in the Dutch,[26] West German,[27] and Austrian[28] legal systems.[29]

Although there is no general statutory recognition of this in Scots or English law, it is likely that the courts in these countries will adopt this view. In principle it is suggested that they would be correct to do so. Before the completion of implantation there may well exist a product of conception, but the mere existence of such a product does not in itself constitute a successful pregnancy. The 'pregnancy' may be non-viable in the sense of the ovum being blighted, as discussed above. And it is to be remembered that pregnancy does not occur in a vacuum, nor indeed in a test tube: rather, pregnancy is a state of being, for a woman. If an egg is fertilized *in vitro*, the woman whose egg was used could not be said to be in a state of pregnancy. Such a woman becomes pregnant when the fertilized egg is re-implanted into her uterus, and it would be logical to define pregnancy in the same way in cases of natural fertilization also. Implantation is a moment of significance, because it is the moment the fertilized egg becomes a part of the woman's body and therefore any anti-pregnancy technique after implantation must be an action directed towards the woman's body. This gives the woman a particular status, that carries with it certain moral rights (more or less extensive) over the embryo, which is now *part of her body*. And it also justifies the law stepping in to provide regulation of potentially hazardous actions upon the woman's body. Before implantation the law has far less justification in stepping in, and the woman herself has no particular status flowing from any change in her body.

Summary

Abortion therefore, as understood by the law, is the destruction of potential human life by the deliberate termination of a pregnancy that has already successfully commenced, this done with the intent that the potential human life be destroyed. This act is prohibited in most of the world's legal systems, except in circumstances that satisfy certain criteria or indications for legality. The next section of this chapter will look at the criteria required by Scots and English law.

The Criteria for Legality in Scots and English Law

The history of the law of abortion in Great Britain, culminating in the Abortion Act 1967 is too well known to require reiteration here,[30] but it must be emphasized that the 1967 Act does not, as is commonly supposed by the layman (and indeed by many health care workers), contain the whole of the law of abortion. That Act exists parasitically (or perhaps symbiotically) on the previously existing law. The law in England and Wales before 1967 was very different from the law in Scotland, and apart from the matters governed by the 1967 Act, it remains very different today.[31]

In English law, s. 58 of the Offences Against the Person Act 1861 declares that any pregnant woman who, with intent to procure her own miscarriage, unlawfully administers to herself any poison or other noxious thing, or who unlawfully uses any instrument with like intent, shall be guilty of an offence, for which the penalty is liability to life imprisonment. S. 58 also provides that any other person may be liable for the same acts, the only difference being that when a person other than the mother is charged, it matters not whether the woman is pregnant: the crime is the same – doing acts with intent to procure abortion – even though practised upon a non-pregnant woman. S. 58 is still in force today.

In Scots law, procuring abortion was, and is, a common law crime,[32] although it has always been accepted in Scotland that there may be circumstances in which it is necessary to procure abortion, such as when it is a 'necessary medical operation'.[33] As was seen earlier in this chapter, abortion cannot be committed in Scots law unless the woman upon whom the abortionist directs her or his acts is – and can be proved to be – pregnant.[34]

The Abortion Act 1967, which applies both in England and Wales and in Scotland,[35] provides an absolute defence to the above offences, so long as the criteria in the Act are satisfied. If they are not, then the crime of procuring abortion or doing acts with intent to procure miscarriage will have been committed.

The Grounds for Abortion

Like many statutes, the Abortion Act 1967 is open to many interpretations and the grounds laid down in s. 1 can be given either a very narrow or very wide construction. Normally the courts very jealously, and rightly, guard their own power to interpret Acts of Parliament. However, uniquely, the English courts have shied away from giving any interpretative guidance concerning this Act. In *R. v. Smith,*[36] Scarman L. J. said that 'the legality of an abortion depends on the opinion of the doctor'. Adopting this approach in *Paton v. Trustees of the British Pregnancy Advisory Service,* Sir George Baker P. had this rather remarkable thing to say:

> My own view is that it would be quite impossible for the courts in any event to supervise the operation of the 1967 Act. The great social responsibility is firmly placed by the law on the shoulders of the medical profession.[37]

He went on,

> Not only would it be a bold and brave judge . . . who would seek to interfere with the discretion of doctors acting under the 1967 Act, but I think he would really be a foolish judge who would try to do any such thing.[38]

This statement was quoted with apparent approval by Sir John Donaldson, M.R., in *C. v. S.*[39] The consequences of this pusillanimity is that we are left with no judicial guidance at all – indeed a denial of judicial competence to give guidance – as to how the grounds laid down in the 1967 Act are to be interpreted. Thus, the medical profession has effectively been left with a free hand to interpret these grounds according to its own ethics, views and prejudices.

The following paragraphs represent a personal opinion on the meaning that the words setting out the grounds for abortion reasonably bear; but it should be remembered that, in the absence of judicial guidance, these views can only be personal.

By s. 1(1) of the Abortion Act 1967 the induced termination of pregnancy will not be a crime if two registered medical practitioners are of the opinion, formed in good faith, that one or more of the grounds for abortion exist in the particular case. The grounds upon which an abortion can be performed are laid out as follows:

> (a) that the continuance of the pregnancy would involve risk to the life of the pregnant woman, or of injury to the physical or mental health of the pregnant woman or any existing children of her family, greater than if the pregnancy were terminated; or
> (b) that there is a substantial risk that if the child were born it would suffer from such physical or mental abnormalities as to be seriously handicapped'.[39a]

Within these two paragraphs there are in fact four separate grounds. This is recognized in the Abortion Regulations 1968[40] which prescribe the form of the certificates that have to be completed for every abortion (see below), specifying, *inter alia*, upon which of the four grounds the abortion is to be performed. The four grounds are:

1. risk to the physical health of the pregnant woman;
2. risk to the mental health of the pregnant woman;
3. risk of foetal abnormality; and
4. the 'non-medical' ground, as it is called in the English Regulations, and the 'socio-medical' ground as it is called in the Scottish Regulations.[41]

The two health grounds reflect the law as it previously existed in both England and Scotland, although the wording of the Act is rather wider than either the English health ground recognized by McNaughten J. in *R. v. Bourne*[42] or the rather nebulous therapeutic exception (apparently based on necessity) recognized by Scots law. All that is required under the Act is that the risk of continuing the pregnancy is greater than the risk involved in its termination. Mason, among others, has pointed out[43] that, with early abortions, the risks of termination will invariably be less than the potential risks of continuing the pregnancy. This will become even more obviously the case when the anti-progesterone drug RU 486, discussed in the next chapter, becomes more widely available for use in abortion, for the use of that drug very much reduces the risks compared with current abortion techniques. However, as an abortifacient that drug is suitable only in the first seven weeks of pregnancy; later on in pregnancy the balance of risk may be more uncertain and it might not be so clear that the risks of pregnancy outweigh the risks of abortion.

The foetal ground contained in paragraph (b) is one that often attracts criticism, particularly from the disabled lobby. Like the other grounds, it is susceptible to widely differing meanings. On the face of it, the terms of this ground are very tightly drawn: there must be a 'substantial' risk that the child would be 'seriously' handicapped. But these are very amorphous concepts and if the issue were ever to be litigated, it is unlikely that a doctor would be criticized for interpreting them too liberally. A 'substantial' risk is likely to be considered simply one that the expecting couple are not themselves willing to undergo. A 'serious' handicap is likely to be considered to be no more than one that is not negligible (a negligible handicap might be, for example, a missing digit, a hare lip, or smallness in size).

The word 'handicap' itself is ambiguous. In one sense, any physical defect is a handicap, although the common understanding of the word refers to a defect that continuously inhibits day-to-day living. A disease or illness should not normally be considered a handicap. Genetic diseases such as haemophilia ought not to be regarded as handicaps if they can be controlled to such an extent that the patient has, to all intents and purposes, a 'normal' life. HIV infection, on the other hand, being both permanent and inhibiting of 'normal' life, may well be considered to be a handicap.

The non-medical or social ground can be gleaned from the first paragraph in s. 1(1), which allows abortions due to risk of injury to health of either the pregnant woman or any existing children of her family, and from s. 1(2), which is in the following terms:

> In determining whether the continuance of a pregnancy would involve such risk of injury to health as is mentioned [above], account may be taken of the pregnant woman's actual or reasonably forseeable environment.

Taken together, these provisions permit abortion when the social or environmental or living conditions of either the mother or her existing children are likely to be worsened by the continuation of the pregnancy. Thus, a woman who cannot economically afford to bear a child or another child will clearly satisfy this condition. But, further, if existing children are disadvantaged (and there will be few families in which an extra child will not to some extent lessen the wealth – both financial and emotional – available to existing children), then the ground will be satisfied.

This is the widest and most loosely drawn of the grounds, and, again, the courts have left it to the medical profession to define, in good faith, what it means. The result, once more, is that the interpretation of the words in this section depends not on the court's application of the normal rules of statutory interpretation, but on the beliefs and prejudices of the medical profession itself. If a professional woman wants an abortion because childbirth would interfere with her career, she is unlikely to have difficulty in obtaining it, since the predominantly white middle-class medical profession regard that as a reasonable request. But if a coloured woman from a non-Christian background wants an abortion because she has discovered that the foetus she is carrying is female, she is likely to have great difficulty in persuading a doctor that this comes within the terms of the Act, since the medical profession generally (but not universally) disapprove of abortion solely for sex selection reasons. Yet it is easy to make out a case to the effect that a woman from an ethnic background that values male children very much more than female children would suffer in her social position if she produces only girls.[44]

It is no aim of the present book to argue that abortion solely for sex selection reasons is ethically acceptable: rather the aim is simply to show that an argument for its legality can easily be supported. This graphically illustrates the dangers that the English courts' denial of their own competence to assist in the interpretation of the grounds laid down in this Act of Parliament can give rise to. Leaving it to the medical profession to interpret the scope of the grounds in the Abortion Act has in fact left it in the hands of each individual member of the medical profession, for the profession as a whole has no considered, standard and enforced view. The availability of abortion therefore depends upon which doctor the pregnant woman has access to: because there are vast variations in availability across the country, the legislation, which is designed to give uniform rights throughout the jurisdictions covered, is frustrated by the power held by individual doctors. It is interesting to remember that inequality of access was one of the main reasons why the abortion legislation in Canada was declared unconstitutional in 1988;[45] yet it is an unavoidable – and surprisingly little criticized – fact of life in Scots and English law as currently applied.

If the law is to recognize a social ground for abortion, then the medical profession really ought to be honest and admit that the interpretation of that ground rests solely in the hands of the individual doctor. This is the single most important factor bolstering the overwhelming power that lies in the doctor's hands, rather than in the hands of the pregnant woman.[46] With abortion, more than any other form of medical treatment, the power structure of the doctor-patient relationship is grossly imbalanced.

The Requirement for Good Faith

One or more of the above grounds must exist before the abortion will be legal, but the law is clearly of the view that the ground need exist only in the perception of two registered medical practitioners, rather than in fact. Not only does the law allow the medical profession to interpret the Act itself, but it will not allow any challenge to that interpretation unless the doctor's good faith can be brought into question. The opinions as to whether the case comes within the terms of the Act must be formed in good faith, but that is all. They need not be accurate, nor even reasonable – all the law requires is that they be honestly held.[47]

A challenge was made to a doctor's good faith in *R. v. Smith*,[48] which remains the only reported case since the passing of the 1967 Act in which a medical practitioner was charged with unlawful abortion. Here, the prosecutor alleged that the doctor had not formed his opinion in good faith. He had made no examination of the pregnant woman, nor asked her why she wanted an abortion, but had told her that she could have one as soon as she paid £150. There was a dispute as to whether a second doctor had seen her. The accused claimed that he had not in fact performed an abortion, but had simply given the woman treatment for a spontaneous miscarriage that she suffered shortly after entering his clinic: this was proved to be untrue, and his perjury here probably went a long way to establish his lack of good faith. The accused was convicted, after the judge's summing up had suggested that, in forming an opinion, it would be 'usual' for the doctor to make some enquiry into the woman's background, and her environmental and personal history. The speed with which the opinion is formed was also stated to be relevant. On appeal, the Court of Appeal accepted this summing up as legally sound, and upheld the conviction. It also rejected the accused's contention that he ought to have been convicted only if the prosecutor could show that his opinion was one which, in the circumstances, no doctor could have entertained. Instead, the Court of Appeal held that good faith was a question of fact and that the evidence must suggest the strong probability that the opinion said to have been reached was formed either in bad faith or not at all. The normal practice of the profession will be relevant here, but not determining. Scarman L. J. said:

> The question of good faith is essentially one for the jury to determine on the totality of the evidence. A medical view put forward in evidence by one or more doctors as to the good faith of another doctor's opinion is no substitute for the verdict of the jury. An opinion may be absurd professionally and yet formed in good faith; conversely an opinion may be one which a doctor could have entertained and yet in the particular circumstances of a case may be found either to have been formed in bad faith or not to have been formed at all . . . If a case is brought to trial which calls in question the bona fides of a doctor, the jury, not the medical profession, must decide the issue.[49]

So, the jury must find good faith in fact, but only in the sense of finding that the doctor genuinely and honestly believed the case to come within the terms of the Abortion Act – as he, the accused, honestly believes it is to be interpreted. Such a belief is unlikely to be considered honest if the doctor has not examined the patient properly.

Who may Carry out Abortions

According to s. 1(1) of the 1967 Act, abortion is not a criminal offence if, in addition to satisfying the other requirements, the termination of pregnancy is carried out by a registered medical practitioner. Many forms of abortion involve more professional health care workers than simply registered medical practitioners. Nurses assist in surgical operations and, in some abortion procedures, do many more of the physical acts required than any doctor. The question of whether this amounts to treatment carried out by a registered medical practitioner was raised in the case of *Royal College of Nursing v. D.H.S.S.*[50] Here, the House of Lords held that a nurse who administers prostaglandin as part of an abortion procedure does not her or himself terminate the pregnancy if the treatment is prescribed, initiated by, and carried out in accordance with the directions of, a registered medical practitioner who accepts responsibility for all stages of the treatment. Abortion is often a team effort, but the law considers the doctor who is in charge of the team to be the person carrying out the abortion, whether or not she or he does the main act or indeed any act necessary to bring about the termination of the pregnancy. The doctor need only carry out the

> . . . physical acts, forming part of the treatment, that in accordance with accepted medical practice are done only by qualified medical practitioners . . . In other words . . . the requirements of [s. 1(1)] are satisfied when the treatment for termination of a pregnancy is one prescribed by a registered medical practitioner carried out in accordance with his directions and of which a registered medical practitioner remains in charge throughout.[51]

The same principles will apply to abortion performed by the administration of antiprogesterones.

The Certificates

Once two registered medical practitioners are of the opinion, formed in good faith, that one of the abortion grounds exist, they must certify that this is so in the form set out in the Abortion Regulations 1968;[52] the forms must be completed before the treatment commences. If the abortion is immediately necessary to save the life or to prevent grave permanent injury to the physical or mental health of the pregnant woman, then s. 1(4) of the Act allows that only one medical practitioner need certify his opinion, and in this case the 1968 Regulations allow the certificate to be completed either before the termination or, where that is not reasonably practicable, within 24 hours thereafter. The practitioners must preserve the completed certificates for three years, after which they may destroy them.

Notification of the abortion must be made within seven days thereafter to the Chief Medical Officer of the Department of Health (England) or of the Welsh Office (Wales) or of the Scottish Home and Health Department (Scotland), in the form set out in the Abortion (Amendment) Regulations 1980.[53] Notification may not be disclosed except for the limited reasons laid down in the 1968 Regulations, as amended by the Abortion (Amendment) Regulations 1976.[54] These reasons include such things as criminal proceedings, bona fide scientific research, and acting with the consent of the woman involved.

Conscientious Objection

Section 4(1) of the Act provides that no person is under a duty to 'participate in any treatment' authorized by the Act to which she or he has a conscientious objection, but conscientious objection must be proved by the person claiming to rely upon it.[55] This section allows people to do what would otherwise be a breach of their contract of employment, although it is clear that the main provisions of the Act effectively close certain career avenues for people who would wish to make use of this section. However, this is a practical rather than a legal point.

Section 4 was at issue in the case of *R. v. Salford Health Authority ex p. Janaway*,[56] in which a typist was dismissed for refusing to type letters for a doctor referring a potential abortion patient to another doctor in order to obtain the necessary second opinion. The typist applied to the court for a declaration that she was entitled to rely upon the conscience clause. However, the Court of Appeal held that that clause was open only to those who would, but for s. 1 of the Act, have been committing an offence under the law relating to abortion, and that a typist in the position of the applicant would not have been subject to any criminal penalties and therefore could not rely upon the section.

The extent of application of s. 4(1) is therefore determined by the criminality of the acts. Nurses, and anaesthetists, who are undoubtedly accessories to the termination of pregnancy, can rely on s. 4(1) and would have a right to refuse to assist in the carrying out of abortions. Secretaries, administrators, hospital porters and the like cannot.

Section 4(2) qualifies the right to conscientious objection by providing as follows:

> Nothing in subsection (1) . . . shall affect any duty to participate in treatment which is necessary to save the life or to prevent grave permanent injury to the physical or mental health of a pregnant woman.

The test appears stricter than that for the legality of abortion itself, in that it is restricted to abortions carried out to prevent 'grave permanent injury': it follows that just because an abortion is carried out for one of the health reasons this does not necessarily exclude the conscience clause. Rather, the right to conscientious objection will be excluded only when the abortion is one to which s. 1(4) applies – that is, when it is an emergency procedure. The issue should arise only seldom in practice, since those who are likely to wish to rely on s. 4 are likely also to have avoided the type of employment that may give rise to these conflicts.

Time Limits in Abortion

Most legal systems that recognize the legality of abortion on the satisfaction of certain criteria or indications place time limits on that legality, so that abortions after such limits will either not be legal at all, or be legal only on much more limited grounds. It is assumed in most jurisdictions that the more advanced the pregnancy becomes the more entitled to protection the foetus becomes: thus while in the early stages the right to protection is so limited that it can easily be overridden by other interests, in the later stages that right becomes much more weighty and therefore more difficult to override.

The question of time limits is one that has proved particularly contentious, and it is also one that the English courts have not been able to avoid. It is a subject that, until recently, was treated very differently in Scotland than in England and Wales; and it has been the cause of high controversy in the US Supreme Court. The position in Great Britain will be examined separately from the position in the USA.

Time Limits in Scots and English Law

Until 1990, one of the most startling differences between Scots and English law was the fact that in England the defences laid down in the Abortion Act 1967 were available for abortions performed only up until the foetus had reached a certain age, while in Scotland the defences in the 1967 Act were available throughout the pregnancy.[57] This was the result of the fact that the Infant Life (Preservation) Act 1929,[58] which had created the offence of child destruction (that is, the destruction of an unborn child that was 'capable of being born alive') did not extend to Scotland, since there was no doubt that the offence created by that Act was already a common law crime in Scotland. The 1929 Act was expressly preserved by the 1967 Act, which had the effect of making the latter's Act's defences available, in England, only until the child was 'capable of being born alive'. That phrase had given rise to much academic controversy,[59] before the Court of Appeal effectively equated its meaning with the concept of 'viability' in the case of *C. v. S.*[60] Once the child reached viability, that is, once it reached the stage of being able to breathe with or without artificial aid, the 1967 defences to its destruction were no longer available, and only the single defence remained, being that the destruction of the child was done solely for the preservation of the life of the mother. In Scotland on the other hand, all the 1967 defences were available throughout the pregnancy.

Since the Human Fertilisation and Embryology Act 1990, however, the position has been the same for both Scots and English law, for that Act simplified the English position in relation to time limits, and also imposed time limits into Scots law for the first time. Under this Act, the four 1967 defences are available up until the end of the 24th week of pregnancy. Thereafter only three defences are available, but they will be available for the whole of the remainder of the pregnancy: (1) that there is a substantial risk that the child if born would be seriously handicapped, (2) that the continuance of the pregnancy would involve grave risk to the life of the pregnant woman greater than if the pregnancy were terminated, and (3) that the termination is necessary to prevent grave permanent injury to the physical or mental health of the pregnant woman.

On the face of it, 'grave permanent injury' is somewhat stricter than 'injury to physical or mental health', suggesting a stricter test after 2 weeks if life is not threatened (as with SI (4) g the 1967 Act). However, given the English courts' reluctance, mentioned earlier, to involve themselves in the interpretation of the abortion defences, it is likely that this defence will similarly be left in the hands of each individual doctor. And it is to be noted that in *R. v. Bourne*,[61] in which a doctor was charged with unlawful abortion and in which the judge held the defence of 'preservation of the life of the mother' applicable, the judge there directed the jury that, life depending upon health, preservation of life included protection of health, either physical or mental. This jury direction has been accepted on a number of subsequent occasions as representing the law.[62] We shall of course have to wait to see how the new rules are applied in practice by the medical profession; but the present writer would not be at all surprised if the practical effect of the new rules were simply that the non-medical ground, or socio-medical ground (see previous section) is available only until the 24th week of pregnancy, while the other three grounds (that is, risk to the life or physical health of the pregnant woman, risk to her mental health, and risk of foetal abnormality) are available for the whole duration of the pregnancy.

The English offence of child destruction survives, but it will now be relevant only for those acts it was originally designed to prohibit, that is destruction of the child in the course of being born. The final question to be asked in relation to time limits is, when do the abortion defences come to an end, which is the same as asking, when does pregnancy itself come to an end? It is clear, as the existence of the 1929 Act recognises, that pregnancy may end at sometime before the birth process is complete: thus the possibility of abortion (and the availability of the defences) must end then also. As Scotland has only recently acquired time limits in abortion, the previous position in that jurisdiction will be instructive.

In Scots law it is clear that if the child is destroyed after having been fully born then the crime is homicide, and the abortion defences are irrelevant. Homicide in Scotland is the destruction of a 'self-existent human life',[63] which was defined in *HM Adv. v. McAllum*[64] as a person who has been fully born and who has an existence separate from its mother.[65] In *HM Adv. v. Scott*[66] the jury was directed that the panel (that is, the accused) would be guilty of murder if her actions resulted in the death of a child which had both breathed and cried. It was also held in this case that it did not matter that the injury from which the child died was inflicted when the child was still partly in the mother's body.[67]

These cases show that homicide cannot be committed until the child is fully born, that is, sustaining its own life (with or without artificial aid) separate from its mother. The taking of breath seems to be required[68] but it is unlikely that the law today will demand (as it previously did) that the child be heard to have cried.

As for the process of birth itself, it is submitted that destruction during that time is neither homicide nor abortion.[69] Destruction of a foetus in the womb is clearly abortion, but in *HM Adv v. McAllum* the Lord Justice-Clerk, having expressly distinguished between abortion and destruction during birth, described them both as 'very serious offences'. And destruction that is not abortion cannot have the abortion defences available to it. It follows that as soon as the foetus commences its journey from the womb to the outside world, that is, the point when spontaneous or induced labour commences, its destruction will amount to a serious, though innominate, crime (or, in England, the crime of child destruction).

Preservation of the life of the mother was a common law defence to abortion in Scotland, and is almost certainly also a common law defence to this innominate crime. *R. v. Bourne*[70] is accepted [71] authority for the proposition that this is a defence to the English crime. If the doctor acts in good faith, 'preserving the life of the mother' is likely to be given a wide interpretation.

In summary, all the 1967 defences are available in the first 24 weeks of pregnancy. Thereafter preservation of the life of the mother (which presumably will be taken to include her physical and mental health) or grave risk of permanent injury, or foetal abnormality, will be available as defences for the remainder of the pregnancy. Once the birth process itself begins, the child may be legally destroyed only to preserve the life of the mother (which again will presumably be taken to include her physical and mental health). If a child is destroyed for any other reason then the crime of child destruction in England and an innominate common law crime in Scotland will have been committed. Once the child is fully born (i.e. once the umbilical cord is cut and the child is living and breathing and is being sustained separately from its mother's body) then its destruction will be homicide.

Time Limits in the USA

The problem of time limits has been inherent in US abortion law since 1973, because of the 'trimester' approach upon which *Roe v. Wade*[72] was based. In that case the Supreme Court held that pregnancy should be divided into three stages, to each of which state legislatures might apply different legal regimes. During the first trimester the pregnant woman's right to her own privacy is compelling, and, effectively, she is therefore allowed abortion on demand. After 'approximately' 12 weeks the second trimester begins and the state may further its legitimate interest in protecting women's health by regulating such matters as where abortions can be carried out, and by whom. During the third trimester, however, the state can, if it wishes, protect the potential human life of the foetus by regulating abortion much more strictly, and even by proscribing it completely (unless the continuation of the pregnancy constitutes a threat to the life or health of the mother). A number of states thereupon passed legislation prohibiting abortion during the third trimester.

In *Roe* the Supreme Court decided that the state's interest in protecting unborn human life becomes compelling (that is, the third trimester begins) when that unborn life becomes 'viable'. However, although the Court indicated when the second trimester begins, it deliberately did not lay down a strict time-limit for the commencement of the third trimester – in other words, for the achievement of viability. Justice Blackmun, giving the Opinion of the Court, held that a foetus becomes viable when it is 'potentially able to live outside the mother's womb, albeit with artificial aid'.[73] Further, viability is the point after which the foetus 'presumably has the capability of meaningful life outside the mother's womb'.[74]

In many respects this approach reflects that subsequently adopted by English law before 1990, for it similarly proceeds on the assumption that the more developed the foetus the greater the legal protection to which it is entitled; further, it is similarly based on the recognition that different foetuses will achieve viability at different rates. It also assumes, as did English law that before the fullest protection is granted the foetus must have acquired an ability to continue living or an ability to have 'meaningful' life, separate from its mother.

However, there are also some fundamental differences between the US and English positions. The Supreme Court did not lay down any point in time after which the foetus is deemed to be viable. Justice Blackmun pointed out that 'viability is usually placed at about seven months (28 weeks) but may occur earlier, even at 24 weeks'.[75] He elaborated somewhat on this statement in the later case of *Planned Parenthood of Central Missouri v. Danforth*,[76] where he said of viability that it was 'a point purposefully left flexible for professional determination, and dependent upon developing medical skill and technical ability'.[77] This is important, because to leave the determination of viability to the medical profession leaves viability itself open to variations brought about by increased medical competence in determining the point, as well as increased medical ability to save for 'meaningful life' earlier and earlier foetuses.[78]

In *Danforth* a number of provisions in a Missouri abortion statute were challenged, amongst them being a provision defining viability as 'that stage of fetal development when the life of the unborn child may continue indefinitely outside the womb by natural or artificial life-supportive systems'. The challenge was founded particularly on the word 'indefinitely' in that definition, but the Supreme Court held that the assumption behind it did not conflict with what was said and held in *Roe*. From this it is clear that, in using the phrase 'capable of meaningful life' in defining viability, the Supreme Court intends to give legal protection to the foetus that can live 'indefinitely' outside the womb.

The Court also made explicit in *Danforth* that which was implicit in *Roe* – that is, that the determination of viability is a matter for the physician to decide in each particular case and is not an issue for which the state can lay down uniformly applicable rules:

> It is not the proper function of the legislature or the courts to place viability, which essentially is a medical concept, at a specific point in the gestation period. The time when viability is achieved may vary with each pregnancy, and the determination of whether a particular fetus is viable is, and must be, a matter for the judgement of the responsible attending physician.[79]

This statement was reaffirmed in *Colautti v. Franklin*,[80] in which the Court also held that neither state legislatures nor the courts could define viability in terms of one or more of the elements that go towards viability, such as ability to breathe, gestational age, or weight.[81] The physician is to decide, bearing in mind the matters he considers of particular significance in the individual case. This contrasts sharply with the English position in *C. v. S.*, which gives overwhelming significance to the ability to breathe, and which refuses to consider any other factor to be relevant.

The issue of viability was again raised in *Webster v. Reproductive Health Services*,[82] in which a later Missouri statute was at issue. The statute prohibited, consistently with *Roe*, abortions in the third trimester, but one of the challenged provisions imposed an obligation upon physicians to undertake certain tests before performing abortions on women 20 or more weeks pregnant, in order to determine whether the foetus to be aborted was viable or not. It was argued that, since testing for viability would show a number of foetuses to be non-viable, to require testing was in fact unconstitutional state regulation of some second trimester abortions, and accordingly was inconsistent with *Roe*. Likewise it was argued that testing would increase the cost of many second trimester abortions, contrary to the Supreme Court's ruling in *Akron v. Akron Center for Reproductive Health Inc*.[83] The Supreme Court (Justice Blackmun with three others dissenting) held that the testing provision as constitutionally sound. Chief Justice Rehnquist (whose opinion on this point was joined by two others)[84] attacked the trimester doctrine upon which *Roe v. Wade* was based, castigating it as 'unsound in principle and unworkable in practice'.[85] He stated that he did not see why the state's interest in protecting potential human life came into existence only on viability. It is difficult to see how this answers the actual challenges made to the Missouri statute, particularly since it was accepted that Missouri could validly choose viability as the point after which abortions could normally be prohibited. Chief Justice Rehnquist then concluded that the requirement of the tests for viability 'permissibly furthers the state's interests in protecting potential human life' and was therefore constitutional.

Although this has been attacked as being assertion masquerading as reasoning,[86] it is difficult to fault the conclusion. If a statute prohibits abortion after viability (consistently with *Roe),* and if viability is to be determined by physicians (*Danforth* and *Colautti),* then to require physicians to perform tests (though only where necessary and where good medical practice allows) in order to help them make that determination does, it is submitted, logically follow. It is certainly not a denial of any constitutional right; rather, it simply ensures that only those with the right can actually exercise it. Justice O'Connor (who agreed with the result) also adopted this approach, although she could not see why the Chief Justice and those who joined him had to attack *Roe v. Wade* in order to come to a conclusion supporting the testing provision. Justice Blackmun pointed out that 'the testing provision, as construed by the plurality, is consistent with the Roe framework and could be upheld effortlessly under current doctrine'.[87] Brennan and Marshall JJ. joined with Justice Blackmun, and since Justice Stevens also took this approach, there is in fact a majority for the view that the upholding of the testing provision in no way compromises *Roe*: any attack on *Roe* in this case is therefore obiter and irrelevant.

The issue is likely to resurface in the not too distant future. One of the most disturbing aspects of the *Webster* ruling, as Justice Blackmun pointed out,[88] is its implicit invitation to states to enact increasingly restrictive abortion laws, which might then be challenged, and potentially upheld, in the Supreme Court. The position in the USA can therefore only be described as being currently unstable.

Notes

1 Mason, *Medico-Legal Aspects of Reproduction and Parenthood*, Dartmouth, Aldershot, 1990; also *Human Life and Medical Practice*, Edinburgh University Press, Edinburgh, 1988.
2 See Keown, ' "Miscarriage": A Medico-Legal Analysis' *Crim. LR* 604, 1984. But see Somerville 'Reflections on Canadian Abortion Law: Evacuation and Destruction – Two Separate Issues'. 31 *U. Tor. LJ* 1, 1981 at pp. 15–16.
3 See Beard, 'Miscarriage or Abortion?', letter to the Editor, *Lancet* 1122, 1985.
4 Gordon, *Criminal Law of Scotland* 2nd edn. Green, Edinburgh, 1978 at pp. 253 and 257. There are a number of other crimes that cannot be committed recklessly, such as perjury, and assault.
5 Glanville Williams, *Textbook on Criminal Law* 2nd edn, Stevens, London, 1983, at p. 293. This is not the position in Scotland: see Gordon, op. cit, note 4 above. The Abortion Act 1967 does not alter this position, and nor does it bring Scots law into line with it: see Norrie, 'Abortion in Great Britain: One Act, Two Laws', *Crim. LR* 475, 1985 at pp. 484–5.
6 See, further, Norrie, op. cit., note 5 above.
7 *Anglicae*, 'accused'.
8 1937 *JC* 41 at p. 45.

9 See Bhiwandiwala *et al*,. 'Menstrual Therapies in Commonwealth Asian Law', 20 *Int. J. Gyn. Obs*. 273, 1982.
10 See Norrie, op. cit., note 5 above.
11 Per Lord Anderson in *HM Adv. v. Anderson* 1928 *JC* 1 at p. 4. See Wilson J to similar effect in *Morgentaler, Smoling & Scott v. The Queen* (1988) 44 *DLR* (4th) 385, at p. 498.
12 Op. cit., note 2 above, at p. 12.
13 Which were, of course, held to be unconstitutional by the Supreme Court of Canada in *Morgentaler, Smoling & Scott v. The Queen* (note 11 above).
14 Although Mason has suggested that any prosecution on such facts is unlikely to succeed: see *Medico-Legal Aspects of Reproduction and Parenthood* op. cit., at p. 160. See also Wright: 'The Legality of Abortion by Prostaglandin', *Crim. LR* 347, 1984
15 368 *NW* 2d 182 (1985)
16 'Selective Reduction and Feticide: The Parameters of Abortion', *Crim. LR* 199, 1988 at p. 203.
17 652 *SW* 2d 61 (1983).
18 Discussed by Price, op. cit., note 16 above.
19 A fact pointed out by Mason, *Medico-Legal Aspects* . . . op. cit., note 1 above at p. 98.
20 Cf. Justice Stevens in *Webster v. Reproductive Health Services* 109 *Sup. Ct*. 3040; 106 *L. Ed*. 2d 410, 1989.
21 Letter to *The Times*, 13 April 1983.
22 Tietze & Henshaw, *Induced Abortion: A World Review, 1986* 6th edn. Alan Guttmachar Institute, New York, 1986.
23 The reproduction process is explained in terms easily understood by the layman by Johnson, 'The Onset of Human Identity' in Bromham *et al*. (eds), *Ethical Problems in Reproductive Medicine*, NAFDP, London 1989.
24 See 'Post-Coital Contraception', 1 *Lancet* 853, 1983; Tietze & Henshaw, op. cit., note 22 above; Yen & Jaffe, *Reproductive Endocrinology, Physiology, Pathophysiology and Clinical Management*, 2nd edn, Saunders, Philadelphia, 1986 at p. 200. See also Cook, 'Antiprogestin Drugs: Medical and Legal Issues', 21 *Fam. Plan. Persp*. 267, 1989 for further medical authority for this proposition. The proposition is the basis for the '14-day rule' suggested by the British Warnock Committee (The Committee of Inquiry into Human Fertilisation and Embryology, (1984) Cmnd. 9314).
25 109 *Sup. Ct*. 3040; 106 *L. Ed*. 2d 410 (1989).
26 Law of 7 May 1981.
27 Law 15 of 18 May 1976.
28 Fed. Law of 23 January 1974.
29 See further, Cook & Dickens 'International Developments in Abortion Laws: 1977–88' 78 *Am. J. Pub. Health* 1305, 1988. In one sense, at least, the law in Scotland and England also accepts this: for the purposes of the Human Fertilisation and Embryology Act 1990, a woman is to be treated as 'carrying a child' when an embryo has become implanted.
30 It is covered well not only in Mason, *Medico-Legal Aspects* . . . op. cit., note 1 above, and by Keown, *Abortion, Doctors and the Law*, Cambridge University Press, Cambridge, 1988, but also in Dickens & Cook, 'Development of Commonwealth Abortion Laws' 28 *ICLQ* 424, 1979. For the position in the United States, one could do no better than refer to Wardle & Wood, *A Lawyer Looks at Abortion*, Brigham Young University Press, Provo, 1982.
31 See Norrie, 'Abortion in Great Britain: One Act, Two Laws', *Crim. LR* 475, 1985.
32 Macdonald *Criminal Law of Scotland*, 5th edn., Green, Edinburgh, 1948 at p.

114; also Gordon, *Criminal Law of Scotland*, 2nd edn, Green, Edinburgh, 1978 at p. 812.

33 Anderson, *Criminal Law of Scotland*, 2nd edn, Bell & Bradfute, Edinburgh, 1904 at p. 76.

34 *HM Adv. v. Anderson* 1928 *JC* 1, *H. M. Adv. v. Semple* 1937 *JC* 41.

35 The Abortion Act 1967 does not apply in Northern Ireland, although the Offences Against the Person Act 1861 does. It follows that, in Northern Ireland, the law today is as it was in England before 1967. See, further, Mason, *Medico-Legal Aspects* . . . op. cit., note 1 above, ch. 5, n.13

36 [1974] 1 *All ER* 376 at p. 378.

37 [1978] 2 *All ER* 987 at p. 991.

38 Ibid. at p. 992.

39 [1987] 2 *WLR* 1108 at p. 1124.

39a The wording and format, but not, it is submitted, the substance of this was altered by the Human Fertilisation and Embryology Act 1990.

40 SI 1968/390 (England and Wales) and SI 1968/505 (Scotland).

41 Mason, *Medico-Legal Aspects* . . . op. cit., note 1 above at p. 106 classifies the four grounds somewhat differently, but the classification given here is that used in the 1968 Regulations.

42 [1939] 1 *KB* 687. Lord Diplock in *Royal College of Nursing v. DHSS* [1981] *AC* 800 at p. 827 pointed out that this ground under the Act was significantly wider than that envisaged by McNaughten J.

43 Mason, op. cit., note 1 above at pp. 106–7.

44 Mason, op. cit., note 1 above at p. 114.

45 *Morgentaler, Smoling & Scott v. The Queen* (1988) 44 *DLR* (4th) 385.

46 That the medical profession has – and has always had – control of abortion is the central thesis of Keown's persuasively argued book, *Abortion, Doctors and the Law*, Cambridge University Press, Cambridge, 1988.

47 In *Rance v. Mid-Downs Health Authority & Anor.*, 5 February 1990, Brooke J. held that he would not have found a doctor liable for professional negligence if he had followed a practice formed on a reasonable belief, shared by many of his colleagues, about the relevant law, even if that belief turned out to be wrong when the law was authoritatively determined by the courts.

48 [1974] 1 *All ER* 376.

49 Ibid. at p. 381.

50 [1981] *AC* 800.

51 Per Lord Diplock at pp. 828/829.

52 SI 1968/390 (England and Wales) and SI 1968/505 (Scotland).

53 SI 1980/1724 (England and Wales) and SI 1980/1864 (Scotland).

54 SI 1976/15 (England and Wales) and SI 1976/127 (Scotland).

55 On the difference between Scots and English law on the issue of proof of conscience, see Norrie, op. cit., note 5 above at p. 475/476.

56 [1988] 2 *WLR* 442, commented on by Grubb in (1989) *CLJ* 17.

57 For a fuller discussion, see Norrie, op. cit., note 5 above.

58 The legislative history of the 1929 Act is described by Keown, in 'The Scope of the Offence of Child Destruction', 104 *LQR* 120, 1988.

59 See, for example, Tunkel, 'Abortion: How Early, How Late and How Legal?' 2 *BMJ* 253, 1979; Bowles & Bell, 'Abortion: A Clarification; 129 *New LJ* 944, 1979; Wright, 'Capable of Being Born Alive?' 131 *New LJ* 188, 1981; Keown, op cit., note 2 above, and op. cit., note 58 above.

60 [1987] 2 *WLR* 1108.

61 [1939] 1 *KB* 687.

62 See for example *R. v. Newton & Stungo* [1958] *Crim. LR* 469; *R. v. Smith* [1974]

1 *All ER* 376 at p. 378; and *R. v. Salford Health Authority, ex p. Janaway* [1988] 2 *WLR* 442 at p. 448.

63 Macdonald, op. cit., note 32 above at p. 87; Gordon, op cit., note 4 above, at p. 727.

64 (1858) 3 *Irv.* 187.

65 Ibid. at p. 201.

66 (1892) 3 *White* 240.

67 Cf. the English decision of *R. v. West* (1848) 2 *Cox CC* 500.

68 Macdonald, op. cit., note 32 above at p. 87; Gordon, op. cit., note 4 above at p. 727. This requirement does not exist in some other legal systems: see for example s. 206(1) of the Canadian Criminal Code.

69 See Gordon, op. cit., note 4 above, at p. 727.

70 [1939] 1 *KB* 687.

71 See note 62 above.

72 410 *US* 113, 35 *L. Ed.* 2d 147 (1973).

73 410 *US* at p. 160, 35 *L. Ed.* 2d at p. 181.

74 410 *US* at p. 163, 35 *L. Ed.* 2d at p. 183.

75 410 *US* at p. 160, 35 *L. Ed.* 2d at p. 181.

76 428 *US* 52, 49 *L. Ed.* 2d 788 (1976).

77 428 *US* at p. 61, 49 *L. Ed.* 2d at p. 800.

78 See Mason, *Medico-Legal Aspects* . . . op. cit., note 1 above at pp. 157–8.

79 428 *US* at p. 64, 49 *L. Ed.* 2d at p. 802.

80 439 *US* 379, 58 *L. Ed.* 596 (1979).

81 Compare the approach of Wilson J. in the Canadian decision of *Morgentaler, Smoling & Scott v. The Queen* (1988) 44 *DLR* 4th 385 at p. 499, for she is happy to leave the decision of when the state's interest in the life of the foetus becomes compelling to the legislature.

82 109 *Sup. Ct.* 3040, 106 *L. Ed.* 2d 410 (1989).

83 426 *US* 416, 76 *L. Ed.* 2d 687 (1979). In *Margaret S. v. Treen* 597 *F. Supp.* 636 (1984) the US District Court had held that a requirement in a Louisiana statute on physicians to perform ultrasound tests to determine foetal age was unconstitutional as it imposed an unnecessary and significant cost on the abortion procedure.

84 The majority for the decision of the Court was made up with O'Connor and Scalia JJ, agreeing with the conclusion but not the reasoning. Justice Scalia 'strongly dissent[ed] from the manner in which [the conclusion] has been reached' – and even more strongly dissented from the approach of Justice O'Connor.

85 He also rather curiously criticized *Roe* because the trimester doctrine and the concept of viability are not found in the text of the Constitution. Bang goes much of American Constitutional Law!

86 Per Justice Blackmun, who also described it as ' "it-is-so-because-we-say-so" jurisprudence'.

87 Justice Blackmun thought that the testing provision was unconstitutional because he interpreted it as demanding tests to be carried out in every case whether or not they were medically necessary or even desirable. The majority interpreted the provision to mean that the tests were to be carried out only if necessary and in accordance with accepted medical practice.

88 'The plurality opinion is filled with winks and nods and knowing glances to those who would do away with *Roe*.'

4 The Legality of Post-coital Birth Control

Introduction

The creation of human life is not an event. Rather, it is a continuing, developing process; unfortunately it is a process that is 'well recognized in medical sciences, but poorly accommodated in the law'.[1] The reason for this is that the law is happiest when dealing with definitions of things or events that can be given strictly defined boundaries: processes on the other hand cannot easily be given strict definitions. Reproduction, indeed, is particularly awkward, for even its commencement (sexual intercourse) and its completion (the birth of a living child) are processes rather than events.

Family planning is the interruption of this process. As was seen in Chapter 2, the law in most jurisdictions permits contraception and sterilization (that is, the prevention of conception) with little or no legal regulation; and as was seen in Chapter 3, the law in most jurisdictions places severe limitations on the availability of abortion (that is, the interruption of the process after pregnancy has commenced). Because the prevention of conception and the termination of pregnancy are subject to very different legal regimes, the law has to draw strict boundaries between them, and we must therefore be aware of when conception is completed and when pregnancy has commenced. For after the completion of conception there can be no contraception, and before the commencement of pregnancy there can be no abortion.

Before the whole reproductive process was understood as well as it is today, it was assumed that the completion of the process of conception and the commencement of the process of pregnancy occurred at the same moment in time. However, today, medical science clearly recognizes that there is a gap between the moment of fertilization (that is, the moment when a single sperm breaks into, and joins with, a woman's egg)[2] and the commencement of a pregnancy (the completion of implantation, as was shown in

Chapter 3). If 'conception' is taken to mean the moment of fertilization then contraception is that which prevents fertilization. But fertilization will occur a number of days before the fertilized egg has made its way to the womb and implanted itself there – in other words, a number of days before the commencement of pregnancy. Indeed with *in vitro* fertilization, conception could occur weeks, or even years, before pregnancy commences. Many birth control methods are designed to take effect during that gap between fertilization (= conception) and pregnancy, and this chapter is concerned with the legality of such methods.

Classifying these methods within boundaries recognized by the law is awkward. In reality, birth control methods designed to take effect during this gap can properly be described neither as contraception, because they do not prevent conception, nor as abortion, because they do not interrupt pregnancy. In recognition of this fact, a new word has been coined to cover these methods. An act or procedure that does not prevent conception but which does prevent gestation can be described as contra-gestation, or 'contragestion'.

Now, 'contragestion' is a word apt to cover a number of long-established birth control methods, as well as new methods that are currently being developed. The IUD, for example, could be described thus, for its effect is not to prevent fertilization but rather to render the uterus inhospitable to the fertilized egg. Likewise the so-called 'morning after pill' seems to render the uterus inhospitable and thus prevents implantation (as indeed is one of the actions of the pre-coital progestogen-only contraceptive pill). The recently developed anti-progesterone RU486 has a double effect: it renders the uterus inhospitable and also dislodges any early implantations that have not been prevented. Likewise, the anti-hCG (human chorionic gonadotrophin) vaccines currently being developed act on the fertilized egg to render it incapable of implantation.

In order to determine the legality of these methods, or to determine which legal regime they come under, we must determine what status (if any) the law accords to the entities such methods are designed to destroy – that is, the fertilized egg that has not yet been implanted.

The Legal Position of the Pre-implantation Embryo

It has been argued by a number of writers that the pre-implantation embryo (or the 'pre-embryo' as it is increasingly being called on both sides of the Atlantic) has the same status in law as the post-implantation embryo, and that destruction of the former is therefore as much abortion as is destruction of the latter.[3] For the reasons given in the previous chapter, this misunderstands the nature of abortion, which involves termination of pregnancy as well as destruction of potential human life. The pre-implantation embryo is potential human life that is not protected by the law of abortion, and so, whether or not it is morally or genetically identical to the post-implantation embryo, its status in law is without doubt different.

Neither is that status affected by the tedious question of when human life begins, for this is not a question that has any direct legal significance (although its answer may affect people's perception of what the law should be). This can be illustrated from the way the issue was dealt with in the US Supreme Court's unsatisfactory decision in *Webster v. Reproductive Health Services*.[4] Here, the preamble of a Missouri statute declared that 'the life of each human being begins at conception'), and that 'unborn children have protectable interests in life, health, and wellbeing'. This was challenged on the ground that it was contrary to the Supreme Court's ruling in *Roe v. Wade*, viz. that the state had no right to adopt one theory of life over another in order to justify its abortion regulations; and for that reason the lower court in *Webster* invalidated the preamble. However, in the Supreme Court the preamble was upheld, the Opinion of the Court being based on the narrowly legalistic ground that the preamble could not contravene the statement in *Roe* because the preamble itself did not purport to regulate abortions. Although this avoids the real argument, it does confirm that the question of when human life begins is irrelevant to the question of the legality of abortion.

Justice Stevens dissented on the ground that the preamble, by apparently investing pre-implantation embryos with 'protectable interests', was an interference with a woman's right to use what he described as 'post-fertilization contraceptive devices', and was therefore unconstitutional under *Griswold v. Connecticut*[5] (see Chapter 2). However, although the Opinion of the Court did not address this point, Justice O'Connor, concurring with the Court, found these possible objections 'simply too hypothetical'. She said:

> It may be correct that the use of post-fertilization contraceptive devices is constitutionally protected by *Griswold* and its progeny but, as with a woman's abortion decision, nothing . . . indicates that the preamble will affect a woman's decision to practise contraception.

Justice O'Connor seems to be equating contraception with contragestion, and she finds that the question of when life begins is not relevant to the legality of either. This finding follows from a redefinition of 'fertilization' and 'conception'. It has generally been assumed in this chapter that the two words mean the same, but this is not universally accepted. If 'conception' refers to the moment a woman conceives, or takes into her womb, rather than the moment when the sperm enters the egg, then contraception would include methods that act after fertilization but before implantation. Contragestion therefore becomes subsumed into contraception and therefore subject to the same legal regime.

This becomes all the more apparent when we examine the position of a very peculiar type of pre-implantation embryo. Nowadays there is an important factual distinction to be drawn between two groups of pre-implantation embryos. First, and vastly more commonly, are embryos created naturally in a woman's body. Secondly, and still highly uncommonly, are embryos created *in vitro* – that is, outside a woman's body. It is suggested that these two groups have such pathological and moral identity that it would be wholly illogical for the law to treat them differently. Much has been written on the status of the *in vitro* embryo,[6] and the conclusions drawn ought logically to apply to *in vivo* embryos also.

The important issue is whether the *in vitro* embryo has such a status that it cannot be destroyed, or experimented upon.[7] Such destruction cannot be abortion, for the reasons given in Chapter 3; nor can it be homicide, for there is no living human person in any sense in which that phrase is used in the criminal law, which requires a 'self-existent human life' before homicide can be committed.[8] As the law protects only the living (that is, live-born) human being, and to a lesser extent the post-implantation embryo, it follows that, in the absence of statutory prohibition, the destruction of any other form of human life or potential human life is legally innocuous.

Some legal systems do of course regulate by statute the treatment of *in vitro* embryos. Cusine reports that there is legislation permitting research in New South Wales and in Victoria.[9] In the case of *Margaret S. v. Edwards*,[10] the Fifth Circuit of the US Court of Appeals held unconstitutional a statute banning experimentation on *in vitro* embryos, because of the vagueness of the word 'experimentation'[11]. The British Human Fertilisation and Embryology Act 1990 permits research upon (and therefore destruction of) *in vitro* embryos up until 14 days after fertilization, which it defines as being completed on the appearance of a two-cell zygote. If it takes legislation to prohibit the destruction of artificially created embryos, the common law is unlikely to prohibit the destruction of naturally created pre-implantation embryos.

In conclusion, it is clear that the law grants no protection to the naturally created pre-implantation embryo. The only significant question concerns abortion, and it follows that the legality of contragestive methods of birth control are to be tested only against the abortion laws. The real issue is whether any of these methods come within the definition of abortion as given in the previous chapter.

Particular Contragestive Methods

In Chapter 3, unlawful abortion was defined as an act (not satisfying the legal defences) that is intended to bring about the destruction of potential human life, through the deliberate termination of a pregnancy that has already commenced. All abortions are contragestive in the sense that they prevent the continuance of gestation, but it does not follow that all contragestive methods of birth control are abortion.

The IUD (intra-uterine device)

This is the longest established contragestive, and probably the most commonly used in the world. According to Potts and Diggory:

> More or less any foreign body placed in the uterus prevents pregnancy in the majority of cases and intrauterine contraceptive devices (IUDs) have a lengthy history. . . . It is surprising, after so many years of use, that it is still not known for certain how IUDs work in human beings. Almost certainly they produce no systemic hormonal effects. . . . The insertion of an IUD post-coitally appears to prevent pregnancy and there is strong empirical evidence that at least one of the actions of the IUD must occur after fertilization.[12]

The most likely explanation of how the IUD works is that its presence increases the level of white blood cells in the uterus, which then attack the fertilized egg as a foreign body. However it works, the result is that the fertilized egg, as happens naturally to a large percentage of fertilized eggs,[13] fails to implant and is lost in the next menstrual flow or is absorbed into the woman's body through phagocystosis. The IUD will also dislodge any embryos that were implanted before its insertion.

Insofar as the IUD prevents implantation there is no crime committed because, for the reasons given above, it does not result in the termination of pregnancy. On the other hand, the dislodging by an IUD of an implanted embryo may well be criminal abortion. However, if the IUD is inserted at such an early time that no-one can tell whether there has yet been implantation, then a prosecutor could not prove that a pregnancy in fact existed. In Scotland a criminal charge could not be brought in these circumstances, for one of the constituent elements of the crime in that jurisdiction is actual pregnancy, which would be missing (or at least – which amounts to the same thing in criminal procedure – not susceptible to proof). So it would follow that a family planner in Scotland could fit an IUD with impunity for so long after intercourse as it remains impossible to establish the existence of a pregnancy.

English law is quite different, for, as explained in Chapter 3, the prosecutor in England does not have to prove the existence of a pregnancy in order to bring a successful charge of unlawful abortion. However, in practice, the position in that jurisdiction is much the same as in Scotland although this result is achieved by a slightly different route. For, while an actual pregnancy does not need to be proved, the prosecutor must nevertheless establish that the accused in fact believed that a pregnancy did exist. This is shown in the case of *R. v. Price*.[14] Here a doctor inserted an IUD into a woman who was three and a half months pregnant. The woman had told the accused that she was pregnant and that she wanted an abortion, but he told her that he did not believe that she was pregnant, and that she could therefore be fitted with an IUD to protect her in the future. She miscarried two days later. A police surgeon who saw the woman shortly before she miscarried gave evidence that, in his view, the woman was 'manifestly' pregnant. The charge of inducing miscarriage under the 1861 Act by use of an IUD was held relevant, and the accused was convicted. The conviction was quashed on appeal, but not because the charge was irrelevant: rather it was quashed on the factual ground that there was not sufficient corroboration that the doctor believed the woman to be pregnant at the time he acted. As Sachs L. J. put it:

> The essential issue for the jury was, did the appellant at the time that he inserted [the IUD] . . . *know or believe* that the patient was pregnant and, accordingly, introduce the instrument with intent to procure a miscarriage.[15]

That belief had not been established, because the woman's evidence against the doctor was the evidence of an accomplice, and the jury should therefore have been warned to treat it with particular care.

Likewise, it must also be remembered that, for a criminal charge to be successful, proof of the doctor's knowledge and intent must be 'beyond reasonable doubt'. Suspicion of pregnancy would not be enough to found a charge, for suspicion does not amount to knowledge or belief. If a family planner fits an IUD some days after an episode of unprotected mid-cycle sexual intercourse, she or he will undoubtedly be aware of the possibility of pregnancy existing, but could have no knowledge or belief in pregnancy. In this case, Dr Price was told by the woman that she was pregnant, and so must have been aware of the possibility that she was: his conviction was quashed because it could not be proved beyond reasonable doubt that his knowledge went any further than that.

Now, most IUDs are fitted pre-coitally, even although it is known, indeed intended, that they will act after intercourse and may act after implantation. But, again, this knowledge is nowhere near that deemed necessary by the Court of Appeal in *Price*. The family planner must be shown to know, or believe, that a pregnancy does (or will) in fact exist, and must fit the IUD with the intent of bringing about an end to that pregnancy. It is suggested that Tunkel is wrong when he suggests[16] that acting in the belief of the mere possibility of pregnancy would evidence sufficient intent to found a charge, for this would not only be inconsistent with *Price*, but would also be inconsistent with the proposition that criminal abortion cannot be committed recklessly.[17]

So, in practice, the law of England is much nearer to the law of Scotland than it might at first appear, for the most satisfactory way of proving that the doctor believed the woman to be pregnant is to show that she is in fact pregnant. Thus, in both jurisdictions, a criminal charge would be successful only if, for example, the family planner had fitted an IUD after receiving a positive result of a pregnancy test. Without a pregnancy being proved in Scotland, or without belief in a pregnancy being proved in England, no charge could successfully be brought for the implantation of an IUD.

Menstrual Extraction

Menstrual extraction is a post-coital procedure whereby the uterine contents are sucked out at around the time the woman would expect to begin menstruating. This may be done for genuinely therapeutic reasons, such as, for example, to assist a woman who suffers from dysmenorrhoea: or it may be done for birth control reasons, – that is, to extract any fertilized or implanted egg that may have been brought into existence by an episode of unprotected intercourse.

A charge of unlawful abortion through the use of such procedures would suffer the same difficulties of proof as those described above for the IUD. As with the IUD, it was pointed out by Bhiwandiwala *et al.* that 'without clear and compelling evidence of pregnancy in the individual case, the doctor may proceed on the presumption that the woman was not pregnant'.[18] However, they also point out that the doctor will be fully protected only when acting in good faith, and they conclude that 'wilful ignorance of pregnancy detectable beyond reasonable doubt by available means may be incriminating'.[19] If a woman asks for menstrual extraction because her period is late, this might be provided, but if it is requested specifically and solely because the woman has recently had mid-cycle unprotected sexual intercourse, it is difficult to accept that the procedure is provided in good faith to assist menstruation. In the early stages it might be impossible to prove pregnancy, but if the procedure is performed at a time when pregnancy could easily be detected and the doctor deliberately fails to make any attempt at detection, then her or his legal position would be much more precarious. The courts are perfectly willing to equate wilful ignorance with knowledge.

Post-coital Pills

High doses of certain contraceptive pills taken very shortly after unprotected intercourse (within 72 hours)[20] have high efficiency rates in preventing pregnancy. These will act in the main after fertilization: 'the altered hormonal environment probably upsets the sequence of events necessary for implantation'.[21] The intention is invariably to render the uterus inhospitable to implantation – that is, to prevent implantation rather than fertilization. For the reasons given above, and consistent with the view of the English Attorney General, expressed to the British Parliament,[22] post-coital pills therefore prevent pregnancy beginning, rather than interrupt already existing pregnancies.

To be criminally liable for abortion in England through the use of such pills, the doctor would have to be shown to believe that a pregnancy existed and that the pills would terminate it; to be criminally liable in Scotland it would additionally have to be shown that a pregnancy did in fact exist. But since these pills are effective contragestives only for 72 hours after unprotected intercourse, and pregnancy could never be established within so short a time, it follows that their use within that time could *never* amount to unlawful abortion.

Anti-progesterones and Anti-hCG Vaccines

Progesterone is a hormone produced by women that is essential to maintain a pregnancy. Without it, the lining of the womb is not able to take and hold a fertilized egg and allow it to develop. There has recently been developed an artificial steroid that temporarily blocks the progesterone receptors in the lining of the womb. As a result of its administration a fertilized egg would not be able to implant, and any already implanted eggs would be shed and lost. This steroid, initially known as RU486, or Mifepristone, can therefore be used as a contragestive agent preventing implantation (like the IUD and the post-coital pill), and also as an early abortifacient.[23] It is already in use in some countries.

Similarly, human chorionic gonadotrophin is a hormone produced by the early developing embryo which is essential to allow it to implant in the uterus. The WHO are funding the development of an anti-hCG vaccine that will encourage the woman's body to mount a hostile immune response to hCG. The neutralization of that hormone will render the embryo unable to implant itself, and the effect is therefore the same as with administration of anti-progesterones.[24]

The legality of both these methods used as contragestives is not in doubt, and the same principles would be applied as for the other methods discussed above that prevent implantation of the fertilized egg.[25] Their use to dislodge very recently implanted eggs would, on the other hand, amount to abortion but, again, the doctor's intent and knowledge will prove crucial. Any action upon very early embryos would be undetectable because their very existence could not be established at least for a number of days after implantation. So even if these methods did act upon very recently implanted embryos, no criminal liability could follow, because the existence of, or belief in, implantation could not be proved.

However, there is a difference between established contragestive methods and anti-progesterones like RU486, for the latter can dislodge the implanted egg at a much later stage when implantation is in fact detectable. If the doctor who administers RU486 is aware that the woman is pregnant (or wilfully ignorant of that fact) and it is administered with the intent to end that pregnancy and destroy the embryo, then there is no doubt that this would amount to abortion, just as late insertion of an IUD with that knowledge and intent would also amount to abortion. As a consequence, the use of RU486 after the doctor knows the woman is pregnant will be legal only insofar as the conditions in the abortion laws are satisfied. Roussel-Uclaf, the creators and developers of this drug, accept this, and are marketing it as an abortifacient rather than as a contragestive.

The provision of anti-progesterones only on satisfaction of the conditions in the appropriate abortion legislation would obviate any potential legal problems, but it does not, of course, silence criticism from the anti-abortion lobby. The evidence shows that anti-progesterones provide a safe and non-invasive method of early abortion, which does not involve either surgery or general anaesthesia or an overnight stay in hospital. The side effects so far reported have been of a minimal and acceptable nature, and are minimized if given in conjunction with a small dose of prostaglandin, which will, in fact, increase the success rate of the procedure.[26] Even if one disapproves of abortion, it has to be accepted that, where abortion is lawful, there is an ethical duty to perform it by the safest and most effective means. Indeed some countries, such as Italy,[27] make it a legal duty to provide abortion and other family planning services in the least hazardous way; and a strong argument could be made in other countries that it would be negligence on the doctor's part to provide a more invasive, more painful and more traumatic method when an easier and safer method is available. Indeed it might even amount to a deliberate infliction of unnecessary injury, just as it would be if a surgeon performs an operation without anaesthesia because he has moral objections to the use of anaesthetics. To deny RU486 when it would work and force women to undergo surgical operations instead is equally unacceptable, both in medical ethics and in law.

Historically the law has tried to protect women's health. Abortion was criminal in large part because of the dangers the operation previously posed to women. And abortion was legalized, particularly in the European countries, when it was realized that women were not inhibited from resorting to the most dangerous forms of 'back-street' abortions.[28] The law ought to continue to protect women's health, and so long as abortion remains legal this means making it as safe – that is, providing it as early – as possible. For its effect on women's health, the development and marketing of RU486 is the most significant medical development in birth control since the discovery of the contraceptive pill itself.

Notes

1 Cook, 'Anti-Progesterones and the Law,' 20 *IPPF Medical Bulletin* 2, 1986 at p. 2.

2 The British Human Fertilisation and Embryology Act 1990, defines fertilization, for the purposes of that Act, to be completed on the appearance of a two-cell zygote.

3 See, for example, Smith & Hogan, *Criminal Law*, 6th edn, Butterworths, London, 1988 at p. 367; Tunkel, 'Modern Anti-Pregnancy Techniques and the Criminal Law' [1974] *Crim. LR* 461, 1974 and 'Abortion: How Early, How Late and How Legal?' 2 *BMJ* 253 (1979); Keown, ' "Miscarriage": A Medico-Legal Analysis', *Crim LR* 604, 1984.
4 109 *Sup. Ct.* 3040, 106 *L. Ed.* 2d 410 (1989)
5 381 *US* 479, 14 *L. Ed.* 2d 510 (1965)
6 See, for example, Cusine, *New Reproductive Techniques; A Legal Perspective*, Dartmouth, Aldershot, 1989 and citations therein. Much of the material is now gathered in Kennedy & Grubb, *Medical Law: Text and Materials*, Butterworths, London 1989, at pp. 655–93.
7 The issue is further discussed by Kluge, 'Experimentation on Human Embryos' in Bromham *et al.*(eds), *Ethical Problems in Reproductive Medicine*, NAFPD, London, 1989.
8 Gordon, *Criminal Law of Scotland* 2nd edn, Green, Edinburgh, 1978 at p. 727, Smith & Hogan op. cit. note 3 above at pp. 310–11.
9 Cusine, op. cit., note 6 above, at p. 140 and note 49.
10 794 *F.* 2d 994 (1986).
11 For a discussion of this and other cases in the USA, see Clapp, 'State Regulation on Fetal Experimentation' 88 *Colum. LR* 1073 (1988).
12 Potts & Diggory, *Textbook of Contraceptive Practice* 2nd Edn, Cambridge University Press, Cambridge, 1983 at pp. 216–18.
13 'Post-Coital Contraception,' 1 *Lancet* 855, 1983, at p. 856.
14 (1968) 2 *All ER* 282.
15 Ibid. at p. 283, emphasis added.
16 'Abortion: How Early, How Late and How Legal?', 2 *BMJ* 253, 1979 at p. 254.
17 See Chapter 3.
18 Bhiwandiwala *et al;*, 'Menstrual Therapies in Commonwealth Asian Law', 20 *Int. J.Gyn. Obs.* 273, 1982.
19 Ibid. at p. 278.
20 See 'Post-Coital Contraception' 1 *Lancet* 855, 1983. At this stage the fertilized egg will have divided but a very few times, and will usually consist of only 16 cells.
21 Potts & Diggory op. cit., note 12 above at p. 202.
22 10 May 1983, *HC* Written Answers, Vol. 42, Col. 236/237.
23 RU486 has uses other than its contragestive one. So, for example, administration leads to complete foetal expulsion within 72 hours in the case of second trimester foetal death *in utero*. See Elia, 'Uses of RU486: A Clinical Update', 20 *IPPF Medical Bulletin* 1, 1986; Nieman *et al.*, 'The Progesterone Antagonist RU486: a Potential New Contraceptive Agent', 316 *New Eng. J. Med.* 187, 1987; Rodger & Baird, 'Induction of Therapeutic Abortion in Early Pregnancy' *Lancet* 1415, 1987; Couzinet *et al.*, 'Termination of Early Pregnancy by the Progesterone Antagonist RU486', 315 *New Eng. J. Med.* 1565, 1986.
24 See Griffin, 'Vaccines for Fertility Regulation' in *Research in Human Reproduction: Biennial Report: 1986–1987*, WHO, Geneva, 1988.
25 Although the rate of success in preventing pregnancy is currently too low, at least in relation to RU486, for this to be a useful contragestive agent.
26 See Rodger & Baird, op. cit., note 23 above.
27 Law No. 194, 22 May 1978.
28 This was recognized as the policy and purpose of the Abortion Act 1967 by Lord Keith in the House of Lords in *Royal College of Nursing v. DHSS* [1981] *AC* 800 at p. 835. In *Morgentaler, Smoling & Scott v. The Queen* (1988) 44 *DLR* (4th) 385, one of the major reasons given by the majority in the Supreme

Court of Canada for holding the Canadian abortion legislation unconstitutional was the fact that the delays the procedure created could have profound detrimental consequences on the woman's physical and emotional well-being. It was found that the legislation defeated the end of protecting the life and health of the pregnant woman, and was therefore unconstitutional. In the USA, on the other hand, the impetus for the legalization of abortion in *Roe v. Wade* 410 *US* 113, 35 *L. Ed.* 2d 147 (1973) seemed to come more from the recognition of the principle of autonomy of the individual – that is, the woman's right to choose.

5 The Rights of the Sexual Partner

Introduction

It should never be forgotten that the process of human reproduction necessarily requires two individuals – one to provide sperm, the other to provide an egg. Family planning is concerned with the interruption of that process and, practically speaking, it can always be effected by a single individual. Reproduction may take two, but birth control only needs one. This fact, combined with the fundamental principle of medical law that the only person who can consent to a medical procedure is the actual subject of that procedure, results in the position that family planning is effectively in the hands of the person whose bodily function is to be interfered with.

One view of the matter is that this is just as it should be. A woman's body may be affected by contraceptive pills, or by the implantation of an IUD and it is she, it might be argued, who should have the sole decision-making powers. Another view, however, is that, since the decision to reproduce (ideally) is a mutual and well considered one, so too ought the decision not to reproduce be mutual. After all, both partners to a heterosexual relationship will be significantly affected in their whole lifestyles whichever way the decision is made, and each may have understandable and recognized desires to become, or not to become, parents: both therefore, it can be argued, ought to have an input into the decision-making process. This argument is raised particularly often in relation to the abortion decision.

Some legal systems have rules that insist that family planning decisions require the consent of both partners, although these are usually framed more as rules of matrimonial law, giving husbands rights of decision over the bodies of their wives.[1] Few, if any, legal systems give such rights to the mere sexual partner of the person who will utilize the family planning method. But even in the absence of express legal provision, the law may recognize significant effects of a disagreement between partners on the issue of family planning.

This chapter will examine the ways in which the sexual partner – that is, the person who is not the direct subject of the family planning treatment – might acquire some legal right to take part in the decision-making process. The issue has reached the courts most frequently in relation to abortion, and to a lesser extent in relation to sterilization; but the principles to be discussed apply, where appropriate and *mutatis mutandis*, to all forms of family planning.

There are a number of different legal bases upon which a claim for partner's rights in the decision-making process can be based.

Matrimonial Rights

The marriage relationship is one that the law generally invests with many more characteristics and consequences than a merely sexual relationship. Marriage imposes rights and duties on both partners and requires the offices of the law both to create the relationship and to bring it to a close. Although sex has a central role to play in marriage,[2] and sexual relations are often described as matrimonial rights, marriage does not in fact give either party the right to insist that the other takes part in any sexual activity. Nor does marriage give the right either to insist that the other reproduce, or take steps to avoid reproduction. Similarly, marriage gives no right to either spouse to have any say in the medical treatment of the other. The law in Scotland and England, and in systems following English law, does not recognize proxy consent to medical treatment (except with parent and child), and any medical practice of consulting one spouse in relation to the medical treatment of the other has no validity or basis in law. A person's bodily integrity is an aspect of the individual's right to autonomy, and this is a personal right which cannot be compromised by a so-called 'right to reproduce' attaching to anyone else. Such a purported individual 'right to reproduce' cannot possibly exist, even within marriage, so long as reproduction requires the bodily functions of two individuals.[3]

The result of this is that, in the absence of legislation requiring spousal consent, family planning can be provided to an individual without consultation with the individual's spouse. However, even in countries like Scotland and England where there is no legislation requiring spousal consent, medical practice can sometimes have the effect of preventing the free availability of certain forms of family planning to married persons. The medical profession has its own ethical rules – or at least practices – in relation to a number of different issues in medicine. Many surgeons will, for example, refuse to perform a vasectomy on a young unmarried man with no children, notwithstanding that the patient might be fully competent to make up his own mind about the issue. Similarly, doctors often insist (although not as often as in the past) on spousal consultation or consent before performing a purely contraceptive sterilization on a married patient; and many consent forms reflect this, notwithstanding that there is no legal requirement for any such spousal participation. This attitude is sometimes justified by reference to professional ethics, but more often by reference to fear of the perceived legal consequences. That fear is generally unfounded, for the law in most jurisdictions does not give one spouse rights over the other which a family planning procedure on the latter would infringe.[4]

However, the courts have traditionally given great weight to common medical practice, and for this reason medical practice can indirectly affect the law's attitudes. This is illustrated by the case of *Bravery v. Bravery*,[5] in which a woman sought to divorce her husband on the ground of cruelty. Her case was based on the husband allegedly having undergone a vasectomy operation against her wishes. The wife claimed that she had not been asked for her consent, but no evidence was led on this point. However, in the absence of evidence one way or the other, Evershed M. R. and Hodson L.J. concluded that she *must* have given consent, for this reason:

> We find it difficult to believe that any surgeon, a member of an honourable profession, would perform an operation of this kind on a young married man, unless he were first satisfied that the wife consented.[6]

On this point, Denning L.J. took a much more realistic approach by pointing out that, since there was no evidence at all that the surgeons had ever asked for the wife's consent, it should not be presumed that she had consented. Although the majority did not hold that there is a legal obligation to obtain spousal consent for a sterilization operation, they were clearly of the view that it would be bad medical practice to fail to do so. If the law were to insist on 'good medical practice' and claim that good practice is to obtain spousal consent, then effectively a veto power is created. However, even if it were common practice to obtain spousal consent, which, in Scotland and England it probably no longer is, it is difficult to see what, in law, could happen to a doctor who did not follow this 'good medical practice'. If no legal right has been infringed – and none is – then no legal consequence will follow. The implication in the majority judgement in *Bravery* is therefore wrong (and probably always has been).

In the USA the question of spousal rights has been raised directly in relation both to sterilization operations, and to abortion. As regards sterilization, the US courts have consistently refused to recognize a requirement that a person wishing a sterilization must obtain spousal authorization thereto,[7] primarily on the ground that a continued ability to reproduce is not to be regarded as an essential feature of marriage.

Much more contentious has been the issue of abortion, and rather stronger claims have been made for a spousal right of veto in relation to this operation, with which, it is said, both spouses have much stronger rights. It is argued that what strengthens these alleged rights is the fact that the partners have interests not only in relation to each other (as with other forms of family planning), but also in relation to an independent existing entity, such being the potential human life of the foetus.

When the US Supreme Court liberalized the American abortion laws in the case of *Roe v. Wade*,[8] it did not comment upon the issue of whether a statute giving a woman's husband some right in the decision-making process would be constitutional, because the statute in *Roe* contained no such provision.[9] It was not long, however, before a statute with just such a provision was directly challenged. In *Planned Parenthood of Central Missouri v. Danforth*,[10] the Supreme Court, by a majority, held unconstitutional a provision in a Missouri statute that gave a husband a right of veto over his wife's decision to abort the child she was carrying (this whether or not the husband was the father). The statute had required the husband's prior written consent to any abortion during the first 12 weeks of pregnancy unless it was necessary in order to preserve the life of the mother.[11] It had been argued by the state in support of this provision that states had an interest in regulating marriages to protect the institution of marriage itself; that a husband has an interest, which ought to be protected, in his wife's child-bearing capacity and that since the decision to change the family structure by having a child was generally set in motion by mutual consent, the decision to terminate such a change should also be taken by mutual agreement.

None of these reasons stands up to close examination. The state may indeed have an interest in protecting the institution of marriage, and in that way the structure of society as presently constituted; but that protection will not be achieved by giving the husband a right in all cases to decide his wife's medical treatment. This might disrupt rather than strengthen the marriage relationship if, for example, the husband is not the father of the child. Similarly, while a husband may have an interest in his wife's child-bearing capacity, the wife has a right to her own bodily integrity, which must be at least as strong as the husband's right: the husband's right would only be stronger if it amounted to a right to control the woman's body, and the law gives no such right. And, finally, it is extremely unrealistic to assume that conception is invariably a matter of deliberate choice and mutual consent. Ideally that is as it should be, and the law ought to encourage this ideal; but the law must also recognize that, in reality, a very large percentage of conceptions are not the result of a careful and mutually considered decision.

The Supreme Court held the spousal consent provision unconstitutional, the majority doing so on a rather narrow ground of constitutional law. They pointed out that *Roe v. Wade* had established that the state has no right to veto a woman's decision to terminate her pregnancy in the first trimester, and they concluded from this that the state could not therefore constitutionally delegate such a right of veto to any other person, not even the woman's husband. Stewart and Powell JJ., in a minority concurring opinion, found the issue rather more difficult than the majority acknowledged, primarily because the Court in previous decisions had recognized that a man's right to father children and enjoy the association of his offspring was a constitutionally protected freedom. However, they ultimately came to the same conclusion as the majority, although on the slightly different ground that *Roe* established a woman's right to decide and that the woman's interest in the pregnancy was far greater than the man's because of the interference upon her body that the pregnancy constituted. Thus a spousal veto which gave a husband greater rights than his wife in cases of conflict was an unconstitutional breach of the rights recognized in *Roe*.

Wardle and Wood[12] are not persuaded by the approach of the majority in *Danforth*, on the ground that the power of veto is not a state interest but a personal interest that the state is entitled to protect. Yet the whole reasoning in *Roe v. Wade* suggests that the state *does* have interests, though of different types, throughout the pregnancy.[13] The Supreme Court in *Roe* emphatically rejected the proposition that the woman's right of decision was absolute, and it recognized that the state may have an interest in preventing an abortion in the later stages of pregnancy. It is therefore not unreasonable to suggest from this that the state has an interest in protecting the woman's free choice in the earlier stages. All the conflicting interests must be balanced, with different weights at different stages being attached to each of these interests. If the state's interest is weaker than the woman's interest during the first trimester, the husband's interest must also be weaker.

A rather more serious criticism of the reasoning of the majority is that it is entirely dependent on the absence of state power during the first trimester. But *Roe* clearly establishes that, in the third trimester, the state does have power to regulate, even prohibit, abortion. Thus there would be nothing constitutionally to prevent the state delegating that power to a spouse at that stage. The opinion of the minority, not being dependent on the issue of delegation, but rather on the greater weight to be given to the woman's interests than the man's in the rights equation, is therefore much stronger in its rejection of absolute spousal veto.

From the above it is clear that marriage, in itself, does not give spouses the right to determine the other's family planning methods. Rather than trying to establish matrimonial rights, partners in many Commonwealth jurisdictions have sought instead to claim remedies that will give them some say in the decision-making process. There are a number of possible remedies that might be used.

Injunction or Interdict

An injunction (interdict in Scotland) is a court order designed to restrain a person from performing a threatened action. The action must amount to a civil or criminal wrong, and the person applying for the injunction must be someone whose legally recognized rights or interests will be adversely affected if the injunction is not granted. If the party against whom an injunction is issued breaches that court order, this will amount to contempt of court and could lead to imprisonment.

To use contraception or to undergo a sterilization operation is not a civil or criminal wrong on the part of the patient, and an injunction would therefore never be available to prevent a patient accepting such treatment. It has been said judicially by an English judge, 'No court would ever grant an injunction to stop sterilization or vasectomy'.[14]

However, abortion is quite different in that it can sometimes amount to a legal wrong; and there have been a number of attempts in various jurisdictions to seek an injunction to prevent a woman carrying out her decision to have an abortion. There are a number of hurdles that any applicant for such an injunction would have to clear, and Commonwealth and other courts have consistently rejected these applications.[15] The hurdles are as follows.

Title to Sue

The first hurdle to be surmounted is to prove that the applicant has title to raise the action. He must establish that he possesses some interest which is entitled to legal protection and which will be denied if the injunction is not granted. Some statutes in the USA expressly confer standing to sue on the father,[16] but the writer is unaware of any such statute in a Commonwealth jurisdiction. Applicants have therefore had to base their claims on some common law right. Most applicants have argued that they have title to sue because they are married to the pregnant woman. For example, in *Paton v. Trustees of the British Pregnancy Advisory Service*,[17] a husband applied to the English court for an injunction to restrain his wife and the British Pregnancy Advisory Service from causing or permitting an abortion to be carried out on his wife without his consent. Sir George Baker P. refused to grant the injunction, saying that a husband has no right to stop his wife having a legal abortion. He held that a father of an illegitimate child would have no rights over that child except insofar as statute states otherwise, and that therefore the plaintiff's claim could only be founded on the fact that he was the mother's husband. But he held further that a husband, simply by being a husband, or by being a husband and a father, has no rights recognized by law. Baker P. said:

> The only way [the plaintiff] can put the case is that the husband has a right to have a say in the destiny of the child he has conceived [sic]. The law of England gives him no such right.[18]

As the plaintiff had no enforceable legal right, he had no title to apply for an injunction to restrain a breach of it.

That conclusion was not challenged in the later English case of *C. v. S.*,[19] which involved an unmarried couple. The father claimed title in this instance on the basis of having a 'personal interest', which was not as high as a legal right, to prevent a threatened crime concerning the life of his unborn child. Heilbron J. held that he had no such interest recognizable in law, as the proposed abortion in the present case was not illegal; and there was no indication that title would have been established even had the court in that case considered the proposed abortion to be illegal.

On the other hand, some Canadian courts have held that a man who was both father and husband, might indeed have sufficient title, *qua* husband, to apply for an injunction to prevent the abortion of his child. In the first *Medhurst* case[20] it was held that the husband of a pregnant woman had sufficient standing to raise the action if the abortion was allegedly illegal, because he was 'a person directly affected' by the abortion legislation. Reid J. said this:

> The husband has a direct interest in the issue of compliance with the law which, in my view, entitles him to bring this application on his own behalf, and his lack of any right to withhold consent or to be consulted does not deprive him of the right to resort to this court to assert or protect that interest. I cannot think of anyone more entitled to the court's protection of that interest than a husband.[21]

The judge here found it 'difficult to think of anyone who could have an interest equal to that of a husband in the pregnancy of his wife',[22] and in support he cited the Supreme Court of Canada's decision in *Minister of Justice for Canada v. Borowski*,[23] which had recognized that a husband would be 'directly affected' by the wife's abortion decision (even though the applicant in that case was neither a husband nor a potential father).

This approach concentrates on the father as being the mother's husband, which is rather illogical. The male interest in a pregnancy surely lies more directly with the father of the foetus than with the husband of the pregnant woman; and since there will always be a father, while only usually a husband, the right to challenge the woman ought logically to attach (if at all) to the man because of his potential fatherhood rather than because of his marriage. Yet Reid J. in *Medhurst* expressly refused to consider the position of the father, and he recognized title to sue only in the woman's husband.

In other cases it has been argued that the unborn child has title to seek an injunction, and actions have been raised on their behalf (normally by the potential fathers). If the abortion is otherwise legal, such a claim would have to be based on the foetus's alleged 'right to life'. In England, an unborn child has been held to have no such right. In *Paton v. Trustees of the British Pregnancy Advisory Service* Baker P. held (although this was *obiter)* that a foetus has no title to seek an injunction, because any rights that English law recognizes as attaching to a foetus are dependent for their legal effect on the child being born alive. The foetus cannot therefore have an enforceable right to life, and consequently a case could never be raised on its behalf.[24] When the husband in *Paton* took his case to the European Commission of Human Rights,[25] he alleged, *inter alia*, that Article 2 of the European Convention on Human Rights, (which guarantees 'everyone' the right to life) was breached by the Abortion Act 1967. The Commission held that the word 'everyone', as used in the Convention, was not intended to cover the unborn child. The approach was accepted by the Court of Appeal in the later English case of *C. v. S.*[26] The same conclusion has been reached in Canada. In *Borowski v. Attorney General for Canada*[27] it had been argued that the legalization of abortion in Canada breached the Canadian Charter of Rights and Freedoms by denying the foetus the right to life, which right is protected by Art. 7 of that Charter. The Saskatchewan Court of Appeal held that when the Charter says 'everyone' shall have a right to life, that word does not include the unborn, because a foetus has never been recognized by Canadian law or the law of any other Western democracy as being a legal person to whom legal rights and protections can attach.

When *Borowski* reached the Supreme Court of Canada,[28] it was decided that the issue as posed in that case was too theoretical, and the Court therefore refused to rule on the rights of the foetus. Shortly thereafter, in *Tremblay v. Daigle,*[29] the Supreme Court did decide the issue, and it unanimously overturned a decision of the Quebec Court of Appeal that had decided that a foetus possessed a civil status entitling it to protection against a mother who wished to abort it for 'insufficient reasons'. The Supreme Court held that any rights the law conferred on the foetus were conditional on its being born alive, and that before then it did not have a sufficient status to give it title to sue to prevent its own abortion.[30]

Injunctions and the Criminal Law

Slightly different considerations would be relevant if the proposed abortion were alleged to be criminal. In the English case of *C. v. S.*,[31] an unmarried man tried to raise an action on behalf of his unborn child, arguing not only that it had a right to life, but also that it had an interest to prevent itself being the victim of a criminal act. The plaintiff based his claim on the allegation that the proposed abortion of a foetus between 18 and 21 weeks old would amount (for the reasons discussed in Chapter 3) to the (English) crime of child destruction under the Infant Life (Preservation) Act 1929. The court dismissed the action on behalf of the child on the ground that it had no *locus standi*, even to prevent a crime, for it was not, until its live birth, a legal person.

Many continental legal systems allow private individuals to restrain breaches of the criminal law. There, and possibly in Scotland also,[32] the *actio popularis* may give private citizens the right to raise actions to prevent the commission of public wrongs. However, there is much doubt as to whether this procedure is available to prevent breaches of the criminal law, and it is unlikely to be a satisfactory means of controlling a pregnant woman's powers of decision in relation to abortion. In most common law jurisdictions no general right exists which allows private individuals to seek restraint of threatened breaches of the criminal law.[33] To have title, the applicant must possess a legal right, attaching to him as an individual, which is threatened or breached. In *Dehler v. Ottawa Civic Hospital*[34] it was held by the Ontario High Court (affirmed by the Ontario Court of Appeal)[35] that the plaintiff in that case, who had raised an action for the protection of all unborn children, had no title as he had no independent right that was being breached by the existence of a law permitting abortion. The English courts would certainly follow this approach.

A father (or indeed any other person) who believes that the performance of a particular abortion will amount to a breach of the criminal law could of course request the law enforcing agencies to act. This is only possible, of course, when the proposed abortion is allegedly criminal. While these agencies can normally act only after the commission of an offence, it is open to the Attorney General in England or the Lord Advocate in Scotland to seek an injunction or interdict to prevent the threatened commission of a crime. In a case before the High Court of Australia,[36], the Attorney General of Queensland stepped in and took over an application for injunction raised by the father. This obviated all difficulties concerning title to raise the action.

But even if title to sue to prevent a criminal act could be established there are still significant problems. An injunction to restrain a woman from undergoing a criminal abortion is, in essence, a civil procedure being used to prevent an alleged breach of the criminal law. This causes difficulties in principle, for not only is the standard of proof between civil and criminal cases different, but the penalties laid down by the criminal law are of a different order from those applicable to a breach of a civil court order: the penalty for the latter may be quite inappropriate for the nature of the crime.

This difficulty was first mentioned in this context in the *Paton* case, although the discussion was *obiter* since there was no challenge to the legality of the proposed abortion in that case. Baker P. did not think that it would be right to issue an injunction to prevent the commission of a criminal abortion. He said:

> Not only would it be a bold and brave judge . . . who would seek to interfere with the discretion of doctors acting under the 1967 Act, but I think he would really be a foolish judge who would try to do any such thing, unless possibly, there is clear bad faith and an obvious attempt to perpetrate a criminal offence. Even then, of

> course, the question is whether that is a matter which should be left to the Director of Public Prosecutions and the Attorney General.[37]

These remarks were repeated and applied in *C. v. S.*, in which it was claimed that the proposed abortion would amount to a breach of the Infant Life (Preservation) Act 1929. Heilbron J. at first instance said:

> Such an injunction should not issue, in any event, on evidence which is conflicting, or uncertain as here, and, in my opinion, for such an injunction to issue there must, most importantly, be strong evidence against the proposed defendant and virtual certainty that what is being complained of constitutes a defined criminal offence. Every case depends on its own facts and circumstances and none more so than this, for the greater the offence the more vital it is, before an injunction issues to interfere with the operative procedures being prepared because of the risk to the health of Miss S., that it is shown that an offence is virtually certain to be committed, if no injunction issues.[38]

The Court of Appeal, the next day, refused an appeal (quoting with approval Baker P.'s comments in *Paton)* and, on the same day, the House of Lords dismissed the plaintiff's petition to appeal to that chamber.

In neither *Paton* nor *C. v. S.* was an injunction considered appropriate, but nor does either of these cases deny absolutely the civil court's right in an appropriate case to issue an injunction to restrain a threatened criminal abortion. Heilbron J. indicated her willingness to issue an injunction if there was 'strong evidence' and 'virtual certainty' that the threatened abortion would be criminal. Baker P. suggested that a case of 'clear bad faith and an obvious attempt to perpetrate a criminal offence' might allow a court to issue an injunction.

Clearly this goes beyond the civil standard of proof required in normal civil court proceedings, and it is a standard that will in most cases prove difficult or impossible to satisfy. In the *Kerr* case, Gibbs C.J. in the High Court of Australia refused to grant an injunction to the Attorney General of Queensland to restrain a woman undergoing an allegedly criminal abortion. He held that 'while there is no doubt that in appropriate cases the courts will grant an injunction to restrain a breach of the criminal law', in the present case he would not do so because it appeared 'quite unjustifiable . . . to assume that the respondent would be convicted by a jury of an offence . . . if she proceeded to have an abortion'.[39] This identifies a very real difficulty with attempting to use this civil procedure to prevent breaches of the criminal law:

in order to issue the injunction, the court would have to assume guilt on the part of the woman and her medical advisers. No court would be keen to assume guilt in the absence of a criminal hearing and all the procedural protections that such a hearing gives.

Public Policy

Even if all the above difficulties could be surmounted, an action might still not be successful. Injunction and interdict are discretionary remedies which the court is not required to grant even if the applicant proves his case. The remedy will not be granted if there are policy reasons against doing so. The courts have identified a number of policy objections to allowing a woman's sexual partner to prevent her undergoing an abortion.

For example, Baker P. in *Paton* pointed out that if the husband in that case were to be successful in his application for an injunction, then it could only be enforced by restraining the mother from carrying into effect a decision concerning her own body. Yet this would go against a fundamental principle of the law:

> The law is that the court cannot and would not seek to enforce or restrain by injunction matrimonial obligations, if they be obligations such as sexual intercourse or contraception . . . No court could ever grant an injunction to stop sterilisation or vasectomy. Personal family relationships in marriage cannot be enforced by an order of a court.[40]

Similarly in *Kerr*, Gibbs C.J. pointed out that even if the applicant could satisfy the standard of proof required,

> . . . there are limits to the extent to which the law should intrude upon personal liberty and personal privacy in the pursuit of moral and religious aims. Those limits would be overstepped if an injunction were to be granted in the present case.[41]

The difficulty with an injunction of this nature is that it affects the personal liberty of the woman, and any sanction for breach of the injunction would therefore be quite unacceptable to the courts. As Baker P. put it in *Paton*:

> No judge could even consider sending a husband or wife to prison for breaking such an order.[42]

The most significant issue of policy is the protection of the woman's human right to decide for herself what will be done to her own body. To allow a husband or any other person to obtain an injunction against a pregnant woman would – certainly if the abortion were otherwise legal – constitute a breach of the European Convention on Human Rights, which, by Article 8, protects the right to private and family life. The unsuccessful plaintiff in *Paton* took the British government to the European Commission of Human Rights,[43] alleging, *inter alia,* that his right to respect for his private and family life had been breached by his wife's aborting their child. The Commission pointed out that the woman too has this right, and that the breach of the man's right was justified 'as being necessary for the protection of the rights of another person' – that is the rights of the woman to respect for *her* private life. The Commission, in an approach reflecting strongly that of the minority concurring opinion of the Supreme Court of America in *Planned Parenthood of Central Missouri v. Danforth,*[45] held that the competing rights of the woman and the man to respect for their family lives had to be weighed up, and that the woman's rights were always stronger. It concluded:

> Any interpretation of the husband's and potential father's right, under Article 8 of the Convention, to respect for his private and family life, as regards an abortion to which his wife intends to have performed on her, must first of all take into account the right of the pregnant woman, being the person primarily concerned in the pregnancy and its continuation or termination, to respect for her private life.[46]

This gives the ultimate answer. The effects that pregnancy has on the woman, her family life and her bodily privacy, are *always* far greater, during the pregnancy, than the effects it has on the man. It is therefore her decision that must prevail at the end of the day.

Judicial Review

Similar reasoning to the above would be applied in relation to applications for judicial review, a procedure that has also been used in a number of Commonwealth courts in attempts to prevent a woman undergoing the abortion she wants. Very basically, if any public body acts or makes a decision that will affect other people, then any affected person may seek judicial review of the act or decision on the ground that it was unreasonable and ought therefore to be overturned. An unreasonable decision or action in this context is determined by the '*Wednesbury* test' – that is, whether the decision is one that is based on irrelevant considerations; one that is so absurd that no sensible person would ever have made it; or one that is made in bad faith.[47] This is a very strict test: the applicant must show not only that the action would be considered unreasonable by the court, but also that the action is such that no reasonable actor would have done it.

In order for a decision or action to be open to judicial review, the applicant must establish that some public element is involved, for judicial review is essentially a public law remedy. A health authority carrying out a statutory function would almost certainly be carrying out a public function, and would thus be open to challenge by this procedure.[48] However, not all decisions within a public body such as, for example, the British National Health Service, would be considered to be public decisions.[49] The problem of deciding whether a decision or action contains a public element is particularly acute in English law, where there is a strict dichotomy between public and private law.[50] In other Commonwealth jurisdictions such a strict dichotomy is not accepted.[51] In Scotland, also, the boundary between public and private law is not so strictly adhered to as in England; and in any case there exists the remedy of reduction of a decision in Scotland, which is open for any administrative or quasi-judicial act, whether it is public or private.[52]

Now, most of a doctor's relations with her or his patients will be purely private matters, with no public element at all. So a doctor's decision to prescribe contraceptives, or a surgeon's decision to perform a sterilization, would not be open to judicial review. The abortion decision, on the other hand, might be public or private depending upon the procedures that have to be undergone in any particular legal system. In Scotland and England, certificates have to be granted by two doctors and then notified to a government department. This is unlikely to be considered to be a public act. The power to grant certificates belongs to doctors as individuals: the Abortion Act 1967 significantly gave that power to doctors and not to health authorities acting through doctors. Judicial review would therefore not be available in relation to these certificates in Scotland or in England[53] (although in Scotland they would be subject to an action of reduction). In other countries where there is more public control of abortion, the conclusion might be different. In Canada before *Morgentaler, Smoling & Scott v. The Queen*[54] therapeutic abortion committees rather than individual doctors decided whether or not a woman could have an abortion, and such decisions were considered to be open to judicial review.[55]

Once it has been determined that the decision is open to judicial review, the applicant must prove he has title to seek it – that is, he must show that some legally recognized interest of his will be affected by the decision. Most applications for judicial review of the abortion decision have been raised by potential fathers, and they have generally failed in the face of the same difficulties as those discussed above in relation to the remedy of injunction or interdict: just because they are *affected* by a decision does not give them a title to challenge that decision.

A different applicant raised the action in the New Zealand case of *Wall v. Livingstone*.[56] Here, the application for judicial review was made not by the father but by a doctor who had examined a pregnant woman and who had decided that she did not come within the terms of the New Zealand Contraception, Sterilisation and Abortion Act 1977. When two of his colleagues later decided that the woman *did* come within the terms of that Act and issued the required certificates to that effect, the original doctor sought to overturn these certificates by way of judicial review. The action failed on the issue of title to sue, the New Zealand Court of Appeal holding that no-one other than the mother would be able to establish sufficient right or interest that was allegedly being affected by the certificates. The Court pointed out:

> Whatever their concerns may be individuals outside the direct ambit of the Act could not possibly show that the exercise of statutory powers under these provisions would operate to their personal advantage or disadvantage. It follows therefore that no individual who is not one of the *statutory participants* could ever be regarded as having a sufficient interest to institute proceedings for judicial review.[57]

The 'statutory participants' in the abortion decision are restricted, the New Zealand court held, to the mother and her medical advisers. The father was implicitly excluded.

A different approach was however adopted in Canada. In the first *Medhurst* case[58] it was established that a father did have title to seek an injunction, and in the second *Medhurst* case[59] the father sought judicial review of the decision of a hospital therapeutic abortion committee to provide his wife with an abortion. The judge in this case, Krever J., was prepared for the purposes of argument to assume title, although he was expressly not prepared to make a definitive pronouncement to that effect.

However, even when the abortion decision can be challenged, and even when someone can be found with title to make the challenge, a further hurdle must be surmounted: it must be shown that the decision was unreasonable in the *Wednesbury* sense given above. It was at this stage that the second *Medhurst* case ultimately failed. Krever J. held that a decision could not be quashed just because there was insufficient evidence to support it: rather the applicant must himself lead evidence to show that the decision is insupportable. Otherwise the court's judgement as to whether an abortion should be performed would be substituted for that of the committee to which Parliament had delegated the task.

> Only if there is no evidence [to support the opinion], or possibly if the opinion could be shown to be perverse, is a court entitled to interfere.[60]

Although Canadian abortion law is currently in a state of flux, the principles in this case would be appropriate for other jurisdictions that allow judicial review of the abortion decision. The policy difficulties with injunction discussed above do not apply here, for (unlike a successful application for injunction) a successful action for judicial review would not constitute any infringement of a woman's fundamental freedoms: all it does is to quash the particular decision and it would be open for the woman to obtain a fresh decision from another doctor in her favour.[61]

Guardianship of the Unborn Child

In some of the cases mentioned above, attempts were made to sue on behalf of the unborn child and, mostly, it was held that the unborn child had no title to sue. However, this does not mean that the unborn child lacks all of the law's protections. It has been argued that the unborn child can have such a status that the law will, in some circumstances, protect it. Certainly this is true in the sense that, as most legal systems do not allow abortion on demand, the potential human life in the unborn child is to that extent protected. Whether it could be protected in any wider sense depends upon whether a foetus is susceptible to certain legal institutions, such as wardship or custody.

For a number of years the possibility of making an unborn child a ward of court had been mooted in the academic literature as a means of protecting a foetus.[62] Any decision relating to a ward of court has to be made in the ward's best interests, and it would almost certainly never be in the best interests of the foetus for it to be aborted, even if it were severely handicapped.[63] However, the Court of Appeal in England decided in the case of *Re F. (In Utero)*[64] that the courts have no jurisdiction to make an unborn child a ward of court.[65] In this case a woman whom a local authority considered wholly unsuited to motherhood became pregnant. So, for its safety, the local authority applied to have the child made a ward of court shortly before it was due to be born.

Although holding that, had such a jurisdiction existed, they would have had no hesitation in exercising it in the present case, the Court of Appeal unanimously held that the English courts had no jurisdiction to ward a child *in utero*. In law, a child only achieves full personhood on birth: the statutory provisions relating to children, such as s. 1 of the Family Law Reform Act 1969, all assume that minority – the earliest form of legal personhood – commences on birth.[66] Further, in principle, the application was misconceived as it was, in reality, an application to control the mother and would therefore create a conflict between the existing legal interests of the mother and those of the unborn child. There would necessarily be, in the words of May L.J., 'an inherent incompatibility between any projected exercise of wardship jurisdiction and the rights and welfare of the mother'.[67] As in *C. v. S.*, the court was very unwilling to allow an application on behalf of one person that could only be enforced by limiting severely the rights and liberties of another. It is this factor that distinguishes the unborn from the born child, and which justifies the court casting 'an immediate cloak of protection' over a live-born child, while denying the right of anyone to interfere with the decision of the doctors and the mother legally to destroy the unborn child.[68] Wardship is therefore not an appropriate procedure to protect an unborn child, and no-one can use it to take away the right and power of decision-making from the pregnant woman.

Not all legal systems recognize the institution of wardship, so even if that procedure could be used to take the decision-making process out of the hands of the pregnant woman, (which it cannot), it would be irrelevant in countries like Scotland, which have no concept of wardship. However, in Scotland (and indeed in England now that the wardship door has been so firmly closed) an application for custody might serve the same purpose if the court could be persuaded to grant custody of the unborn child to someone other than the pregnant woman. The right of custody carries with it the right to make the important decisions concerning a child's future – for example, its name, religion, place of residence, education and medical treatment. One of the usual consequences of the right to custody is the right to physical possession, but there is no reason in principle why one person may not have the right physically to possess a child while another exercises the other custodial rights concerning the child.[69]

Now, clearly, a decision to undergo an abortion is a 'matter of real importance' affecting the future of the foetus, and if the court could be persuaded to grant *de iure* custody over a child in the womb to the father, or a third party, even while *de facto* custody must, of necessity, remain with the pregnant woman, then he could expect to be consulted on that important decision. In an old Scottish case, *Murray v. Merschall*,[70] the Court of Session decided that a father could appoint, by will, a tutor over his child in the womb but not yet born at the time of the father's death, but it is unclear from the short report what rights the tutor could exercise before the child's birth or even whether the appointment took effect on the death of the father or the birth of the child.

This is a doubtful precedent today, for the exercise of any 'right' by the guardian would necessarily involve controlling the pregnant woman: while it may have been socially and legally acceptable in sixteenth-century Scotland, the Scottish courts today are far more likely to follow the English approach of giving precedence to the personal liberty of the woman, the right to which she does not lose merely by becoming pregnant. On the other hand, in the USA, there are a number of decisions in which women have been forced, against their wills, to undergo caesarian sections, or have been compulsorily hospitalized, for the alleged benefit of the unborn child.[71] The English cases discussed above suggest firmly that such an approach would not be adopted in England.

And, of course, the claim for custody would also fail on the ground that the court would not be persuaded that a foetus is a child over whom parental rights can in any way be exercised. In Scotland a child in the womb can have certain rights, but, as in England, these rights only crystallize once the child has been born alive. People do not become parents, in either lay or legal terms, until the moment of birth. While a pregnant woman clearly exercises *de facto* rights of decision concerning the foetus she is carrying, this is not, while the child is still in the womb, the exercise of 'parental rights'.

Indirect Effects of Unilateral Family Planning Decisions

From the above it is clear that, in the law in most jurisdictions, a decision to accept any form of family planning procedure is a matter for the single individual who will have to undergo the procedure, rather than for the sexual partner who may be affected by it. No-one other than the person whose body is affected, either by hormonal, mechanical, or surgical means, may make the decision. This is as it should be. If a woman is pregnant, her interests in her own body are far greater than the potential father's interests. It cannot be denied that it is socially unfortunate for the parties to disagree on such an important issue, but the fact remains that if there is a disagreement, say, as to whether to have an abortion or not, one partner must prevail. There is no compromise.

To argue in favour of a father's right to prevent an abortion, through whatever legal procedure, is to argue in favour of a control over a woman's body that not even the courts are currently willing to exercise, far less give to another person.

However, although the decision to accept a family planning procedure is to be made only by the person whose body is involved, this is not to say that the way the decision is made will not have legal effects. If there is real disagreement between the two partners, and one acts in some way against the wishes of the other, then a number of legal consequences can follow.

Matrimonial Relief

If the sexual partners are married, a disagreement about family planning may have significant matrimonial consequences. For example, if a man insisted on wearing a condom, or on practising coitus interruptus, in the knowledge that his wife wished to have children, and knowing that the denial of this opportunity caused her great distress, then it could be argued that this amounted to behaviour such that it is unreasonable to expect the wife to continue living with him. This would justify a divorce under s. 1(2)(b) of the (English) Matrimonial Causes Act 1973 and s. 1 (2)(b) of the Divorce (Scotland) Act 1976. In the English case of *Bravery v. Bravery*[72] the Court of Appeal said that it would not be difficult to construct a case of grave cruelty towards a wife founded on the progressive hurt to her health caused by an operation for sterilization undergone by her husband in disregard of, or contrary to, the wife's wishes and 'natural instincts'.[73] Although there is no reported Scottish or English decision to this effect, it is probably also the case that a wife's decision to undergo an abortion in the face of her husband's strong opposition might, in some circumstances, amount to behaviour such that the husband could no longer reasonably be expected to live with her.

However, as with the refusal of sex itself,[74] the mere fact of undergoing an abortion or sterilization operation, or utilizing some contraceptive method, without spousal consent would not in itself be regarded as being unreasonable, and the dissatisfied spouse would have to establish some other element to satisfy the test in s. 1(2)(b) of the English or Scottish Act. Just because the spouses disagree, even on an issue as fundamental to their futures as whether or not to have children, this should not justify matrimonial relief. But if, for example, the decision to avoid reproduction could be shown to have been taken simply to spite the other partner, or in disregard of the known strong desire of the other, this might be sufficient. On the other hand, if a woman obtains an abortion or undergoes a sterilization purely for health reasons, then this is not likely to be held unreasonable behaviour. Indeed, her husband's opposition in these circumstances is more likely to be deemed to be unreasonable. Between these two extremes, where most cases will probably lie, it is impossible to lay down categorical rules, except to state that the spousal opposition will be one of the factors taken into account by the court in determining whether the adoption of a family planning method is behaviour such as to justify a divorce. The onus, as always, is on the claimant to establish that the behaviour is such as to come within the terms of s. 1(2)(b).

It is to be remembered that any matrimonial consequences are, of course, irrelevant in relation to unmarried couples.

Maintenance and Aliment

The financial obligation to look after a child or provide for its maintenance, although once significantly affected by the question of whether the child was legitimate or not, does not, in many jurisdictions, now depend upon marriage between the parents. Many legal systems (including Scotland and England) impose a duty on both parents to provide for their children, whether or not the parents are married to each other. However, a consequence of imposing an obligation to maintain or to aliment a child upon both parents, when the decision to reproduce can be taken or frustrated by only one partner, is that in effect one partner's unilateral decision can have significant financial consequences for both. Historically, of course, the law has assumed that the obligation to aliment a child is the price to be paid for indulging in sexual intercourse; but with the freedom conferred by the wide availability of family planning services, this rationale breaks down.

If the financial consequences of heterosexual activity *can* be avoided, then the question arises of whether both parties have a *duty* to avoid them on behalf of the other. This question was raised (by the sheriff) in the Scottish decision of *Bell v. McCurdie*.[75] Here the sheriff held that a woman's failure to use the contraceptive pills that she possessed would diminish her paramour's liability to aliment the resulting child. He said:

> In my opinion, in this modern day and age when a young girl knows about contraception, and has a supply of contraceptive pills available for her own use, and readily embarks on a regular course of sexual relations with her boyfriend, she must be taken in law to have voluntarily assumed the risk of falling pregnant, and can only

> have herself largely to blame if that unfortunate event occurs subsequently.[76]

The sheriff pointed out that s. 1(2) of the then extant Illegitimate Children (Scotland) Act 1930 allowed the court to determine the shares of aliment to be provided by each parent according to all the circumstances of the case and he held that the relative failure of a duty to take contraceptive precautions was one of those relevant circumstances. Although he found that the boyfriend, in the present case, also had a duty to take contraceptive measures himself if he wished to avoid the consequences (that is, the legal consequence of having to pay aliment), he held that the girl was more to blame; thus he fixed the aliment payable by the father at the nominal figure of £1 per week.

However, this decision was overruled, unanimously, by the Second Division of the Inner House of the Court of Session, and Sheriff Gow's approach to the issue of aliment was strongly disapproved. It was pointed out that the action for aliment was an action on behalf of the child, not to provide the mother with extra cash, and therefore the relative blameworthiness between the mother and father was irrelevant since the award in reality was one between the father and the child. Statute has since rendered this decision otiose in Scotland;[77] but it is to be commended to other jurisdictions as a means of denying any possibility of one partner in a sexual relationship using the obligation to maintain or aliment a child as a threat to strengthen a demand that the other bends to her or his will on the question of contraceptive usage.

Custody Decisions

The use or non-use of family planning techniques ought to have no effect on other court decisions, such as the determination of custody of children in divorce proceedings. It has been argued in some American cases that the fact that a woman has sought or undergone an abortion is a factor to be taken into account in determining the relative claims between her and her husband for custody of their existing children.[78] It is to be hoped that courts strongly resist this suggestion. By recognizing the legality of abortion, the law has recognized the acceptability of a woman's decision to seek an abortion and it would be quite contrary to principle for the courts to turn round and use that decision to the woman's detriment by holding it relevant to its determination of the worth of the woman's claim to custody of her existing children. The decision to undergo an abortion, often made for the benefit of existing children (and indeed in Scots and English law a statutory ground for the legality of abortion),[79] ought to have no effect on the assessment of the woman's suitability to be awarded custody. Decisions concerning contraception and sterilization are equally irrelevant to the issue of custody.

Right of Consultation

It is sometimes argued that the other partner, even though she or he has no right of veto, ought nevertheless to be given a right of consultation in the family planning decision-making process. It has been suggested that a father of a foetus ought to be informed about the mother's decision to abort it, and ought to be given the opportunity to make his feelings known. The common law in neither Scotland nor England recognizes such a right, and it could only arise in these countries through statute. No such statute currently exists, and the Abortion Act 1967 concerns only the relationship between the pregnant woman and her medical advisers.

A number of jurisdictions in the USA have enacted spousal notification requirements, and the validity of such a statute was upheld by the US Court of Appeals in *Scheinberg v. Smith*,[80] on the ground that such a requirement added more to the protection of the integrity and dignity of family life than it took from the woman's right to secure an abortion. Wardle and Wood find it 'refreshing to see a court attempt to balance conflicting interests and distinguish between absolute prohibitions and mere inconveniences' and consider this a 'sensible approach' for the court to adopt.[81]

There are, however, a number of practical problems with such a requirement. First, given society's, and increasingly the law's, acceptance of unmarried couples, it is difficult to see the moral force in a requirement to consult the spouse rather than to consult the father. If the husband is different from the father, then any consultation requirement is hardly likely to encourage matrimonial stability. Secondly, is the law to accept the woman's word as to whom the father is? If the woman is unmarried and two men claim to be the father, who determines, or how is it to be determined, which of the two is to be consulted? Thirdly, a requirement for consultation that does not include a right to determine may frustrate a man who has strong views but is legally powerless to give effect to them. It is an empty gift to allow a man to be consulted but to deny any legal force to his opinion. Fourthly, a man may abuse any right of consultation with psychological or physical or financial pressure on the woman, and so turn the right of consultation effectively into a right of veto. Cook and Dickens point out[82] the important fact that, in a number of societies in the world, women find it impossible, for social reasons, to go against the wishes of their husbands: even in societies we like to regard as sophisticated, such practical pressure can be much more real than any legal pressure.

In reality, any spousal consultation requirement is one more hurdle to a woman's free choice, because it provides a means of influencing her by potentially illegitimate means. The practicalities of enforcing such a requirement, and its inherent danger, suggest that it is not the satisfactory compromise that some American courts see it as.

Conclusion

Family planning is regarded by the law as a matter for one individual. The person, normally the woman, who must adopt the invasive medical procedure, is the person with the sole right to decide whether to accept that procedure. The fact that acceptance of a family planning method will affect the sexual partner is not sufficient to give the sexual partner any rights at all in the decision-making process. Individual free choice is a round hole into which the square peg of joint decision-making will not go. Our decisions in very many areas of life affect other people to a greater or lesser extent – but that does not, in itself, give such people a moral, far less a legal, claim to take over the decision-making process.

The law in Scotland and England recognizes no right of veto nor any right of consultation, but it does allow for matrimonial relief if there is real and abiding disagreement on the issue of reproduction, which is, of course, fundamental to the nature of many marriages. This probably provides a sensible compromise. The person whose body is physically affected by the family planning procedure, whether contraception, sterilization or abortion, has the sole right of deciding whether to adopt that procedure. However, if their partner feels that this deprives them of the basis of the relationship, the law should not (and it does not) insist on the maintenance of that relationship. The disgruntled partner can be set free to seek the fulfilment of her or his sexual or reproductive urges elsewhere.

Notes

1 See Cook & Maine, 'Spousal Veto Over Family Planning Services', 77 *Am. J. Pub. Health* 339, 1987.
2 This is discussed further by Mason, *Medico-Legal Aspects of Reproduction and Parenthood*, Dartmouth, Aldershot, 1990 at pp. 1–12.
3 This proposition is more fully discussed in Chapter 7.
4 Indeed, in some jurisdictions statute expressly denies spouses the right to be consulted in family planning decisions, so getting round the medical profession's misapprehension of the law: this is the case, for example, in Quebec and Ontario: see Dickens, 'Reproduction Law and Medical Consent' 35 *U. Tor. LJ* 255 (1985) at p. 267.
5 [1954] 3 *All ER* 59.
6 Ibid. at p. 62.
7 See Cook & Maine, op. cit., note 1 above at p. 341.
8 410 *US* 113, 35 *L. Ed.* 2d 147 (1973).
9 For earlier *US* cases, see Shipley, 'Women's Right to Have Abortion Without Consent of, or Against Objections of Child's Father'. Annotation 62 *ALR* (3d) 1097.
10 428 *US* 52, 49 *L. Ed.* 2d 788 (1976).
11 The statute also contained a requirement that the woman consent in writing, but this was held to be not unconstitutional.
12 Wardle & Wood, *A Lawyer Looks at Abortion*, Brigham Young University Press, Provo, 1982 at pp. 82–3.
13 410 *US* at p.154, 35 *L. Ed.* 2d at p. 178, for example, the Court talks of the "important state interests in regulation", and it expressly repeats this at 410 *US* at 162, 35 *L. Ed.* 2d at p. 182.
14 Per Baker P. in *Paton v. Trustees of the British Pregnancy Advisory Service* [1978] 2 *All ER* 987 at p. 990.
15 See Cook & Dickens, 'International Developments in Abortion Laws: 1977–88', 78 *Am. J. Pub. Health* 1305, 1988 at p. 1307.
16 See, for example, Public Act No. 82–280, Section 11–107.1, 1985 (Illinois).
17 [1978] 2 *All ER* 987.
18 Ibid. at p. 992.
19 [1987] 2 *WLR* 1108.
20 *Medhurst v. Medhurst* (1984) 9 *DLR* (4th) 252.
21 Ibid. at p. 259.
22 Ibid.
23 (1981) 130 *DLR* (3d) 588, discussed by Pickard, 'Why Joseph Borowski Has Standing,' 36 *U. Tor. LJ* 19, 1986.
24 This was followed by the High Court of Australia in *Attorney General of Queensland ex rel. Kerr v. T.* (1983) 46 *ALR* 275.
25 *X. v. United Kingdom* (1980) 3 *EHRR* 408, *ECHR* 19 BR 244.
26 [1987] 2 *WLR* 1108.
27 (1987) 39 *DLR* (4th) 731 (Sas. C. A.).
28 (1989) 57 *DLR* (4th) 231.
29 (1990) 62 *DLR* (4th) 634..
30 In West Germany the opposite conclusion was reached in a case that did not go to appeal: see the judgement of the *Arbeitsgerichtshof*, 15 March 1984, reported in 38 *Neue Juristische Wochenschrift* 2201, 1985.
31 [1987] 2 *WLR* 1108.
32 But see *MacCormick v. Lord Advocate* 1953 *SLT* 255; Yorke, The Legal Personality of the Unborn Child', 1979 *SLT* (News) 158, at p. 160.

33 Lord Diplock in *Gouriet v. Union of Post Office Workers* [1977] 3 *All ER* 70 at p. 100 said:

> . . . a court of civil jurisdiction is concerned with legal rights only when the aid of the court is invoked by one party claiming a right against another party to protect or enforce the right or to provide a remedy against the other party for infringement of it, or is invoked by either party to settle a dispute between them as to the existence or nature of the right claimed.

34 (1979) 101 *DLR* (3d) 686.
35 (1980) 117 *DLR* (3d) 512.
36 *Attorney General of Queensland ex rel. Kerr v. T.* (1983) 46 *ALR* 275.
37 [1978] 2 *All ER* at p. 992.
38 [1987] 2 *WLR* at p. 1120.
39 (1983) 46 *ALR* at p. 277.
40 [1978] 2 *All ER* at p. 990.
41 (1983) 46 *ALR* at pp. 277/278.
42 [1978] 2 *All ER* at p. 991.
43 *X. v. United Kingdom* (1980) 3 *EHRR* 408, *ECHR* 18 BR 244..
44 Commission Judgement, para 26.
45 428 *US* 52, 49 *L. Ed.* 2d 788 (1976).
46 At para 27. Cf. Krever J. in *Re Medhurst* (1984) 7 *DLR* (4th) 335, who said (at p. 342):

> I have to balance the interest of the applicant, which is certainly not to his life or health, against the interest of the respondent wife in avoiding delay which is surely a risk to her health and life. I think that precedence must be given to the interest of the respondent wife.

47 *Associated Picture Houses Ltd v. Wednesbury Corp.* [1948] *KB* 223.
48 *R. v. Secretary of State for Social Services, ex p. Walker, The Times*, 26 November 1987; *R. v. Central Birmingham Health Authority, ex p. Collier, The Times* 6 January 1988.
49 See *R. v. Ethical Committee of St. Mary's Hospital ex p. Harriott* (1988) *Fam. Law* 165, in which the court refused to decide whether or not judicial review would lie against a consultant in obstetrics and gynaecology who had refused to accept the applicant onto her IVF programme within the National Health Service.
50 A dichotomy 'pronounced in categorical terms' (Wade, *Administrative Law*, 6th edn, Clarendon Press, Oxford 1988 at p. 672) by the House of Lords in *O'Reilly v. Mackman* [1983] 2 *AC* 237.
51 See Wade op. cit., note 50 above at p. 678.
52 See Walker, *Civil Remedies*, Green, Edinburgh, 1974 at p. 163–71. See also Bradley, 'Administrative Law', Stair Encyclopaedia of the Laws of Scotland 1:325.
53 Conversely a doctor's decision to *refuse* to grant the certificate would likewise not be open to judicial review in England and Scotland.
54 (1988) 44 *DLR* (4th) 385.
55 See *Re Medhurst* (1984) 7 *DLR* (4th) 335. Cf. the English law of *R. v. Ethical Committee of St. Mary's Hospital ex. p. Harriott*, note 49 above in which it was held that an informal non-statutory committee's decisions were not subject to judicial review. The court however recognized that in some (unspecified) circumstances such a committee's actions might be subject to this remedy.
56 [1982] 1 *NZLR* 734.
57 Ibid. at pp. 740–1 (emphasis added.)

58 *Medhurst v. Medhurst* (1984) 9 *DLR* (4th) 252.
59 *Re Medhurst* (1984) 7 *DLR* (4th) 335.
60 Ibid. at p. 341.
61 See the comments of Reid J. to this effect in *Medhurst v. Medhurst* (1984) 9 *DLR* (4th) at p. 264.
62 See, for example, Phillips, 'Wardship and Abortion Prevention', 95 *LQR* 332 1979; Lyon & Bennett, 'Abortion – Whose Decision?', 9 *Fam. Law* 35, 1979.
63 Cf. *Re B. (A Minor)* [1981] 1 *WLR* 1412 in which the Court of Appeal refused to hold that it would be in the best interests of a Down's Syndrome child to refuse it life-saving medical treatment.
64 [1988] 2 *WLR* 1288.
65 In South Africa it has been held that a *curator ad litem* could not be appointed over an unborn child to represent its interests when its mother wishes to have it aborted: *Christian League of Southern Africa v. Rall* 1981 (2) *SALR* 821. The decision of the Family Court of Halifax, Nova Scotia, in *Re Simms & H.* (1979) 106 *DLR* (3d) 435, that a guardian *ad litem* could be appointed over an unborn child must now be regarded as overruled by the Supreme Court of Canada's decision in *Tremblay v. Daigle*, (1990) 62 *DLR* (4th) 634.
66 See also *D. (A Minor) v. Berkshire County Council* [1987] 1 *All ER* 20, in which Woolf L. J. said, at p. 30, ' "a person" denotes someone who is living, not someone who has yet to be born.'
67 [1988] 2 *WLR* at p. 1298. On the other hand, the Ontario court seemed willing to hold that the protection of the child from parental abuse might justify controlling the mother: see *Re Children's Aid Society of Kenora* (1983) 134 *DLR* (3d) 249.
68 See Fortin, 'Legal Protection for the Unborn Child' (1988) 51 *Mod. LR* 54 at p. 71, who points out this 'stark contrast'.
69 This was accepted in the Scottish case of *Robertson v. Robertson* 1981 *SLT* (Notes).
70 (1555) *M.* 16226.
71 See *Jefferson v. Griffin Spalding County Hospital* 274 *SE* 2d 457 (1981). This issue is discussed further in Kolder *et al.*, 'Court-Ordered Obstetrical Interventions' 316 *New Eng. J. Med.* 1192, 1987 who point out that, in 11 states in the USA, courts have ordered women to undergo caesarian sections, and in two states courts have detained women in hospital. These cases are critically analysed by Gallagher in 'Prenatal Invasions and Interventions: What's Wrong with Fetal Rights?', 10 *Harv. Women's LJ* 9, 1987.
72 [1954] 3 *All ER* 59.
73 Ibid. at p. 62. It was further held by the majority that since it was not established that the wife had not consented, the relief sought would not be granted in this case.
74 See *Dowden v. Dowden* [1978] 8 *Fam. Law* 106.
75 1981 *SLT* 159. For a discussion, see Bates, 'Aliment, Negligence and the Future of Illegitimacy', 1982 *SLT* (News) 131.
76 1981 *SLT* at p. 160.
77 S. 4(3) (b) of the Family Law (Sc) Act 1985, which provides that in determining the amount of aliment it should award, the court shall not take account of any conduct of a party unless it would be manifestly inequitable to leave it out of account. The equivalent English provision (s. 12A of the Guardianship of Minors Act 1971) does not contain any such direction.
78 See, for example, *Jones v. Smith* 278 *SO* 2d 339 (1973). The Florida District Court of Appeal rejected this argument.
79 See Chapter 3.
80 659 *F.* 2d 476 (Court of Appeals, 5th Cir. 1981).

81 Wardle & Wood, *A Lawyer Looks at Abortion*, Brigham Young University Press, Provo, 1982 at p. 82.

82 Cook & Dickens, *Issues in Reproductive Health Law in the Commonwealth*, The Commonwealth Secretariat, London 1986 at pp. 26–7.

6 Family Planning and the Child

Introduction

It is a fact that many people wish were not true, but true it is, that children, as well as adults, have sexual feelings and desires and sexual experiences. Few would deny that it is not in the best interests of children to indulge in sexual activity with another person at an early age. There is increased risk of disease, such as cervical cancer for girls who start sexual intercourse early; and there can be emotional difficulties arising from the physical relationship itself. A child even at 10 years or younger can, through sexual intercourse, reproduce, causing immense social and financial difficulties. But to accept that early sexual activity is undesirable is by no means sufficient to prevent it happening, or to prevent its unfortunate consequences. Children (and adults) do many things that are undesirable and can potentially harm them (although neither should it be forgotten that sexual activity can give pleasure as well – even to children). Society clearly and rightly disapproves of sexual relations with children and the law in most jurisdictions reflects this through criminal law prohibitions. However, these prohibitions are designed to be more protective than inhibitive. That protection is normally aimed at girls rather than boys, a fact that historically reflected society's (and the law's) assumption that a girl's virtue had a quantifiable economic value. However, this protection can still be justified today since the unfortunate physical, mental and social consequences of sexual intercourse can be far greater for girls than for boys.

The fact is that there will always be children who indulge in sexual intercourse and thus expose themselves to risk. To recognize that neither criminal law prohibition nor the physical risks involved will inhibit such behaviour entirely is an acceptance of reality rather than a counsel of despair. The real question therefore becomes how to protect children who do foolish things from the dangers associated with that foolishness.

Adult women are of course subject to the same risks from sexual intercourse, but they can seek to avoid the most obvious one, pregnancy, with the help of the family planner. That help, practically speaking, might as easily be supplied to children. But there are significant social and legal differences between adults and children (who as we shall see are, for this purpose, in Scotland and England those under the age of 16), and these differences create immense legal difficulties for the provision of family planning advice and treatment for children. Sex with an adult is, generally speaking, not criminal; sex with a girl under 16 is. The adult can, generally, provide her or his own consent to family planning; the child under 16 may not have the capacity to do so. The adult is free from the dominion of her or his parents; the child's wishes may be constrained by parents exercising their legal rights. These differences have created a great deal of difficulty for the law, as is shown both in the USA, where parental participation statutes in abortion have been subject to numerous constitutional challenges, and in England, where the *Gillick* saga ended with an authoritative pronouncement on some of the contentious issues, and a disturbing silence on others.

The criminality or otherwise of the provision of family planning treatment for children was examined in Chapter 2. This chapter will look at the necessity to obtain consent for such treatment, and who, in law, is entitled to provide it.

Consent and the Child

The general rule of law is straightforward and unambiguous: before any medical examination or treatment can be carried out the health care worker must obtain the consent of the patient or of someone else legally entitled to give that consent. Examination or treatment without consent amounts to an assault in law, but consent, at least to the broad nature of the medical procedure undertaken, will provide an absolute defence to an action for assault against the medical practitioner.[1]

This applies to family planning as to any other form of medical practice. Usually, only the patient has the right to give consent but, if the patient is a child, then the parents or those exercising parental rights may consent on its behalf, and, if the court exercises a jurisdiction over the child, the court may do so also. In the absence of statute, no other person has any right whatsoever to consent to medical treatment on behalf of someone else. Whenever proxy consent is given, whether by a parent or by the court, the decision to consent must be made on the basis of the child's best interests.

The fact that one person is legally entitled to consent to medical treatment does not in itself deny all other persons this right, and it is easy to imagine situations in which more than one person can consent on behalf of one patient. There may be two custodial parents, or the patient may be a child who has legal capacity to consent (see below) at the same time as someone else also has the right to consent. In these situations there may, of course, be disagreement but, from the doctor's point of view, in the absence of a statutory requirement to obtain extra consents,[2] so long as consent is given by one person legally entitled to give that consent, and (probably) so long as the child does not object to the treatment, the doctor will be protected from any legal challenge on the basis of assault of the patient.[3]

Consent of the Court

Many legal systems allow courts to exercise a wardship jurisdiction, whereby the court protects the ward and makes all important decisions concerning the ward's life and lifestyle. In England the court can exercise wardship jurisdiction over minors, but the jurisdiction ends on the ward's attaining the age of 18 and entering majority. Children are not wards of court until a particular procedure has been gone through to make them wards. In some other countries, such as Canada, jurisdiction can in some cases extend into majority. Some legal systems, such as Scots law, do not recognize the concept of wardship.

When the child is a ward of court, and a decision concerning the child has to be made, then if the decision is significant for its life or lifestyle (such as, for example, where it is to live, how it is to be educated, or what religious training it is to receive) the court is the only body able to grant consent. This applies even for wards over 16, who in English law would otherwise be able to decide these matters themselves,[4] for wardship takes away all other rights of decision-making in these significant matters that anyone else may have. If the decision is not significant, but rather concerns some minor matter (such as, for example, what clothes to wear or what hairstyle to adopt), then the court's consent is sufficient and valid, but it is not necessary and another person may grant consent. With medical treatment, either the child's guardian or the court can consent to matters such as the removal of a rotten tooth, but only the court could consent, for example, to the termination of life-supporting treatment of the ward.

Certain family planning procedures are clearly so significant that the court's consent would always be required. For example, sterilization of a ward will not be allowed except with the permission of the wardship court, and no other person may consent to that operation.[5] Abortion, too, will clearly come within this category. In *Re P. (A Minor)*[6] a 15 year-old girl, who already had a child, was made a ward of court and Butler-Sloss J. authorized the termination of her second pregnancy. In *Re G-U*[7] a girl of 16 who was a ward of court became pregnant, and the local authority who had care and control of her (that is, exercising some parental rights over her) arranged for her pregnancy to be terminated. The court held that this was the correct thing to do as it was clearly in the best interests of the child; but it pointed out that the operation had technically been unlawful as the court had not been asked for its consent. It was emphasized by Balcombe J. that, in future, the court's permission should always be sought for such operations. He said:

> A child who is a ward of court, even in the care of a local authority, may not have anything major done in its life without the leave of the court. It is difficult to think of anything which can be much more important to a young woman of 16 or 17 years of age than the termination of a pregnancy.

Abortion and sterilization are clear examples of a significant step in the ward's life. Many forms of contraception are less clearly so and it is therefore less obvious that the court's authority should always be sought. Although Parker L.J. in the Court of Appeal in *Gillick v. West Norfolk & Wisbech Area Health Authority*[8] considered that all contraceptive treatment would require the permission of the wardship court, it is suggested that this is going too far. Certain contraceptive methods (such as, for example, the use of the condom) are not particularly significant to the life and well-being of the user, and it is suggested that a 17 year-old boy who is a ward of court can safely be sold or given condoms without the supplier asking the court's permission. On the other hand, different considerations may come into play if the boy is 12, for sexual intercourse at that age is probably far more significant to the future well-being of the child than sexual intercourse at age 17.

The issue has been raised in a small number of English cases. In *Re P. (A Minor)* (above) the court authorized not only an abortion, but also the fitting of an IUD into a 15 year-old ward of court. Butler-Sloss J. seems to be of the opinion, in that case, that the court's consent was not strictly necessary and that the local authority, which had care and control of the child, could itself have authorized both the abortion and the fitting of the IUD. However, she clearly believed that in cases of doubt it was quite proper to go to court. After the decision in *Re G-U* (above) it is clear that, in relation to abortion, the court's permission must always be obtained.

The matter has not been discussed in relation to oral contraceptive pills, or the cap. The fact that the pill may have long-term health consequences suggests that the court's consent is probably (one can put it no higher) necessary. The cap is reversible and has less problems associated with its use: therefore the court's consent is probably (one can put it no higher) not necessary.

Unlike abortion and sterilization (and the supply of condoms) most other forms of family planning fall into a grey area and it will be unclear whether the court's authority is necessary. The age of the ward, the invasiveness of the treatment, and its permanence, are all relevant factors. In cases of doubt it would be wise for the family planner always to ask the court, because although the court's consent may not always be necessary, it is always sufficient. It must be emphasized that the above relates *only* to children who are wards of court.

In Scotland there is, of course, no wardship procedure, but the court may become involved through an application concerning the exercise of parental rights. S. 3(1) of the Law Reform (Parent and Child) (Scotland) Act 1986 allows the court to make any order it thinks fit in relation to parental rights. The application must be one concerning 'parental rights' and is therefore more appropriately dealt with in the next section.

Consent of the Parents

When the child is not a ward (as will normally be the case) or the court is not otherwise involved, a general rule of medical law in most jurisdictions is that parents may consent to any medical treatment for their children. This is an exercise of parental rights, and it entitles the parents to consent to any family planning advice, examination or treatment, subject to the limitation discussed below. This power to consent flows from the parents' right of custody of the child.[9] Custody is the right to have day-to-day care and control of the child,[10] and from that right flows the rights (and duties) required to exercise it properly, such as the right to consent to medical treatment. In English law parents have a right of custody until the child achieves the age of 18, and therefore they possess the right to consent to medical treatment until that age (subject to the limitation discussed below). At age 16, the child will acquire a statutory right to give personal consent (see below) but that provision does not deny a concurrent right of the parents to consent until age 18.[11]

Scots law is very different. In Scotland, childhood is (at the moment) divided into two, following the Roman law classification of persons. First, there are pupils (girls up to the age of 12 and boys up to 14), who are protected and controlled by tutors (normally the parents of course). Tutors have the right to make decisions (subject to the limitation discussed below) over both the pupil's property *and* person. Secondly, there are minors (between 12 or 14 and 18) who are protected by curators (again normally the parents), who make decisions concerning only the child's property.[12] Minors have the right to deal with their own bodies as they choose, including the right to decide about their own medical treatment; but this right is subject to certain protective statutory exceptions, and in particular is subject to the fact that parents have custody of children up until the age of 16, and through that right may be entitled to have some control over the child's person.[13] In Scots common law custody applied only to pupil children,[14] until it was extended by statute to 16, and it follows that control of the person of the child, being an attribute of either pupillarity or custody[15] cannot be extended beyond age 16, because by that time both pupillarity and the right of custody have ended. Parents' rights to consent to medical treatment do not therefore extend beyond 16, as they do in England.

However, in both Scotland and England, the parent's power to consent at any age is limited to treatment that satisfies the welfare test – that is, to treatment that is in the child's best interests – and it follows that they may only consent to family planning treatment if that treatment satisfies that test. However, the law does seem to accept a presumption that the parent will be acting in the best interests of the child,[16] and it is only if the parent's decision is challenged that the court will exercise a supervisory role and ensure that the parent's decision does in fact accord with the welfare of the child. If the court decides that the parents have made a wrong decision, the court itself will determine what is in the child's best interests, and decree accordingly. So, in the English case of *Re B. (A Minor)*[17] where the parents of a child and its doctors agreed that it would be in the best interests of the child *not* to be given life-saving treatment, the Court of Appeal held that they were wrong and ordered the treatment to be given.

In Scotland, if there is any doubt as to whether consenting to a particular treatment is a proper exercise of parental rights, any interested person may make an application to the court under s. 3(1) of the Law Reform (Parent and Child) (Scotland) Act 1986, and the court may make any such order relating to parental rights as it thinks fit. The court order may either declare that consenting to the proposed treatment is a proper exercise of parental rights, or that it is not, and the test the court will adopt in making this determination is laid down in s. 3(2) as follows:

> . . . the court shall regard the welfare of the child involved as the paramount consideration and shall not make any order relating to parental rights unless it is satisfied that to do so will be in the interests of the child.

This is also the test that the English courts adopt in determining whether parents are exercising their parental rights properly.[18]

It is often quite difficult to tell whether family planning treatment is, or is not, in the child's best interests, for it is seldom necessary, in the sense of being life-saving, and it is seldom wholly elective in the way that, say, cosmetic surgery generally is. This, however, need not inhibit parents who wish to consent on behalf of their children, for it is a misunderstanding of the welfare test to say that it is satisfied only by treatment that unquestionably enhances a child's best interests. Parents are not duty-bound always to do what is wisest for their children, for that would deny them the right to do neutral things: the position is rather that they cannot do that which is detrimental. Parents will always have a certain element of discretion. So, for example, while the wise parent will always have her or his child vaccinated, a refusal to consent to vaccination will be tolerated by the law because that is not necessarily detrimental to the child's best interests. Similarly, parents may consent to a baby boy's circumcision, even though it is a medically neutral operation and does not necessarily positively further the child's interests.

Rather, the court's supervisory role is to ensure that the parents do not consent or withhold consent when the child's interests would positively suffer. The Quebec Court of Appeal put it thus:

> It is not up to the court to substitute itself for the person having parental authority and to decide in his place. The court's role is to correct a decision which is *clearly* wrong.[19]

In this case, the court refused to overturn a mother's decision to withhold consent to further chemotherapy for her three year-old daughter who was dying of cancer, because it had not been shown that her refusal was invalid in that it was against the child's interests. It follows that parents can consent to family planning treatment, even when it is unclear that that would further the child's interests, so long as the treatment would not positively harm the child. If it would positively harm the child then the parent's consent is invalid, and may be challenged in court. A case in which the parent's consent was overturned by the English court for that reason is *Re D. (A Minor)*.[20] There, a mother wished her mentally disabled 11 year-old daughter to be sterilized, but the court held that this decision was clearly wrong and refused to sanction the operation.

One situation in which parental consent will almost certainly be detrimental to the child would be when the child herself refuses to accept the treatment. If, for example, a young girl became pregnant and the parents wished her pregnancy to be terminated, but she refused, to force her to undergo the operation would almost certainly amount to an assault, notwithstanding the parents' consent. There are two possible rationales for this conclusion. First, it could be argued that any pregnant girl (however young) is old enough to decide for herself that she does not want an abortion (which is not the same as saying that she is old enough to decide that she does want an abortion). This, however, is a patent fiction, for some very young girls are simply too immature to make the decision one way or another; indeed, the US District Court decisively rejected such an argument in *Baird v. Bellotti*.[21] Secondly, and more plausibly, one might follow McLean's suggestion[22] to the effect that 'best interests' 'might equally reasonably be taken to mean vindication of free choices': in other words, the denial of the child's choice can in itself be contrary to the child's interests (certainly in a matter as fundamental as abortion). It is difficult to argue against the proposition that it would never be in the best interests of a child to force her against her wishes to terminate her pregnancy. While one may force a resisting five year-old on to the dentist's chair for the removal of a rotten tooth, it is a different order of things completely to compel a resisting pregnant girl, even one who resists irrationally, to have an abortion. As Williams put it:

> The only acceptable opinion is that if the girl understands what an abortion is, the doctor can perform it at her request even if she is under 16; if she refuses to consent, the doctor cannot do it . . . and in neither event is it (on a rational view of the law) necessary for the doctor to enquire whether the girl appreciates all the consequences of taking one course of action or the other.[23]

Williams also points out that the same principle would apply to sterilization operations and, one may assume, to contraceptive treatment also. As a general rule, therefore, a family planner should assume that parental consent satisfies the welfare test only when the child also consents to the proposed treatment. Dickens reports an interesting Canadian case in which an adolescent was granted an injunction against her parents to prevent them exerting pressure on her to terminate her pregnancy.[24] This is a clear recognition that such pressure is against the interests of the child.

With the opposite situation – that is, of the child wishing the operation and the parent refusing – the matter will depend not on the parent's rights, but on the child's capacity to consent, for if the child can consent to the operation, and does, then this would be a sufficient defence to any charge of assault against any health care worker who relied upon it. The child's capacity to consent is, however, the issue that has proved most troublesome for the courts.

Consent of the Child

The age at which a person is considered to be an adult for the purposes of providing personal consent to medical treatment depends upon the provisions of law in the relevant legal system. Some jurisdictions deal with the matter legislatively. So, for example, in South Australia the Consent to Medical and Dental Procedures Act 1985 allows children of any age to consent as if they were adults, so long as, in the doctor's opinion, they are capable of understanding the nature and consequences of the treatment, *and also* so long as the procedure is in the best interests of the patient. In England, a person has the statutory right to consent as if she or he were an adult, from the age of 16 years, and this includes family planning treatment.[25] In Scotland there is no statutory provision, but a parent's right of custody ends at 16 and therefore the inherent right of minors[26] to deal with their own persons is liberated from the constraints of custody. For the child under 16 the question of capacity to consent is left open in the English legislation, and may therefore be affected (as in Scotland) by the existence of parental rights over the child, particularly the right of custody.[27]

In Scotland there is some authority at common law to suggest that a child's consent may be valid in law even when it is under the age of 16, so long as the child sufficiently understands the nature of the act to which consent is given. In *Murray v. Fraser*,[28] in an action for damages for seduction of a girl under 16, the Inner House of the Court of Session held that the fact that the pursuer was under the age of 16 did not relieve her of the necessity of proving that her consent had been induced by arts or deceit (that is, she had to prove that her consent was invalid, her age on its own not being sufficient to do so). Lord Salvesen said, 'seduction . . . is not necessarily to be inferred from the mere fact that a man has had connexion with a girl under sixteen'.[29] Similarly, it has been held in Canada that, where a child is capable of appreciating fully the nature and consequences of a particular operation or of particular treatment, that child can give effective consent thereto.[30]

In relation to family planning treatment it would follow from the position in Scotland and Canada that the child could give legally valid consent so long as she or he were of sufficient mental maturity to appreciate the nature of the treatment and its significance. It was this proposition that was vehemently denied in relation to English law by the plaintiff in *Gillick v. West Norfolk & Wisbech Area Health Authority*.[31]

In *Gillick*, the plaintiff sought a declaration from the court that advice, given by the Department of Health and Social Security to area health authorities, that contraceptive and abortion advice and treatment might exceptionally be provided for girls under the age of 16, at a doctor's clinical discretion and without parental consent or knowledge, was illegal. Woolf J. rejected her claim on the ground that there was nothing in law to show that a person under the age of 16 could not give personal consent to medical treatment, and that the validity of such consent depended upon the person's intelligence and understanding of the proposed treatment. The Court of Appeal overturned Woolf J., and granted Gillick the declaration she asked for, on the ground that the provision of contraceptive or abortion advice or treatment without parental consent or knowledge breached the parents' right to determine the way in which the child is brought up, including in particular the right to determine the place and manner in which the child's time is spent. Legally this decision was, to say the least, peculiar, for it declared an act unlawful, while at the same time provided no sanction for that unlawfulness.[32]

The House of Lords overruled the Court of Appeal, by a narrow majority, and held that a girl under 16 can indeed (sometimes) consent to her own medical (including family planning) treatment and that for a doctor to provide this without parental consent does not necessarily breach any parental right, nor any provision of the criminal law. Unfortunately, the circumstances in which the doctor may rely upon the child's consent to such treatment are not free from ambiguity, for within the majority there were significant differences of approach.

Lord Fraser pointed out that contraceptive treatment is, in essence, no different from any other form of medical treatment, and that therefore if Gillick's arguments were correct in relation to contraception, they must also be correct in relation to all other forms of medical advice or treatment or examination of the child's body. But he found that conclusion,

> . . . so surprising that I cannot accept it in the absence of clear provisions to that effect. It seems to me verging on the absurd to suggest that a girl or a boy aged 15 could not effectively consent, for example, to have a medical examination of some trivial injury to his body or even to have a broken arm set.[33]

Consequently,

> Provided the patient, whether a boy or a girl, is capable of understanding what is proposed, and of expressing his or her own wishes, I see no good reason for holding that he or she lacks the capacity to express them validly and effectively and to authorise the medical man to make the examination or give the treatment which he advises.[34]

Of course, not every child from the earliest age will be able to consent, and the test favoured by Lord Fraser is the one used by Woolf J. at first instance, following the Canadian decision of *Johnston v. Wellesley Hospital*[35] – that is, that consent will be valid so long as the child has sufficient understanding and maturity to understand the nature of the act to which consent is being given. Up to this point, Lord Scarman followed the reasoning of Lord Fraser (with the majority being completed by the concurring speech of Lord Bridge).

But on the question of how, or whether, the existence of parental rights affects the child's capacity to consent, Lord Fraser took a fundamentally different approach from Lord Scarman (Lord Bridge again agreeing with both!). The potential influence of parental rights can be seen in the Canadian case of *C. v. Wren*,[36] in which it had been argued that, in determining the child's maturity (in order to apply the *Johnston* test to a case in which a 16 year-old had consented to the termination of her pregnancy), the fact that the child disagreed with the parents' wishes raised an inference of immaturity. This argument was rejected, but the fact that it was raised at all does illustrate that the existence of parental rights can have some influence on the determination of the child's capacity. Lord Fraser in *Gillick* accepted that the child's capacity is indeed affected by parental rights.

He pointed out that parental rights 'exist for the benefit of the child and they are justified only in so far as they enable the parent to perform his duties towards the child'.[37] These rights, he said, may only be exercised in a way consistent with the best interests of the child, and he concluded from this that if the parents' rights to control children or make decisions on their behalf is to be overridden this can only be done if it is in the child's best interests to do so. Lord Fraser put it thus:

> Once the rule of the parents' absolute authority over minor children is abandoned, the solution to the problem in this appeal can no longer be found by referring to rigid parental rights at any particular age. The solution depends upon a judgment of what is best for the welfare of the particular child.[38]

In other words, the existence of parental rights affects the child's capacity by restricting that capacity to consent to treatment that furthers the best interests of the child. Lord Fraser clearly did *not* put the under-16 year-old in the same position as the over–16 year-old. The latter, but not the former, may consent to treatment that is positively detrimental (such as, for example, the *inter vivos* donation of non-regenerative tissue, or, possibly, a sterilization). But the child below 16 has no real *choice,* in the proper sense of that word, *because a person who can choose is a person entitled to choose unwisely*. Lord Fraser's speech is therefore not authority for the child's right to choose her or his medical treatment, but is rather authority for the much more limited proposition that a doctor can rely upon the child's consent in some circumstances – that is, when the child satisfies the understanding test *and* the treatment satisfies the welfare test. Curiously, Lord Templeman, although one of the minority, adopted a remarkably similar line of reasoning to Lord Fraser, taking the view that the mature minor can consent to treatment in her or his own best interests, but dissenting as to the result because he believed that contraceptive treatment could never be in a child's best interests. It is clear, however, from his memorable statement, 'there are many things which a girl under 16 needs to practise but sex is not one of them',[39] that he was confusing the benefits and disadvantages of having sex with the benefits and disadvantages of contraception.[40]

Lord Fraser put the patient under 16 even further apart from patients over 16, by laying down not only that the welfare test must be satisfied, but also that a number of other criteria must be satisfied. He listed them as follows:

> (1) that the girl (although under 16 years of age) will understand [the doctor's] advice; (2) that he cannot persuade her to inform her parents or to allow him to inform the parents that she is seeking contraceptive advice; (3) that she is very likely to begin or to continue having sexual intercourse with or without contraceptive treatment; (4) that unless she receives contraceptive advice or treatment her physical and mental health or both are likely to suffer; (5) that

> her best interests require him to give her contraceptive advice or treatment or both without the parental consent.[41]

Lord Scarman took a fundamentally different approach, because he considered that the existence of parental rights can have no bearing on the child's capacity to consent, once the child has satisfied the maturity condition. Parental rights, according to Lord Scarman,

> . . . exist *only* so long as they are needed for the protection of the person and property of the child.[42]

Consequently,

> Parental right *yields* to the child's right to make his own decisions when he reaches a sufficient understanding and intelligence to be capable of making up his own mind on the matter requiring decision.[43]

The law's protection, through the welfare test, is given only for so long as it is needed, and it is not needed once the child has sufficient maturity to decide for itself. So while Lord Fraser allowed the doctor to rely on a child's consent in only limited situations, Lord Scarman went further and allowed the child not only to consent to that which is in its best interests, but also to choose – which could be a choice of something against the child's interests (or refusal of treatment which is in the child's best interests). The only qualification Lord Scarman made is that the child must understand fully, and he listed a number of factors relevant to the making of that determination:

> It has to be borne in mind that there is much that has to be understood by a girl under the age of 16 if she is to have legal capacity to consent to such treatment. It is not enough that she should understand the nature of the advice which is being given: she must also have a sufficient maturity to understand what is involved. There are moral and family questions, especially her relationship with her parents; long-term problems associated with the emotional impact of pregnancy and its termination; and there are risks to health of sexual intercourse at her age, risks which contraception may diminish but cannot eliminate. It follows that a doctor will have to satisfy himself that she is able to appraise these factors before he can safely proceed upon the basis that she has at law capacity to consent to contraceptive treatment.[44]

This is not a list of extra criteria that the under–16 year-old must satisfy, but rather is an elaboration of the one criterion Lord Scarman agreed with Lord Fraser about, viz., the necessity for a proper understanding of what is being consented to.

Williams criticizes this part of Lord Scarman's reasoning on the ground that, by making sexual intercourse with a girl under 16 a crime irrespective of consent, Parliament has decided and laid down that it is *never* wise for the under 16 year old to have sex. But the point is that while it may not be wise, the girl may still want to do it, and there is no inconsistency between a criminal law prohibition and the civil law recognizing that a girl, who is mature enough to understand what is wise and what is not wise, may decide to do that which is not wise. Lord Scarman required only that the girl has the *capacity* to make a wise decision, not that she actually does so (unlike Lord Fraser who held that the law accepts only consent to wise proposals).

The present writer has previously suggested[45] that Lord Scarman's approach is to be preferred to that of Lord Fraser, on the ground that once the child reaches the age of understanding she or he has, by definition, reached the age of understanding the consequences of doing something not in her or his own best interests, and consequently ought to be allowed the right of choice as well as simply the right to consent to that which satisfies the best interests test. In other words, the mature child should have the right to refuse consent, even when that is against the child's interests, just as adults have this right. The need for protection by the welfare test, which arises from the child's lack of understanding, disappears when the child gains understanding.

But there are more fundamental problems in law with Lord Fraser's approach. Legally, it is difficult to see the validity of the criteria he laid down (except the 'understanding' one). One has to ask, what would happen in law if one of the other criteria were not satisfied in any particular case? The answer, as Williams perceptively points out,[46] is nothing. Take as an example the second of Lord Fraser's criteria. A doctor who concluded that the child fully understood the nature of contraception and the dangers of sexual intercourse, but who did nothing to try to persuade the child to inform her parents, would breach Lord Fraser's guidelines. But such a doctor would not be open to legal challenge. The girl could have no action for assault, since, if she satisfies the maturity condition, her consent would have been based on an understanding of the broad nature of the procedure.[47] If the doctor gives proper information, such as would satisfy the *Sidaway* standard,[48] then there would similarly be no action for negligence available against the doctor, based on a failure to disclose sufficient information. Likewise, the parents could not take an action against the doctor for breach of parental rights, for these 'rights' are not such as to give a remedy for their breach:[49] rather they are more in the nature of duties.

The legal validity of Lord Fraser's extra criteria was examined in the Canadian case of *C. v. Wren*,[50] where it was held that the consent of a 16 year-old girl to an abortion was a valid defence in law to an action for assault, notwithstanding that she had not given full consideration to the ethics of abortion and the nature of the child-parent relationship. Lord Fraser's criteria, the court concluded, were merely ethical rather than legal; and the court in fact assumed that this was how Lord Fraser himself saw them. That court was right. In the very next paragraph to that in which he had laid down his list, Lord Fraser pointed out that a doctor who fails to follow these guidelines

> . . . would be failing to discharge his professional responsibilities, and I would expect him to be disciplined by his own professional body accordingly.[51]

There is no mention here of any legal sanction, because there is none.

The only truly legal requirement mentioned by Lord Fraser is that the child be mentally mature enough properly to understand what is involved, for a breach of this requirement, unlike the others, *would* have legal consequence – that is, a charge of assault based on lack of valid consent. Lord Scarman spent much of his speech elaborating this sole legal requirement, although he too went further than is strictly necessary, or indeed practicable. His list of what is to be understood was far more detailed than is generally regarded as necessary to prevent an action for either assault or negligent disclosure against a doctor. If the level of detail he envisaged is required for children, then it would follow logically, but would be ludicrous to suggest, that before parents could agree to contraceptive treatment for their children, they too would have to possess the capacity to understand all these matters. Few adults take these matters into consideration in relation to their own sexuality (far less that of their children), for the sexual urge remains the human instinct over which we have least control and in response to which we often act most foolishly: it is therefore wrong to expect children to be capable of wisdom where adults often are not.

In fact, it is suggested that this part of Lord Scarman's speech is, like Lord Fraser's criteria, no more than a sop to Gillick and her followers.[52] Recognizing the sharp divisions highlighted by this case, the majority in the House of Lords tried – vainly – to bring the two sides together, not by charting a middle course (for there was none) but by emphasizing that although the plaintiff lost her case, nevertheless her sincerity was not questioned and her fears not wholly unfounded. Lord Fraser and Lord Scarman tried to reassure those whom they had decided against, and this explains much of their speeches. They were not wrong in attempting that reassurance, for it has served to emphasize the serious nature of the decision to provide family planning treatment to the young. Their mistake was in thinking that anything but complete victory would satisfy the plaintiff and her supporters.

Parental Consultation

While the *Gillick* case is clearly authority for the proposition that mature minors can consent to their own family planning treatment, it does not deny parents all rights in the decision-making process. Lord Fraser in particular does not see parental rights disappearing totally just because a child is mentally mature: as shown above, his concept of the doctor's ethical duties is clearly influenced by residual parental rights. Lord Templeman too, although he was in the minority in the actual decision, is strongly influenced by parental rights, and he considered it perfectly lawful for family planning services to be provided if the doctor consulted with the parents and obtained their agreement. He based this conclusion on the fact that parents are the natural and legal guardians of their children, and that the parent exercising custody rights over a child has a variety of powers 'from control and supervision to guidance and advice'.[53] Similar statements were made by Lord Denning in *Hewer v. Bryant*,[54] when he envisaged the right of custody as dwindling from a right of control to 'little more than a right to give advice'.

This suggests that, at lowest, a custodial parent, although she or he may not be able to prevent a child obtaining family planning services, will always have the right to give guidance and advice to her or his child. Thomson suggests that there is authority for this proposition in Scots law also. He argues from the old case of *Harvey v. Harvey*[55] that, in Scotland, the custodial parent has a right, flowing from the right of custody,

> . . . to give friendly and affectionate counsel and aid to a minor to prevent the minor making a decision, *inter alia* in relation to his or her person, which because of the minor's inexperience and immaturity would be against the child's interests.[56]

Thomson concludes from this that, if the parents have a right to give advice, then the children have a duty to seek that advice, and therefore that while parents may not have the right to prevent the child obtaining family planning treatment, they always have the right to be consulted.

It is suggested that this, admittedly tentative, conclusion is wrong, for the following reasons. First, such a conclusion cannot be deduced from *Harvey v. Harvey*, because that case was expressly based on the child's 'inexperience and immaturity', and therefore the comments in that case are inappropriate for the mature minor. Secondly, such a proposition would go against the whole thrust of the *Gillick* decision. There would have been no need for their Lordships in that case to specify a duty on the doctor to 'try to persuade the girl to tell her parents' if in all cases the parents had a right to be consulted, for the child would then be in breach of such a 'right' by failing to consult. Thirdly, it is difficult to see what remedy the parents would have if their 'right' to give advice were denied. They would only suffer loss, if at all, if they could show that their advice would certainly have been followed, but whether or not it is followed is a matter for the child. And, in any case, it is difficult to visualize what loss the parents would suffer: it would be contrary to principle to recognize a remedy in the absence of any substantive loss.

The position, it is submitted, is as follows. Family planners have an ethical duty to try to persuade their (mentally mature) child patients to consult with their parents. If the child does so, the parents have a right to give such advice as they think proper. The parents have no right to insist that the advice be followed, and there is no breach of any legal duty if the advice is not followed. Nor is there any breach of a legal or ethical duty if the patient ignores the doctor and does not seek parental advice. If the family planner fails in her or his ethical duty by failing even to attempt to persuade the patient to talk to the parents, no legal consequences follow, although there may be professional disciplinary consequences to be faced.

The issue of parental consultation in Scotland and England is not affected by the nature of the medical treatment involved. The *Gillick* case is strong authority for the view that all forms of family planning treatment, and other medical treatment, are to be dealt with in the same way. In the USA, on the other hand, the medical procedure of abortion is regarded as something very different from all other medical procedures,[57] thereby justifying far greater legal regulation. Indeed, the issue of parental consultation in the abortion decision has proved one of the most contentious for the US Supreme Court.

Parental involvement in the abortion decision was first discussed by the Supreme Court in *Planned Parenthood of Central Missouri v. Danforth*,[58] which involved a statute that required parental consent to the abortion of unmarried girls under 18. This was struck down by the Supreme Court on the same ground as the requirement for spousal consent in the same statute,[59] viz., that the state had no blanket power to veto a pregnant woman's decision to undergo an abortion and therefore it could not delegate that power to any other person (such as a parent). However, the Court was more equivocal on the issue of parental consultation rather than parental consent. Four justices dissented, on the ground that the state was entitled to protect minors against making important and irreparable decisions without parental consultation and consent, and two of the concurring justices suggested that a statute that encouraged parental counselling and therefore family stability would not necessarily be unconstitutional.

A parental consent requirement was again challenged in *Bellotti v. Baird*.[60] The statute there differed from that in *Danforth* in that it provided an alternative to parental consent which the pregnant girl could rely upon, in the form of a judicial order, but again the statute was held unconstitutional. Four justices held that the possibility of judicial authorization did not save the statute since that still amounted to the delegation, to a third party, of a right of veto in the abortion decision; but they postulated *(obiter)* that a parental notification provision might not be unconstitutional. Four other justices, while agreeing with the result, found the present statute unconstitutional because it permitted judicial authorization to be withheld even when the child was mature. And they postulated (also *obiter)* that a parental notification statute would be unconstitutional.

The split reasoning in *Bellotti* adds to the confusion in this area of American jurisprudence; but it is clear from that case and from *Danforth*, first, that a blanket requirement of parental consent to abortion is not constitutional and, secondly, that a parental consultation requirement would not be challengeable on the same grounds and might, therefore, be looked at more leniently. The stability of the family relationship has long been a value constitutionally favoured by the Supreme Court.[61] In *Danforth* it had been held that a parental veto would not strengthen the family relationship; but in *H. L. v. Matheson*[62] the Court decided that a parental notification provision would strengthen the family, and because it did not delegate any power of veto, such a requirement was constitutionally valid. However, that decision is limited in a number of ways. The plaintiff in that case had not alleged that she was a mature minor and so it was assumed that she had standing only to sue on behalf of the immature minor who was unmarried and living with, and dependent upon, her parents. Thus it is unclear whether the holding in this case would apply to a requirement that a mature minor, or one not dependent on her parents, consult with her parents, and whether it would apply to a minor whose best interests were not best served by parental notification. Indeed, Powell and Stewart JJ. joined in the Court's opinion only on the understanding that these questions were left open, and concluded that statutes such as this would be valid only when they provide an alternative decision-maker to whom the pregnant girl can have recourse if she believes that she is mature enough to make the abortion decision independently. The three dissenters in this case pointed out that the statute did not really require parental consultation, but only parental notification, which could be satisfied by a mere telephone call minutes before the operation. Thus, they held, the statute was not efficacious in encouraging counsel and advice.

Parental consultation, it is submitted, is a flawed concept. According to Justice Marshall in *Matheson*:

> . . . [it] hardly seems a legitimate state purpose where the minor's pregnancy resulted from incest, where a hostile or abusive parental response is assured, or where the minor's fears of such a response deter her from the abortion she desires.[63]

In relation to both abortion and contraception, and on both sides of the Atlantic, parental consultation is particularly flawed in relation to the mature minor (the only person to whom it is relevant since the immature minor cannot consent in any case): the whole point about being a mature minor is that, by definition, one is able to make up one's own mind about things. It certainly does not show a lack of maturity that a person is unwilling to talk to their parents about their sex life – very few of us are.[64] Maturity includes the ability to choose who to consult. Counsel and advice help when voluntarily sought; when they are imposed they can be resented and be counterproductive. Also, a right to give advice without a right to insist that it be followed would be frustrating to a strong-willed parent; and, from the child's point of view, for the law to insist on parental notification when the parent has no further right might seem little more than spiteful. A child who is mature enough to give consent to her own contraceptive or abortion treatment is a child who is mature enough to decide whether seeking parental advice will be a help or a hindrance. The law ought not to insist upon imposing a procedure that is efficacious only when voluntarily sought.

Confidentiality

The issue of confidentiality was almost totally ignored by the English courts in *Gillick*; yet, as has been pointed out,[65] for a young girl this is often the most pressing issue of concern. The General Medical Council takes the view that entitlement to confidentiality follows capacity to consent, and consequently that only those girls the doctor determines are mentally mature enough to consent are protected by confidentiality. The rationale behind this approach seems to be that if the girl is too young to understand, then she is best protected by having her parents informed.

The fallacy of this is that any person's understanding clearly varies according to what has to be understood. A girl who can understand contraception may not understand the full consequences of a sterilization;[66] similarly, the girl who does not understand contraception may understand fully well that she does not want her parents to be told that she sought it. However, it must be said that a doctor who acts on a genuine belief that a young girl may best be protected by having confidentiality breached is highly unlikely to be found guilty by a court of breach of confidence. The right of confidentiality is by no means absolute, and the public interest may supersede it.[67] On the other hand, the thrust of the *Gillick* case is to suggest that the public interest in preventing teenage pregnancies is best served by not inhibiting young girls from seeking contraception. That interest would be furthered by guarantees of confidentiality, even for the immature, except in the most extreme circumstances, for as has been pointed out,

> Unless confidentiality is extended to those who lack . . . capacity it must be anticipated that a significant number of even mature minors will not run the risk of being judged immature.[68]

Lord Fraser gave at least tacit recognition to this fact.[69]

Historically, breach of confidence has been considered a serious professional misdemeanour, and the law has little strong authority on the issue. For the person seeking help in this intimate area of medicine, confidentiality is fundamental, and it is therefore not at all satisfactory that the law should have no ready answer.

Notes

1 See Chapter 9.

2 A requirement found in many *US* jurisdictions in relation to abortion: see

Cook & Dickens, 'International Developments in Abortion Laws: 1977–88', 78 *Am. J. Pub.Health* 1305, 1988.

3 Authority for this proposition can be found in the Canadian case of *C. v. Wren* [1986] 35 *DLR* (4th) 419, and in the Australian case of *K. v. Minister for Youth and Community Services* [1982] 1 *NSWLR* 311 at p. 321.

4 S. 8(1) of the Family Law Reform Act 1969.

5 Per Heilbron J. in *Re D. (A Minor)* [1976] 1 *All ER* 326 at p. 335 and per Lord Templeman in *Re B. (A Minor) (Sterilisation)* [1987] 2 *WLR* 1213 at p. 1218.

6 (1981) 80 *LGR* 301.

7 [1984] *FLR* 811.

8 [1985] 2 *WLR* 413 at pp. 424/425.

9 Thomson, *Family Law in Scotland*, Butterworths, London, 1987 at pp. 159–60; McLean, *A Patient's Right to Know: Information Disclosure, The Doctor and the Law*, Dartmouth, Aldershot, 1989 at pp. 35–6.

10 And so in the Australian case of *Dept. of Social Security v.Van Luc Ho* [1987] 77 *ALR* 491 it was held that a father in Australia could not be said to have custody of the children he had left behind when he fled Vietnam.

11 S.8(3) of the Family Law Reform Act 1969 expressly preserves any right to consent that existed before the passing of that Act.

12 See Norrie, 'The *Gillick* Case and Parental Rights in Scots Law' 1985 *SLT* (News) 157 for institutional authority.

13 See Thomson, op. cit., note 9 above, at pp. 170–2.

14 See Custody of Children (Scotland) Act 1939, s.1; Maxwell, *The Practice of the Court of Session*, Scottish Courts Administration, Edinburgh, 1980 at p. 475.

15 Thomson, 'Parental Rights in Scots Law: Another View' 1985 *SLT* (News) 223.

16 See, for example, Eveleigh J. in the Court of Appeal in *Gillick v. West Norfolk & Wisbech Area Health Authority* [1985] 2 *WLR* 413 at p. 443.

17 [1981] 1 *WLR* 1412.

18 Guardianship of Minors Act 1971, s. 1.

19 Per Chevalier J. in *Couture-Jacquet v. Montreal Children's Hospital* (1986) 28 *DLR* (4th) 22 at p. 31, emphasis added.

20 [1976] 1 *All ER* 326. The case came before the court under the wardship procedure: see Chapter 7.

21 393 *F. Supp.* 847 (1975).

22 McLean, op. cit., note 9 above, at p. 49.

23 Williams, 'The Gillick Saga', *New LJ* 1156, 1985 at p. 1181.

24 'Reproduction Law and Medical Consent' 35 *U. Tor. LJ* 255, 1985 at p. 277.

25 Family Law Reform Act 1969, s. 8(1). Many other jurisdictions have the same rule, with either the same or different ages laid down: see Giesen, *International Medical Malpractice Law*, Martinus Nijhoff, Dortrecht, 1988 at p. 447.

26 Scottish minors, that is, by which is meant those below the age of 18 and above the ages of either 12 or 14.

27 Thomson, 'Parental Rights in Scots Law: Another View' 1985 *SLT* (News) 223.

28 1916 SC 623.

29 Ibid. at p. 635.

30 *Johnston v. Wellesley Hospital* (1970) 17 *DLR* (3d) 139. See also the Australian case of *K. v. Minister for Youth and Community Services* [1982] 1 *NSWLR* 311. For other jurisdictions see Giesen, op. cit. note 25 above, at pp. 437–48.

31 [1983] 3 *WLR* 859 (QBD), [1985] 2 *WLR* 412 (CA), [1985] 3 *WLR* 830 (HL).

32 It can be argued that there was, in fact, no such sanction: see Norrie, 'The Gillick Case and Parental Rights in Scots Law', 1985 *SLT* (News) 157. See

also Williams, op. cit., note 23 above, at p. 1157, who describes the Court of Appeal's conclusion on this point as 'intolerably loose thinking'.

33 [1985] 3 *WLR* at p. 839.
34 Ibid. at p. 839–40.
35 (1970) 17 *DLR* (3d) 139.
36 (1986) 35 *DLR* (4th) 419.
37 [1985] 3 *WLR* at p. 841.
38 Ibid. at p. 843.
39 Ibid. at p. 869.
40 For further criticism of Lord Templeman's approach, see Norrie, 'Gillick Again: The House of Lords Decides' 1986 *SLT* (News) 69.
41 [1985] 3 *WLR* at p. 844.
42 Ibid. at p. 853, emphasis added.
43 Ibid. at p. 855, emphasis added.
44 Ibid. at p. 858.
45 1986 *SLT* (News) 69 at p. 71.
46 Williams, op cit, note 23 above, at p. 1180. See also Brazier, *Medicine, Patients and the Law*, Penguin, Harmondsworth, 1987 at p. 229, who describes Lord Fraser's criteria as 'pious hopes'.
47 And thus would satisfy the consent requirements discussed in Chapter 9.
48 Discussed in Chapter 9.
49 Bromley, *Family Law*, 7th edn, Butterworths, London, 1987 at pp. 285–7.
50 (1986) 35 *DLR* (4th) 419.
51 [1985] 3 *WLR* at p. 844. See also Lord Scarman at p. 860 to similar effect.
52 Cf. Williams, op. cit. note 23 above, at p. 1182, who talks of Lord Fraser's 'public-relations anxieties'.
53 [1985] 3 *WLR* at p. 868.
54 [1969] 3 *All ER* 578.
55 (1860) 22 *D.* 1198.
56 'Parental Rights in Scots Law: Another View', 1985 *SLT* (News) 223.
57 See, for example, Powell J. in *Bellotti v. Baird* 443 *US* 662, 61 *L. Ed.* 2d 797 (1979) who talks of 'the unique nature of the abortion decision' at pp. 642 and 812.
58 428 *US* 52, 49 *L. Ed.* 2d 788 (1976).
59 See Chapter 5.
60 443 *US* 662, 61 *L. Ed.* 2d 797 (1979).
61 See the discussion in Wardle & Wood, *A Lawyer Looks at Abortion*, Brigham Young University Press, Provo, 1982 at pp. 77–90.
62 450 *US* 398, 67 *L. Ed.* 2d 388 (1981).
63 450 *US* at p. 446, 67 *L. Ed.* at p. 422.
64 As Lord Fraser pointed out in *Gillick* [1985] 3 *WLR* at p. 844.
65 Brazier, op. cit., note 46 above, at p. 231.
66 Per Woolf J. in *Gillick* at first instance [1983] 3 *WLR* 859 at p. 869.
67 *X. v. Y.* [1988] 2 *All ER* 648; *W. v. Egdell* [1989] 1 *All ER* 1089.
68 Montgomery, 'Confidentiality and the Immature Minor', *Fam. Law* 101, 1987, at p. 103.
69 [1985] 3 *WLR* at p. 844.

7 Birth Control for the Mentally Disabled

Introduction

The mentally disabled are as entitled to enjoy sexual relations as the rest of us,[1] subject only to their requiring protection from exploitation. Many mentally disabled people do not have the capacity to understand the relationship between sex, pregnancy and childbirth, but can nevertheless understand, and desire, the physical pleasure that sex gives. An increasing recognition of this, together with a greater willingness to allow the mentally disabled to explore and experience social intercourse, has given such people much more opportunity than in the past to enter into sexual relations.

In common with other women who enter into sexual relations, the mentally disabled woman who does so runs the risk of pregnancy. That risk might be considered all the more serious for such a woman if her disability prevented her from being able properly to bring up the child: for it would then inevitably be removed from her, and she would have had to suffer the pains of pregnancy and childbirth without any of the benefits that parenthood normally brings.

If society recognizes that the mentally disabled ought to be allowed to have sex, then logically it should also recognize that these people ought to be allowed to be protected from the unwelcome consequences of sex. Birth control will give the mentally disabled no protection from sexual exploitation (though realistically neither should it make that exploitation any more likely), but it will give the protection for which it is designed – protection from unwanted pregnancy.

However, the obtaining of valid consent for birth control treatment presents a serious legal difficulty. As will be seen in Chapter 9, no family planning treatment may lawfully be given to an individual unless that individual provides consent to the actual treatment given.[2] And, as was seen in Chapter 6, the only exception to this rule is that parents or persons with parental rights over children may provide consent to medical treatment – including family planning treatment – for a child, although the parental right of consent is limited to treatment that is not against the interests of the child. It follows that, for the mentally disabled adult (by which is meant for the purposes of this chapter any adult person whose mind functions so abnormally as to make that person incapable of understanding a proposed medical procedure), no-one can give the consent that the law requires to the family planning treatment; and for the mentally disabled child, consent can only be given in the exercise of the parental right and duty to act for the welfare of the child.

This might suggest that a mentally disabled person, who can validly enter into a sexual relationship, may have medical birth control closed to them, just as, for example, the altruistic donation of blood or organs might be closed to them:[3] the legality of organ donation is based on free and rational choice, and should not be permitted in the absence of such choice. Elective family planning is also a matter of choice. However, it is submitted that birth control is *not* closed to the mentally disabled, although finding the legal justification has caused many jurisdictions great difficulty.

Few countries have dealt with this problem legislatively. New Zealand, however, provides an exception. S. 4 of that country's Contraception, Sterilisation and Abortion Act 1977, expressly allows for the provision of contraceptive treatment to any female 'if that female is mentally subnormal' without her consent. A mentally subnormal female is defined to mean a person suffering from

> . . . subnormality of intelligence as a result of arrested or incomplete development of mind to the extent that she is incapable of living an independent life or of guarding herself against serious exploitation or common physical dangers or to the extent that she is incapable of understanding the effective use of contraceptives or the desirability or need for their use.

The type of contraceptive treatment is not limited in the statute (which talks of the administration of 'any contraceptive'), and hormonal, mechanical or barrier methods may therefore be provided. By s. 4(3), only registered medical practitioners may fit IUDs or administer contraceptives by injection. The only condition that has to be satisfied before any contraceptive can be administered is that 'it is considered in the best interests of the female to do so'. Since the statute makes a clear distinction between contraception and sterilization (they are covered in different parts of the Act), it is likely that surgical sterilization for contraceptive purposes is not covered by s. 4, and will therefore be subject to the general requirement for consent.

Unfortunately, few other jurisdictions have provided statutory authority for the provision of birth control treatment to the mentally disabled, and the courts in most countries have had to find some common law justification for giving treatment that is now being seen not only as acceptable but, increasingly, as highly desirable. The issue of providing family planning treatment to the mentally disabled has come before the courts in a number of jurisdictions, although almost exclusively in relation to sterilization. It is, however, important to remember that the problem does not only arise in relation to that surgical operation, for the lack of consent and the legal problems that are created thereby exist for all forms of medically supplied birth control – indeed all forms of medical treatment.

Due to the diversity of approach between different countries, it will be necessary to examine the case law from a number of jurisdictions separately. Different courts have provided different insights into essentially the same problem, and a proper understanding of the position in one legal system is often assisted by an understanding of how other jurisdictions tackle the issue.

English Law

English law, like other common law jurisdictions, treats children very differently from adults. A minor in English law is a person under 18. A minor over the age of 16 can consent to her or his own medical treatment,[4] and a minor under the age of 16 may provide her or his own consent to such treatment if she or he fully understands what is involved.[5] Parents, or those exercising parental rights, may consent on behalf of a person under 18, although if there is a conflict between a parent and a child able to give personal consent, the child's wishes will almost certainly prevail.

There is, in English law, a further classification of children into those who are wards of court and those who are not. Wardship can last up until the age of 18, and once a child is warded, its own right to decide, as well as its parents' right to decide, are superseded by the court's right to make decisions concerning all 'important' matters. If the child is *not* a ward of court, then she or he can provide personal consent, subject to the satisfaction of the *Gillick* criteria.[6]

Adults cannot be made wards of court in English law, and no-one has the right to give proxy consent to medical treatment on behalf of adults.

These principles apply to the mentally disabled as to the non-disabled person.

Children

A mentally disabled child, if she or he is unable to understand birth control, will not be in a position to give consent to such treatment. But the parent of such a child can consent, and, if the child is a ward of court, so can the court. However, neither court nor parents have an unfettered discretion, and both must make the decision on the basis of the welfare of the child.[7] The test is variously described as the welfare test, or the best interests test, or the interests test, but in law all these phrases have substantially the same meaning.[8] If the child is likely to be sexually active and would suffer from becoming pregnant, to a greater degree than would be caused by providing birth control treatment, then it would be for such a child's welfare to be given that treatment.

Most forms of reversible contraception are less harmful than unwanted pregnancy (an assessment made by many millions of competent adults every day), and if a doctor comes to that conclusion in relation to a particular mentally disabled child, then contraceptive treatment may lawfully be consented to by the parents, or, if the child is a ward, by the court. Abortion may also be consented to on this basis: that operation, to be legal at all, will often be deemed to be in the patient's interests, and if so, proxy consent on behalf of the pregnant child may be given,[9] and relied upon by the doctor.

The real difficulties in law are caused by sterilization, for this is an irreversible procedure that involves a significant surgical invasion into a person's body. Unlike contraception and abortion, sterilization of the mentally disabled is usually factually very different from sterilization of the non-disabled. With a non-disabled person sterilization is normally contemplated only after the patient has had a number of children, and is comparatively old. With the disabled, however, sterilization is often proposed to protect them from having any children at all, and is often suggested at a much earlier age. It is therefore much more difficult to determine whether the operation will be for the welfare of the patient. Sterilization of mentally disabled children has been discussed in two important English cases.

In *Re D. (A Minor)*[10] Heilbron J. was asked to authorize, in the exercise of the wardship jurisdiction, the sterilization of an 11 year-old girl who suffered from a mild mental impairment, which gave her a dull intelligence and emotional instability. Her mother feared that the child, who had precocious physical development, would be seduced and give birth to a baby which she would not be able to look after. Pregnancy and childbirth in these circumstances would, it was claimed, be very much against the interests of the ward. The evidence, however, showed that her mental condition would probably improve, and although she would always be to a certain extent mentally backward, it was accepted that by the time she was an adult she would have sufficient mental capacity to give a valid consent to her own marriage. Heilbron J. considered this to be a decisive factor, and refused to authorize the sterilization. The welfare of the child would be better served by keeping her options open and allowing her – possibly in consultation with a future husband – to make up her own mind about her own medical treatment. Thus it was held that it would not be in her best interests to be subjected to an irreversible procedure to protect her from potential hurts which might never arise, especially when this would involve the denial of a 'fundamental human right' which she would probably be able to decide upon herself in the future. It is clear that had some reversible form of contraception, whether hormonal or mechanical, been proposed (and been practicable), the court would have been much more likely to authorize the provision of that treatment.

The opposite conclusion was reached by the House of Lords in the later case of *Re B. (A Minor) (Sterilization)*.[11] That case involved a 17 year-old-girl, called Jeanette, who suffered from a moderate degree of mental impairment. She had the speech of a two year-old and the understanding of a six year-old (the girl in *Re D.*, at the age of 11, had the mental maturity of a child of 9½). Jeanette was at times moody, unco-operative and violent, and she had recently shown signs of sexual awareness. But she was wholly incapable of understanding the processes of sex, pregnancy and childbirth, and had no maternal instincts. If she were to give birth, she would require to have heavy sedation, probably a caesarian section, and would be likely to pick at her wounds. As an epileptic, and a person of unpredictable moods, a daily course of contraceptive pills was deemed impracticable. Her mental condition ruled out mechanical methods of contraception such as the coil or the cap.

The local authority, which had care and control over the child, and consequently (in English law)[12] parental rights over her, was willing to consent to the operation of sterilization, to protect her from any possible pregnancy; but unsure of its legal authority to provide that consent (in other words, afraid that it might be accused of not acting in the best interests of the child), it had the child made a ward of court and asked the High Court to provide the necessary consent. A guardian *ad litem* was appointed and he opposed the giving of consent. Bush J., a unanimous Court of Appeal, and a unanimous House of Lords all held that consent should be given and that the sterilization operation should be carried out. Lord Hailsham, Lord Bridge and Lord Oliver (with all three of whom Lord Brandon agreed) pointed out that, in wardship, the first and paramount consideration is always the welfare of the ward. Lord Hailsham said that this was the only matter to be taken into account, and that no issue of public policy could be relevant in such a case. All three emphasized in particular that the question of eugenics (the sterilization of those disabled through genetic factors in order to 'improve' the human stock) was utterly irrelevant and not to be taken into account. They accepted that pregnancy would be a disaster for this ward, and that any child born to her would immediately have to be removed. The ward had no maternal instincts, and physically the birth-giving process would be much more difficult for her than for other women. As reversible forms of contraception were, for various reasons, inappropriate, sterilization, being a last resort, was in the ward's best interests and ought therefore to be authorized. Lord Bridge put it thus:

> It is clear beyond argument that for her pregnancy would be an unmitigated disaster. The only question is how she may best be protected against it. The evidence proves overwhelmingly that the right answer is by a simple operation for occlusion of the fallopian tubes . . .[13]

Again, had contraception been appropriate (which it was not)[14] it is likely that that option would have been considered to be more in the ward's best interests than surgical sterilization.

The best interests test has been long established as the sole and paramount criterion for determining issues affecting children, and the wardship courts in *Re D.* and *Re B.* had no other option but to adopt that test. However, what the courts in these cases failed to do was to lay down guiding principles that would help later decision-makers determine what is, or is not, relevant to the application of that amorphous test.[15] Suggested principles are given at the end of this chapter.

Adults

Both parental rights and wardship, which are to be exercised for the protection of the child, come to an end when the child reaches the age of 18. But the mentally disabled do not lose their need for protection just because they attain that age. For many years there was much doubt in English law as to whether or not the courts have an inherent jurisdiction, emanating from the Crown's role as *parens patriae* to protect those, such as the mentally disabled, who cannot look after themselves.[16] In *Re B. (A Minor) (Sterilisation)* the House of Lords held that it was not necessary to answer this question, since the patient in that case was a ward who would clearly benefit from immediate treatment. However, Lord Oliver was prepared to assume, but not prepared without fuller argument to hold, that the *parens patriae* jurisdiction over adults still existed.[17]

Shortly after *Re B. (A Minor) (Sterilisation)* was decided, a judge at first instance was faced with an application for consent to perform an abortion and a sterilization upon a woman beyond the age of wardship. In *T. v. T. and Another*[18] a 19 year-old woman with a mental age of three and no hope of improvement was discovered to be pregnant and her mother and her doctors wished to terminate the pregnancy and to sterilize her to protect her from any future pregnancy. Wood J. found that in law there was no-one able to consent to such operations, not even the court; but he nevertheless authorized these operations even in the absence of consent. The precise basis of this holding is not at all clear. Wood J. accepted that any surgical procedure without consent is *prima facie* an act of trespass to the person, and that the only defence to such a wrong in the absence of consent is that of 'necessity' – that is, the existence of an immediate threat of injury, which treatment would prevent or cure (as in, for example, the unconscious road accident victim).[19] However, he went on to hold that 'necessity' was not sufficiently precise as a test, and instead held that doctors would not be acting unlawfully if they took 'such steps as good medical practice "demands" ', by which he meant to envisage a situation where, based upon good medical practice, there really were no two views about what course was best. It is difficult to identify any real distinction between 'medical demand' and 'necessity', and the former ought probably to be regarded as a more precise formulation of the latter. Wood J. ended his judgement with a plea for a speedy restoration of the prerogative *parens patriae* jurisdiction.

The issue was again discussed in *F. v. West Berkshire Health Authority*[20] in which the extent of the *parens patriae* jurisdiction over adults is fully examined.[21] This case involved a 35 year-old woman with a mental age of four. She had entered into a sexual relationship with a male patient in the hospital in which she lived, and took pleasure from it. Those in charge of her did not want to bring this non-exploitative relationship to an end. Reversible contraception was either not practicable or positively detrimental to her health, and in order to protect her from the problems of pregnancy, an application was made to the court to authorize her sterilization. Once again, all the judges who heard the case were unanimously of the view that no-one had the right to give consent, but that the operation should nevertheless go ahead; and the importance of this case lies in the search for a basis on which treatment without consent would be valid.

It was held initially that the *parens patriae* jurisdiction no longer existed for adults, and so some other basis had to be found. Necessity as a test seems to have been considered too strict or too rigid, although it was accepted that this may be the foundation of the jurisdiction eventually exercised. Lord Bridge pointed out that if necessity alone were the criterion this would deprive many mentally disabled patients of beneficial treatment.[22] Lord Goff seemed to be more attracted by necessity, although he held that there does not need to be an emergency facing the patient before treatment can be described as 'necessary',[23] thus giving a wider meaning to 'necessity' than was assumed in, for example, *T. v. T*. Another test that was regarded as important was the *Bolam* test, which is normally used in actions for negligence and requires the doctor to act with the standard of the ordinary skilled man exercising and professing to have that skill. Indeed Lord Brandon[24] and Lord Goff[25] seemed to suggest that this test imposes a duty on doctors to sterilize when it would be good medical practice to do so. This must surely be going too far, for in most cases good medical practice does not *demand* one course of action over another, as is expressly recognized in *Bolam* itself.

But the test preferred by all the judges in the House of Lords is that of the best interests of the patient. This of course is the test used in relation to children, and there is certainly tidiness in having the same test for adults. There is even, unlike in the speeches in *Re B.*, some indication as to how that test is to be determined. Lord Brandon said:

> The operation or other treatment will be in their best interests if, but only if, it is carried out in order either to save their lives or to ensure improvement or prevent deterioration in their physical or mental health.[26]

Lord Goff had tried to equiparate the best interests test with the necessity test, and even with the *Bolam* test, but this simply will not work. The best interests test is not the same as either. Clearly there will be a large area of overlap, and most, if not all, actions that are both 'necessary' and good medical practice will also be in the best interests of the patient. Yet not everything that is in the best interests of a patient can be regarded as 'necessary', even in the extended sense of that word favoured by Lord Goff. Inherent in the *Bolam* test is a recognition that there may be more than one proper course of action, which takes it away from the 'necessity' or 'medical demand' test postulated in *T v. T*. Non-therapeutic circumcision of a baby boy, for example, might sometimes satisfy the welfare test, since that test takes account of family, religious, and ethnic background; but it could seldom be claimed that that procedure is necessary in the sense of being medically demanded as the only proper course. It is accepted medical practice both to circumcise, and not to circumcise.

Necessity, even in the wide sense, assumes a high degree of certainty, which simply does not exist in most cases. The New Jersey Supreme Court discussed the appropriateness of necessity as the test for authorizing non-consensual sterilization in the case of *Re Grady*[27] and rejected it on the ground that there will usually be many different, though still proper, courses of action available, and that a necessity test could be used to justify treatment *against* (as opposed to in the absence of) a patient's express wishes.[28] In few cases could it be claimed that only one course of action is proper. This might just be apt in cases like *T. v. T.* where the woman was already pregnant, or even in *F. v. West Berkshire Health Authority* itself where the woman had already entered into a sexual relationship. But in other cases in which women are not in sexual relationships, but may some time in the future be so, it would be impossible to say that family planning treatment is 'necessary' in any proper sense of that word.

Nor is the *Bolam* test at all appropriate. Although an important aspect of that test is to recognize that there may be more than one proper course of treatment, it is inappropriate here since it is designed to test the *standard* of treatment given, not its legality, which is an issue that is determined at an earlier stage.

So, the best interests test, applied to children, is now also to be applied to mentally disabled adults. The other tests mentioned in *F.* do not receive majority support and, for the reasons given above, are not appropriate for the type of treatment at issue.

The Best Interests Test in Canada

Canadian law is more straightforward in this area than English law, because the courts in that country accept that the *parens patriae* jurisdiction extends into adulthood. It follows that, for both the mentally disabled child and the mentally disabled adult, the same test will be applied. That test is the best interests test, identical to the one used in England. Suggestions that the Supreme Court of Canada adopts a different test are, as will be seen, unfounded.

In relation to children, there is no question but that, as in English law, the first and paramount consideration is the welfare of the child. In *Re K. and Public Trustee*[29] the British Columbia Court of Appeal authorized a hysterectomy to be performed on a 10 year-old girl who was severely mentally handicapped. The case involved a child, and consequently the court adopted a best interests approach: indeed it overruled the trial judge because, *inter alia*, he had based his decision more on the rights of the handicapped in general than on the best interests of the particular child in question. The Court of Appeal based its authorization of this serious operation on the fact that the girl was said to suffer a phobic aversion to the sight of blood, and was incapable of managing the hygienic aspects of menstruation: it was therefore in her best interests to have the source of this trauma removed. The court emphasized that the operation was in the child's best interests, not because of its birth control effects, but for the prevention of the onset of menstruation. That was simply another problem that sterilization could remove.[30]

The Supreme Court of Canada was asked to authorize the sterilization of a mentally disabled adult in the case of *Re Eve*.[31] That Court, after a lengthy and erudite discussion of the concept, held that the court's *parens patriae* jurisdiction did extend to adult incompetents in Canada, and that, as in wardship, it had to be exercised for the benefit of the patient, not for the benefit of others.

The woman in this case, known as Eve, was 24 years old and was moderately retarded. There was, however, no evidence that childbirth would be any more difficult for her than for any other woman, although certainly any child she might have would be removed immediately after birth as she was wholly incapable of bringing up a child. The Supreme Court held that the real purpose of the operation was to relieve Eve's mother of anxiety, and of the practical realities of looking after any child Eve might give birth to, and it concluded therefore that 'non-therapeutic' sterilizations could *never* be authorized in a court of law.

This conclusion came in for harsh – and ill-informed – criticism in the English House of Lords case of *Re B. (A Minor) (Sterilisation)*. The reasoning and conclusion in the Canadian case were there described as 'unhelpful' and 'meaningless'. Lord Hailsham went so far as to describe the conclusion of the Supreme Court as

> . . . totally unconvincing and in startling contradiction to the welfare principle which should be the first and paramount consideration in wardship cases.[32]

La Forest J, speaking for the whole court in *Re Eve* had said:

> The grave intrusion on a person's rights and the certain physical damage that ensues from non-therapeutic sterilization without consent, when compared to the highly questionable advantage that can result from it, have persuaded me that it can never safely be determined that such a procedure is for the benefit of that person. Accordingly the procedure should never be authorized for non-therapeutic purposes under the *parens patriae* jurisdiction.[33]

Lord Bridge in *Re B.* quoted this passage and replied:

> This sweeping generalisation seems to me, with respect, to be entirely unhelpful. To say that the court can never authorise sterilisation of a ward as being in her best interests would be patently wrong. To say that it can only do so if the operation is 'therapeutic' as opposed to 'non-therapeutic' is to divert attention from the true issue, which is whether the operation is in the ward's best interest, and remove it to an area of arid semantic debate as to where the line is to be drawn between 'therapeutic' and 'non-therapeutic' treatment.[34]

These criticisms are based on the assumption that the Supreme Court of Canada was intending to lay down a different test from the well-established welfare test to be applied in determining whether sterilization ought to be authorized. This is however an unfounded assumption, and a proper and careful reading of La Forest J.'s carefully thought-out judgement indicates that the Supreme Court was intending to apply a best interests test in identical form to the one used by the English courts.

An analysis of the structure of La Forest J.'s judgement shows this. The Supreme Court had been asked to adopt a substituted judgement test rather than a best interests test to determine the issue – that is, to determine how the court thought the patient would have decided the issue had the patient been competent, rather than determining the question according to the court's views of the best interests of the patient. La Forest J. examined both tests, but he rejected the substituted judgement test in favour of the best interests test, holding that the exercise of the *parens patriae* jurisdiction was limited to doing what was in the best interests of the incompetent. This was the real test, and it was not for the court to make the choice on behalf of the individual, 'between two alleged constitutional rights – the right to procreate or not to procreate'.[35]

Other parts of his judgement indicate clearly that he was applying the best interests test. He pointed out that there were two main purposes of the proposed operation: to protect Eve from the trauma of giving birth and the resulting obligations of being a parent, and to protect her mother from anxiety and the practical realities of looking after Eve's possible child. Since the evidence showed that pregnancy and childbirth would be no more difficult for Eve than for any other woman[36] (this in stark contrast to the position of the girl in *Re B.*) the only extra element was the protection of Eve's mother. Now it is clearly not in a person's best interests to undergo a serious surgical operation simply to relieve another person of anxiety, and that was the sense in which La Forest J. described the operation as being non-therapeutic. On saving Eve's mother of anxiety he said this:

> The *parens patriae* jurisdiction cannot be used for her benefit. Its exercise is confined to doing what is necessary for the benefit and protection of persons under disabilities like Eve . . . So we are left to consider whether the purposes underlying the operation are *necessarily for Eve's benefit and protection.*[37]

He decided that the purposes were not for Eve's benefit and protection and he described them as being non-therapeutic. There is no difference between this and saying that they were not in Eve's best interests.

The criticisms of the Supreme Court's judgement levelled by the House of Lords in *Re B.* are not valid. The best interests test, though long established, suffers from being amorphous and unpredictable. Of its nature, it has to be subjective, but this allows for different courts to take different views as to what course of action will be best. The House of Lords in *Re B.* glibly stated that the welfare of the patient is the sole consideration, without giving any guidance as to how that is to be determined,[38] while what the Supreme Court in *Re Eve* attempted to do[39] was to lay down guidelines for the proper application of this test. The major guidance given by the Supreme Court was that the effect on the patient is the only relevant effect for determining the patient's welfare. If the operation is for the benefit of someone other than the patient (such as the parent, the carer, or the state itself) then it is 'non-therapeutic', and not directed to the benefit of the patient; it cannot therefore be authorized as being in the best interests of that patient. La Forest J said:

> I cannot agree that a court can deprive a woman of [the privilege of giving life] for purely social *or other* non-therapeutic purposes without her consent.[40]

The italicized words emphasize that this is all the court meant by the phrase 'non-therapeutic'.

If the word 'therapeutic' is interpreted widely, then this is important guidance. For if one accepts that therapy can include the prevention of future hurts as well as the treatment of existing hurts, then the identity of approaches between the House of Lords and the Supreme Court becomes even more apparent. Lord Oliver disapproved *Re Eve*.

> . . . *if* . . . the expression 'non-therapeutic' was intended to exclude measures taken for the necessary protection from future harm of the person over whom the jurisdiction is exercisable.[41]

But the point is that there is nothing in the Supreme Court's judgement that does exclude such measures. Neither the Supreme Court nor the House of Lords would accept Pope Paul VI's definition of 'therapeutic sterilization', given in *Humanae Vitae* as operations 'in which the impediment to procreation is not directly willed'. In *Re K. and Public Trustee* the British Columbia Court of Appeal criticized the trial judge in that case for limiting 'therapeutic' treatment to 'treatment of an existing as opposed to an anticipated disease, illness, disability or disorder'.[42] A therapeutic abortion is one designed to prevent future hurts, both physical and mental,[43] and it is no abuse of language to extend this description to contraception and sterilization with an identical purpose.

So the guidance given by the Supreme Court in *Re Eve,* for the application of the best interests test, is sensible and helpful. Whether the proposed procedure is for the benefit of the patient or for someone else is not the only criterion to be taken into account in applying that test (as will be seen at the end of this chapter), but it is one of the most important.

Scots Law

Although there are no cases directly in point from the Scottish courts, it is possible to predict the approach that Scots law is likely to take.

So far as children are concerned, there is of course no wardship procedure, although the Scottish courts have historically exercised a protective jurisdiction over children in Scotland, as affirmed in, for example, *Docherty v. McGlynn*.[44] The courts may therefore grant consent on behalf of children up to the age of 18. Parents, in the exercise of their right of custody, may grant consent on behalf of children up to the age of 16.[45] The welfare test, accepted in Scots law as it is in English law, must be satisfied. It follows that any birth control treatment could be given to a mentally disabled child on satisfaction of that test and with the consent of either the court or the parent, where appropriate. Indeed it may be (although there is no authority for this) that the courts would allow parents to consent on behalf of mentally disabled children between the ages of 16 and 18, since the test to be applied is the same as for the court's consent.

In circumstances in which a doctor wishes to provide family planning treatment to a mentally disabled minor, but is unsure whether the best interests test is satisfied, or whether she or he can rely on the parents' consent, then the court's authority should be sought. Thomson[46] suggests two ways in which this can be done (although he also goes on to suggest that the court's authority must *always* be sought: see below). First, in the exercise of its inherent protective jurisdiction, the Court of Session may grant a declaration (declarator) that the proposed treatment is not unlawful or that the parental consent is valid. Secondly, either the Court of Session or the Sheriff Court may under s. 3(1) of the Law Reform (Parent and Child) (Scotland) Act 1986 make 'any order relating to parental rights as it thinks fit'. An order could therefore be obtained to the effect that parental consent to the provision of contraceptives, or the performing of a sterilization or abortion operation, is a proper exercise of parental rights. The court would of course grant such an order only on the basis that it was in the best interests of the child.

In relation to adults, there is (as in English law) no-one, not even the court, who has an inherent right to grant consent on behalf of an incompetent. Certainly treatment would probably be considered legal if it were 'necessary' or 'medically demanded' in the sense used in *T. v. T.*[47] in England, this on the same basis that emergency treatment may lawfully be given to someone who is unconscious. There is no authority allowing the Scottish court itself to authorize non-consensual treatment just because it is in the best interests of an adult incompetent, although an action for declarator might be competent, allowing the court to declare that the proposed treatment is not unlawful even in the absence of consent. More likely to be required, however, is a procedure that *does* have authority: it is open to the Court of Session to appoint someone who can provide the missing consent. A tutor-dative has rights of control over both the estate *and* the person of an incompetent (there is no analogous institution in English law) and while such a tutor will normally be appointed for children, the court may, exceptionally, appoint such a person over adults. A tutor-dative would be bound to act on the same principles as governs tutors of pupil children. In *Morris, Pet.*,[48] parents of a handicapped man of 20 applied for, and were appointed, tutors-dative of their son; and they were given a list of express powers, including the right to consent to any health care that was in the boy's best interests. So, in Scotland, once a tutor-dative is appointed, that person could consent to any birth control procedure, including abortion and sterilization operations, when it is in the best interests of the incompetent.

Non-consensual Sterilization in the United States

Sterilization of the mentally disabled has had a discreditable history in many countries of the world, particularly in the USA where, in the early years of this century, many statutes were passed allowing sterilization of persons for public policy reasons, to save the public purse, and to enhance the human gene pool (for which, of course, read the White Anglo-Saxon gene pool).[49] In the famous case of *Buck v. Bell*[50] a statute authorizing the sterilization of mentally disabled women to prevent them bringing more children into the world to be a burden on the state was upheld by the US Supreme Court, 'for no more compelling reason than to prevent another generation of "imbeciles" '.[51]

Although the eugenics movement in the United States has largely been discredited, many of the early statutes remain in force, and *Buck v. Bell* has never been overruled. However, the American courts, particularly since the end of the Second World War, have been much more cautious about allowing non-consensual sterilization, for any reason.

Many jurisdictions within the USA statutorily allow judges to authorize sterilization, for a variety of reasons – some for social policy reasons, others solely on the ground of the interests of the mentally disabled person. Some jurisdictions allow sterilization only of those who are institutionalized, while other states confer more general powers on the courts.

In many other jurisdictions, however, no express statutory power is granted to judges to order or authorize sterilization. There is much diversity of opinion about whether the courts in these jurisdictions nevertheless possess an inherent equitable jurisdiction to sanction non-consensual sterilization.[52] For many years few courts claimed that they possessed such a power; indeed it was feared that judges who acted in the absence of statutory authority would lose their judicial immunity and be liable for damages for assault if they ordered non-consensual sterilization. The threat of judicial liability was substantially weakened by the US Supreme Court in 1976,[53] and since then a variety of approaches to the problem has emerged. Some courts continue to hold that, in the absence of statutory authority, they have no power to authorize or order non-consensual sterilization of the mentally disabled,[54] but other courts do accept that they possess this power. There is, however, little consensus as to when such a power should be exercised.

Some courts recognize only a very limited power to order sterilization. For example, the Maryland Court of Appeals in *Wentzel v. Montgomery General Hospital*[55] held that it could authorize a sterilization, but only if this were necessary, in the sense of being 'medically essential'. This approach is substantially the same as that adopted by Wood J. in the English case of *T. v. T.*,[56] and, like the approach in that case, would limit the power to situations that are absolutely clear-cut and in which there is no room for doubt as to what to do for the best.

Other courts recognize a rather wider power. A majority of courts, recognizing an inherent equitable jurisdiction, accept, as the Canadian courts have done, that the *parens patriae* jurisdiction extends into adulthood and therefore allow judges to authorize sterilization on the basis of the best interests of the incompetent. There is, however, another approach, adopted by a small number of US jurisdictions, called a 'rights analysis' approach or a 'substituted judgement' test. Giesen describes this test as follows:

> The goal should be to make a substituted judgment for the patient by choosing the option which the patient would choose if he were competent. A decision must not be based on what most people would choose, or on what the court believes to be the wisest choice.[57]

The most influential example of this approach is that of the Supreme Court of New Jersey in the case of *Re Grady*.[58] Here, the parents of a 19 year-old girl suffering from Down's Syndrome wished her to be sterilized, for they felt that this would give her the chance of a richer and more active life, as she would not then have to be prevented from having normal social, and possibly sexual, relationships with other people. The Supreme Court of New Jersey held that there is a constitutionally protected right to contraceptive sterilization (this being complementary to the constitutionally protected right to reproduce); and it further held that this right attaches to everyone. It is not to be denied to the mentally disabled just because they cannot choose to exercise it. Consequently, when the person cannot choose personally, someone else must make that choice, basing the choice *not* on the best interests of the person, but rather on their assessment of how that person would have decided had the person been competent and in full possession of the facts. Implicit in this approach is a recognition that rational people have the right to act against what a court of law might regard as their own best interests. The Supreme Court of New Jersey, in adopting this approach, was following its earlier and more famous decision in *Re Quinlan*,[59] in which it had held that a woman in a coma on a life-support machine was not to be denied the right to switch that machine off, and that the parents of the woman, being in the best position to know what she would have chosen, could make the decision for her. In *Re Grady*, the Court held that, in relation to a sterilization operation, the Court rather than the parents was in the best position to judge how the incompetent would have decided, and on that basis it authorized the sterilization.

The substituted judgement approach can easily be criticized as being 'legal legerdemain', and it is clearly 'obviously fiction'[60] to say that the court's consent is the consent of the patient. But the rights analysis aspect of this approach is a refreshing judicial recognition that rights are not to be denied to the mentally disabled just because they do not understand them. It also provides a strong answer to the frequently made claim that non-consensual sterilization is the denial of the so-called 'right to reproduce'. The rights analysis approach recognizes that different, competing, rights must be balanced against each other, and that there is also a right *not* to reproduce while having sex. The precise weight to be given to the 'right to reproduce' has been subject to much debate in all jurisdictions faced with the issue of non-consensual sterilizations.

Sterilization and the 'Right to Reproduce'

While the problem of lack of consent applies equally to contraception as to abortion and to sterilization, this has caused substantial difficulties for the courts only in relation to sterilization operations. The reason for this seems to be the irreversibility of sterilization. It is claimed that everyone has a 'right to reproduce', and it might follow that the non-consensual removal of this capacity amounts to a denial of that important right. Some argue that only personal consent could ever justify the denial of that right (by the removal of that capacity).[61] This, of course, does not necessarily follow, since the right could be effectively denied by non-consensual means other than the removal of the capacity, for example by incarceration in a single-sex institution.

However illogical it may be, it is nevertheless true that the idea of sterilizing a person without consent does frequently meet with a negative emotional response, unlike non-consensual contraception, or even abortion (which, in its own way, is also irreversible). This response finds voice in the claim for a 'right to reproduce'; and it is not difficult to find apparent legal support for such a right. The European Convention on Human Rights for example protects, by Article 12, 'the right to marry and found a family'. A number of the judges in the cases discussed above appear to recognize a right to reproduce. In *Re Eve* the Supreme Court of Canada talks of the fundamental right and the great privilege of having children. The Supreme Court of New Jersey in *Re Grady* talks of the 'basic liberty' to procreate. Likewise in *Re B. (A Minor)* Lord Hailsham and Lord Bridge maintain that Heilbron J. in *Re D. (A Minor)* was correct to describe the right to reproduce as a 'basic human right';[62] and Lord Templeman talks of the 'fundamental right of a girl to bear a child'.[63] Similar remarks are made in *F. v. West Berkshire Health Authority*.[64]

However, although apparently recognizing such a right, the courts do not seem to have much difficulty in side-stepping its consequences. In *Re B. (A Minor)*, for example, the House of Lords disposed fairly summarily with the 'fundamental rights' argument, Lord Hailsham saying of the 'right to reproduce':

> This right is only such [i.e. a basic human right] when reproduction is the result of informed choice of which this ward is incapable.[65]

Similarly, Lord Oliver said:

> The right to reproduce is of value only if accompanied by the ability to make a choice and in the instant case there is no question of the minor ever being able to make such a choice or indeed to appreciate the need to make one.[66]

These dicta would seem to suggest that a right only attaches to an individual if that individual understands the nature of that right and can choose to exercise it. Yet this cannot be correct, for it would at a stroke deny the mentally disabled of all the rights the law gives them, such as the right to life, the right to confidentiality, and the right to proper medical treatment, just because they cannot *understand* such rights and choose to exercise them.

A more persuasive line of reasoning is given in the US cases that adopt a rights analysis approach. In *Re Grady*[67] it was recognized that neither the right to reproduce nor the right not to reproduce should be denied to the mentally disabled just because they cannot choose to exercise them. Some other person must make the choice, balancing the two competing rights. Similarly, although the Canadian courts reject the *Re Grady* approach, they do nevertheless recognize that the right to reproduce can be ignored if that is necessary to protect a more important right. This is illustrated by Anderson J.A.'s words in *Re K. and Public Trustee.*

> I wish to emphasize that the rights of children under our Constitution include the right to be protected against unnecessary pain and suffering and the right to forego other constitutional rights in order to avoid unnecessary pain and suffering. To have insisted on a meaningless retention of the right to reproduce, would have been, in the circumstances of this case, a direct breach of the right of infant K to be protected against unnecessary pain and suffering.[68]

But there is a much stronger ground for resisting claims based on a fundamental rights argument: *there is no right to reproduce.*[69] To claim that there is diverts attention from the true and important rights that the law must give its protection to. There are three such rights that *do* exist.

Reproduction requires heterosexual sexual activity. If an individual can find a willing partner in sexual intercourse, she or he has a right to have sex, but has no right to demand that the partner takes no contraceptive measures; conversely a man cannot demand that the woman he impregnates undergoes an abortion.[70] The important freedom is therefore a sexual rather than a reproductive one. Putting it another way, the right to have sex does not carry with it the right to reproduce.

Reproduction involves parenthood as well as the creation of a new human person. The law protects the right[71] to care for and nourish and bring up a child, rather than the sterile desire to have one's genetic material used to create human life.[72] Article 12 of the European Convention on Human Rights protects *not* the 'right to reproduce', but rather the right to 'found a family'. Had the wards in *Re B.* or *Re Eve* or *Re Grady* become pregnant and given birth, their babies would have been taken away from them, and it would have been utterly false to say that they had 'founded families'.

Reproduction requires procreative capacity. As some people are born without that capacity, it is as meaningless to talk of such persons having a right to reproduce as it is to talk of the dead's right to life. But a person who does have procreative capacity has the right to keep that capacity, as an attribute of bodily integrity.

So the three important rights which together are often falsely referred to as the right to reproduce are: 1, the right to sexual freedom; 2, the right to family life; and 3, the right to bodily integrity. The right to sexual freedom is not infringed by sterilization. Indeed often it will be enhanced: so in *F. v. West Berkshire Health Authority*[73] the sterilization was proposed expressly in order to allow the woman to continue the sexual relationship into which she had entered. The right to family life is similarly not infringed by sterilization if the person is born without the capacity to exercise that right. A person who is born without the capacity to care for and bring up a child is not being denied the right to found a family by law, but rather has been deprived of the capacity for parenthood (in its full sense) by nature. Nor is the right to bodily integrity necessarily infringed. We all – the mentally disabled included – have the right to be protected from unwarranted surgical interference. But bodily integrity can often be enhanced by surgical interference. A gangrenous leg can be amputated from a person unable to consent, in order to preserve life. If sterilization can be shown to protect a person from greater hurts than the operation itself, then that surgical interference enhances, rather than infringes, bodily integrity.

It was postulated in *Re Grady* that, since pregnancy and childbirth will always cause pain and anguish, it could be considered always to be in the best interests of mentally disabled women to be protected from pregnancy if their children would be removed, so denying them of any of the benefits of parenthood. It is unlikely that the British or Canadian courts would go that far, for in both *Re B. (A Minor) (Sterilisation)* and in *Re Eve* it was emphasized that a very relevant factor in both cases was whether or not pregnancy and childbirth would be any more difficult for the respective women in these cases than for the 'normal' woman. However, it is suggested that to prevent birth control treatment (including sterilization) from being given to a woman who will have all the normal physical trauma, pain and anguish of pregnancy and childbirth, and then have the child immediately removed so denying her the pleasures of parenthood, is not the protection of a privilege or a right, but exactly the opposite.

The Role of the Courts

The decision to sterilize any person who cannot give personal consent to the operation is clearly a very serious and significant step. In *Re D.*, Heilbron J. said: 'I cannot conceive of a more important step than that which was proposed in this case'.[74]

The courts in many jurisdictions have been asked to judge the legality of providing non-consensual treatment and, in the jurisdictions discussed above, the courts have held that, in certain circumstances, abortion and sterilization (and by implication contraception) can lawfully be given without consent. However, in relation particularly to sterilization it has been suggested that the courts ought to go much further than this. It is sometimes suggested that for *every* operation of sterilization for which consent cannot be obtained, the court must be asked to authorize it. Lord Templeman in *Re B. (A Minor) (Sterilization)* made this suggestion, although only in relation to children, saying: 'Sterilization of a girl under 18 should only be carried out with the leave of a High Court judge'.[75]

This received the support of a majority in the House of Lords in *F. v. West Berkshire Health Authority*, despite this being the least logical part of that important case. It will be remembered that the House of Lords decided there that the legality of sterilization was to be determined by whether or not the treatment was in the patient's best interests. The Court also held that judicial involvement cannot affect this: in Lord Goff's words, 'the present position is that the lawfulness of medical or surgical treatment cannot, in the case of adults, depend on the approval of the High Court'.[76] However, the judges did all hold that such approval, as a matter of practice, should always be sought. Indeed, Lord Griffiths wanted to create what he recognized would be a new rule of law, rather than a matter of practice, to the effect that for this type of operation to be legal at all, the court's authorization was always required: only thus could the public interest in the legality of such procedures be recognized.[77] The majority did not accept this, but they did hold that court involvement is very highly desirable, even though that can have no effect on the actual legality of the procedure.

There are many supporters for the view that the courts should always be involved in the decision-making process. Thomson, for example, recommended this course to the Scottish courts after *Re B.* but before *F.*[78] He argues that the court should always be involved because, with proposed sterilization operations, it will invariably not be clear wherein the best interests of the patient lie, and this should therefore be a matter for the courts. Thomson argues (in relation to children) that a person exercising parental rights cannot validly consent 'where the proposed treatment is arguably against the interests of the incapax'.[79] This would mean that parents or carers could only consent when it is quite clear that they are acting for the patient's welfare, and would deny them that right in any circumstance of doubt. This clearly puts carers in a difficult position as it would force them to go to court whenever there is more than one possible course of action available. In relation to sterilization, further support for the suggestion comes from the New Jersey Supreme Court in the case of *Re Grady*,[80] where the court held that, in a substituted judgement approach, the person or body in the best position to judge what the incompetent would have wanted is to be trusted to make the decision. In relation to discontinuation of life-support treatment it held that the parents or family of an incompetent would be in that position; but in relation to sterilization, it held that only the courts would be in a position to make a proper judgement.

The Canadian courts reject the *Re Grady* approach and, in relation to children, are happy to trust parents. The courts there start off with a presumption that the parents' decision will be in the child's best interests[81] and it is only when that decision is challenged will they themselves make the determination[82] (at which point using no presumption one way or the other).[83] They also recognize that there are certain reasons of policy why the courts should not always have to be involved. In *Re K.*, Anderson J.A. said:

> In my view, if the course followed here becomes normal practice, the fate of children like Infant K. may well be prejudiced. Even the most loving and caring parent would hesitate before becoming involved in major litigation. Firstly, most parents could not afford to become involved in such litigation. Secondly, apart from expense, the parents have to face the emotional hurdles confronting them in a case of this kind. The burden of going through ordinary litigation is a heavy one for the litigants. It is a doubly heavy burden in a case of this kind. Thirdly, there is a complete loss of privacy by both the parents and the child. The intimate details of their life are exposed to public scrutiny.[84]

In Scotland, too, the court has shown willingness to trust other people, and does not insist that in cases of doubt (of which sterilization proposals are by no means the only example) the determination must always be left to the court. In *Morris, Pet.*[85] the Court of Session appointed parents to be tutors-dative over their mentally disabled adult son and granted them power to consent to any medical treatment that was in the son's best interests. The Court did *not* insist that the parents always ask the Court to determine where the best interests of the incompetent lie, and it unambiguously gave the right to make that determination to the tutors it appointed. The court appoints the tutor, and the tutor makes the decisions. (These decisions are of course open to review, the possibility of which a prior declarator of the court would avoid).

In English law, however, notwithstanding the clear lack of any sanction for failure to follow the advice of the House of Lords in *F.*, surgeons would clearly be unwise to perform non-consensual sterilizations without a judicial declaration that this would be in the patient's best interests. The motivation behind this conclusion in *F.* is clear from the speeches in that case. Without judicial involvement the medical profession in consultation with the patient's close relatives may come to the wrong decision and, if so, the decision will generally not be reversible. The spectre of the earlier case of *Re D.* was hanging over the House of Lords in *F.* In that case a mother of an 11 year-old girl and her medical advisers had agreed in good faith and after careful consideration that the girl should be sterilized, and it was only the intervention of a social worker that allowed the court to prevent the operation. Lord Brandon in *F.*, without referring to *Re D.*, pointed out that if the court were not involved there would be a greater risk of the decision being made wrongly.[86] Lord Griffiths said that *Re D.* 'stands as a stark warning of the danger of leaving the decision to sterilise in the hands of those having the immediate care of the woman'.[87] And Lord Goff describes *Re D.* as a 'vivid illustration' of the fact that a 'highly qualified medical practitioner, supported by a caring mother' may come to an insupportable conclusion as to what is in the patient's best interests.[88]

Perhaps Lord Griffiths is the most logical after all, for he would create a new rule of law that court authorization must be obtained before the operation is considered lawful. The other noble judges ask the carers of the mentally disabled to come to court for authorization that is not strictly necessary in law if the consent satisfies the best interests test. There is no sanction for failure to do so (unless the decision can be shown to be wrong) and in cases like *Re B.* and *F.*, where there really was no doubt as to where the interests of the patients lay, it can certainly be argued that the involvement of the court is not only legally unnecessary, but practically a waste of time and money.

It is to be remembered that this non-legal requirement would appear appropriate only for sterilization operations, as the judges in *F.* were at pains to distinguish this from other medical procedures, on the ground of its irreversibility. It remains to be seen whether similar considerations are to be applied in relation to abortion.

Factors Relevant to the 'Best Interests' Test

It will be seen from the above discussion that, in determining whether a mentally disabled person ought to be given treatment without that person's consent, the best interests of the person will in most jurisdictions be the deciding factor. Consent may be given, where appropriate, on that basis, and treatment will be lawful on that basis. The application of this test is certainly an exercise in paternalism, but it is to be remembered that, as Dickens perceptively points out, 'not all paternalism is offensive or an insult to autonomy'.[89] The application of the test is also, to a large extent, unpredictable due to its amorphous nature, and each case must be considered independently and on its own merits.[90] Nonetheless, it is possible to identify a number of factors in relation to birth control treatment that are clearly relevant to the decision. Similarly, a number of factors are clearly irrelevant. None is deciding, and each will have greater or lesser weight depending upon the facts of each particular case.[91]

First, and most important, is the assessment that the patient is so mentally disabled that she or he is unable to understand the implications of the proposed treatment. There is an infinite gradation of mental disabilities, and an inability to understand one form of treatment cannot necessarily be taken to indicate an inability to understand another. As the New Jersey Supreme Court put it in *Re Grady* 'the fact that a person is legally incompetent for some purposes does not mean that he lacks capacity to make a decision about sterilization'. Contraceptive treatment will require far less ability to understand than an abortion or a sterilization. For each, the general principle is the same: ability to understand imposes a necessity to obtain personal consent, and the best interests test becomes irrelevant.

Secondly, and following on from this, the possibility must be considered that, some time in the future, the disabled person will have improved sufficiently to acquire an understanding they do not at the moment possess, or that medical science will have improved sufficiently to cure or alleviate the person's disability. If this possibility exists, then this is a strong indication that the patient's best interests will be served by adopting temporary, reversible, birth control methods rather than an irreversible procedure like sterilization. In *Re D.*[92] the evidence showed that the girl would improve sufficiently eventually to be able to make up her own mind about sterilization, and this was the deciding factor in the judge's assessment that it would not be in the girl's best interests to be sterilized.

Thirdly, it should be shown that pregnancy and childbirth or abortion will cause the woman trauma or physical or psychological harm greater than that caused by the birth control technique proposed: and if sterilization is proposed the courts are likely to insist that the harm is greater than it would be with other, non-disabled, patients. Every form of medical treatment carries risks and many cause pain and have side-effects. This is true for hormonal contraception, and mechanical birth control methods such as the IUD, although it is likely to be less so for barrier contraceptives like the cap. The risk of these effects must be balanced against the potential damage that pregnancy can cause. It would only be in a person's best interests to be given any form of family planning treatment if the treatment itself causes less harm than that which it is designed to avoid. The greater the potential harm in pregnancy, the more invasive the medical treatment to avoid it may be. For this reason, it is unlikely that sterilization would be a suitable option except in the most extreme circumstances where other, less invasive, forms of birth control must be ruled out for some reason.

Fourthly, in considering the nature of the harm, the likelihood of its occurring is significant. If the mentally disabled woman has no social opportunity for sexual relations with a man, then the actual trauma of surgery is more likely to outweigh the *potential* benefit of sterility. Keeping a woman on a contraceptive pill throughout her reproductive life *just in case* she has sex and becomes pregnant may well be a greater bodily invasion than not trying to avoid a remote possibility that might never occur. On the other hand, if the woman is likely to have sex and become pregnant, the need for contraception or sterilization immediately becomes much more pressing. So *F.*, in which the woman had already entered into a sexual relationship, was a clear case for sterilization; *Re D.*, in which the child seldom left her mother's side, was not. To accept the possibility of an abortion as a last resort may be less of an invasion of a woman's privacy than subjecting her to a sterilization or oral contraceptives for three decades in order to cover for a remote possibility that she might become pregnant. This may be particularly so with new forms of non-surgical abortion, such as the administration of anti-progesterones (discussed in Chapter 4). While abortion remains legal it would be invalid – in the context of the best interests test as currently applied – to raise moral objections to that procedure.

Fifthly, although this may be difficult, fertility really ought to be established before sterilization or contraception is contemplated. In *Re Grady* the New Jersey Supreme Court said this:

> There need be no showing that pregnancy is likely. The court can presume fertility if the medical evidence indicates normal develop-

ment of sexual organs and the evidence does not otherwise raise doubts about fertility.[93]

Finally, once all the above considerations have been taken into account, it must also be established that the treatment accords with good and acceptable medical practice. Significant non-consensual treatment such as abortion and sterilization, is not, as Heilbron J. pointed out in *Re D.*, a matter within a single doctor's sole clinical judgement.

The above are relevant considerations that, where appropriate, must be taken into account by a doctor in determining whether proposed birth control treatment would be in the patient's best interests and, if so, what that treatment should be. There are various other factors that will be affected by the decision to provide birth control, but which must not be allowed to affect the decision itself. A doctor making a decision to provide birth control treatment on the basis of an irrelevant consideration is opening her or himself up to claims for civil liability for assault. The following are factors that will be affected by the decision, but which are irrelevant to the making of that decision.

First, society itself may be affected by a decision to provide birth control to a mentally disabled person. But, in our culture, society has no right to affect the position of the individual in relation to reproduction. Eugenics, state resources, and the general good of society are quite irrelevant to the best interests of the individual.

Secondly, the ease with which the operation or procedure can be carried out from the provider's point of view is irrelevant. Sterilization may be financially cheaper in the long run than a contraceptive regime, but that is not a consideration to be taken into account in determining the patient's welfare.

Thirdly, and following on from this, the benefit of the proposed treatment to the carers of the mentally disabled person is not a relevant consideration, except, as pointed out by the British Columbia Court of Appeal,[94] insofar as this affects the disabled person. If the burden on the carer becomes too great, the care itself may diminish. But, generally, the best interests test is unashamedly selfish, and the effect of any decision on those around the disabled person is not to be taken into account. One has to be especially careful here to ensure that social convenience does not underlay a claim that a proposed sterilization is therapeutic.[95] The clearest judicial support for this comes from the Supreme Court of Canada in *Re Eve,*[96], for the basis of the decision in that case was that the only real purpose of the proposed sterilization was to relieve the patient's mother of anxiety, and the possible burden of looking after any potential child. The benefit to a patient's mother does not justify surgical interference on a child. This was also accepted in *F. v. West Berkshire Health Authority*, where, in particular, Lord Jauncey said this:

> In the case of the long term incompetent, convenience to those charged with his care should never be a justification for a decision to treat.[97]

So too it is irrelevant that other people may be affected. The position of the potential sexual partner of the patient should not be taken into account. A sharp problem could arise in relation to sterilization of males. In *AL v. GRH*,[98] the Indiana Court of Appeals refused to authorize the vasectomy of a 15 year-old mentally disabled boy who had recently shown signs of sexual awareness. The decision was based on the ground that the operation would benefit those he had sex with, rather than himself. But it may be that benefit could have attached to such a boy if, in practical terms, the operation encouraged his carers to allow him more social and sexual freedom and he is relieved of the risk of financially supporting any offspring. How the courts in other jurisdictions will deal with an application to authorize a non-consensual vasectomy remains to be seen.

Notes

1 This fact is implicitly recognized by the House of Lords in *F. v. West Berkshire Health Authority* [1989] 2 *All ER* 545. See also Gunn, *Sex and the Law: A Brief Guide for Staff Working in the Mental Handicap Field*, 2nd edn, FPA Education Unit, London, 1987; and Groves, 'Sex Education for Mentally handicapped People', 299 *BMJ* 999, 1989.

2 S. 63 of the (English) Mental Health Act 1983 allows treatment without consent to be given to the mentally disabled, but only treatment for their mental condition: this would *not* include birth control treatment.

3 See Norrie, 'Human Tissue Transplants: Legal Liability in Different Jurisdictions', 34 *ICLQ* 442, 1985 at pp. 454–456. Organ removal was permitted by *US* courts from a 7 year-old child in *Hart v. Brown* 29 *Conn. Supp.* 368, 289 A. 2d 386 (1972); and from a 27 year-old mentally retarded ward in *Strunk v. Strunk* 445 SW 2d 145; 35 ALR (3d) 683 (1969).

4 Family Law Reform Act 1969, s. 8.

5 *Gillick v. West Norfolk & Wisbech Area Health Authority* [1985] 3 *WLR* 830 establishes that it is possible for a child fully to understand (and thus to consent to) contraceptive treatment; although Woolf J. at first instance ([1983] 3 *WLR* 859) did point out that it would be highly unlikely that the court would ever accept that a child under 16 would have sufficient maturity fully to appreciate the nature and consequences of an irreversible contraceptive sterilization.

6 See Chapter 6.

7 S.1, Guardianship of Infants Act 1971.

8 Per Lord Hailsham in *Re B. (A Minor) (Sterlisation)* [1987] 2 *WLR* 1213 at p. 1214.
9 See Chapter 6.
10 [1976] 1 *All ER* 326.
11 [1987] 2 *WLR* 1213.
12 In Scotland a local authority with care and control over a child does not automatically have parental rights, and would have to apply for these under s. 3(1) of the Law Reform (Parent and Child) (Scotland) Act 1986, or assume parental rights under s. 16 of the Social Work (Scotland) Act 1968.
13 [1987] 2 *WLR* at p. 1217.
14 The only possible drug treatment for this ward would have required a daily dose, which, due to her emotional problems, might not always be possible to administer: see Lord Oliver at p. 1221.
15 As Meyers put it, 'saying the treatment was not in the child's "best interests" was conclusionary rather than an aid to analysis': 'Selective Non-Treatment of Handicapped Infants', in *McLean, Legal Issues in Human Reproduction*, Dartmouth, Aldershot, 1989 at p. 129.
16 For a discussion of this point, see Grubb and Pearl, 'Sterilisation and the Courts', *CLJ* 439, 1987.
17 [1987] 2 *WLR* at p. 1223.
18 [1988] 2 *WLR* 189.
19 See further Chapter 9.
20 [1989] 2 *All ER* 545 (HL).
21 Particularly in the Court of Appeal, [1989] 1 *All ER* 764.
22 [1989] 2 *All ER* at p. 548.
23 Ibid. at p. 567.
24 Ibid. at p. 551.
25 Ibid. at p. 567.
26 Ibid. at p. 551.
27 85 *NJ* 235, 426 *A.* 2d 467 (1981).
28 Indeed Handler J., although concurring, felt obliged to give a separate opinion because he felt that the majority's opinion did not disapprove necessity strongly enough. See also *Re K. and Public Trustee* (1985) 19 *DLR* (4th) 255 at p. 276, where necessity as a test was also disapproved by the British Columbia Court of Appeal.
29 (1985) 19 *DLR* (4th) 255.
30 Although an appeal was taken from this decision, (1985) 4 *WWR* 757, the Supreme Court of Canada refused to hear it because the operation had been carried out immediately after the decision of the Court of Appeal: see Finch-Noyes, 'Sterilization of the Mentally Retarded Minor: the *Re K.* Case', 5 *Can. J. Fam. Law* 277, 1986 at p. 279.
31 (1986) 31 *DLR* (4th) 1. Both this case and *Re K.* are discussed by McLean, *A Patient's Right to Know: Information Disclosure, The Doctor and the Law*, Dartmouth, Aldershot, 1989, at pp. 63–5.
32 [1987] 2 *WLR* at p. 1216.
33 (1986) 31 *DLR* (4th) at p. 32.
34 [1987] 2 *WLR* at p. 1217.
35 (1986) 31 *DLR* (4th) at p. 36.
36 Ibid. at p. 30: 'In the present case, there is no evidence to indicate that failure to perform the operation would have any detrimental effects on Eve's physical or mental health'.
37 Ibid. at p. 31 (emphasis added).
38 It is interesting to compare this approach with that of the same court, differently constituted, in *Gillick*, where much detailed guidance is given by

Lord Scarman and Lord Fraser. In *F. v. West Berkshire Health Authority* Lord Brandon attempted to define briefly, what he meant by 'best interests' (see [1989] 2 *All ER* 545 at p. 551).

39 As other Canadian courts have also attempted: see, for example, the judgements in the British Columbia Court of Appeal in *Re K. and Public Trustee* (1985) 19 *DLR* (4th) 255.

40 (1986) 31 *DLR* (4th) at p. 34, emphasis added.

41 [1987] 2 *WLR* at p. 1223.

42 (1985) 19 *DLR* (4th) at p. 267.

43 *R. v. Bourne* [1939] 1 *KB* 687.

44 1985 *SLT* 237.

45 See Chapter 6.

46 'Sterilization of Mentally Handicapped Children', 1988 *SLT* (News) 1, at pp. 3–4.

47 [1988] 2 *WLR* 189.

48 Unreported, but discussed by Ward, 'Revival of Tutors-Dative', 1987 *SLT* (News) 69.

49 Similar statutes were in force in Canada until the early 1970s: see Dickens, 'Retardation and Sterilization' 5 *Int. J. Law Psy.* 295, 1982 at pp. 303–304, and 'Reproduction Law and Medical Consent' 35 *U. Tor. LJ* 255, 1985 at pp. 255–6.

50 274 *US* 200, 71 *L. Ed.* 1000 (1927).

51 In the words of Pashman J. in the New Jersey Supreme Court in *Re Grady* 85 *NJ* 235, 462 A. 2d 467 (1981).

52 See McIvor, 'Equitable Jurisdiction to Order Sterilizations' 57 *Wash. LR* 373, 1982. See also the cases reported from various US jurisdictions in *Annual Review of Population Law*, UNFPA, Cambridge MA, 1988 at pp. 27–30.

53 *Stump v. Sparkman* 435 *US* 349, 55 *L. Ed.* 2d 331 (1976).

54 See, for example, *Re Tulley* 146 *Cal. Rptr.* 266 (1978). See further, Giesen, *International Medical Malpractice Law*, Martinus Nijhoff, Dortrecht 1988 at p. 454.

55 293 *MD* 685, 447 *A.* 2d 1244 (1982).

56 [1988] 2 *WLR* 189.

57 Giesen, op. cit, note 54 above, at p. 451.

58 85 *NJ* 235, 426 *A.* 2d 467 (1981).

59 70 *NJ* 10, 355 *A.* 2d 647 (1976).

60 Per La Forest J. in *Re Eve* (1986) 31 *DLR* (4th) 1 at p. 35.

61 See, for example, Freeman, 'For Her Own Good', 84 *Law Soc. Gaz.* 949, 1987.

62 [1987] 2 *WLR* at p. 1216 and p. 1217.

63 Ibid. at p. 1218.

64 [1989] 2 *All ER* 545.

65 [1987] 2 *WLR* at p. 1216.

66 Ibid. at p. 1223.

67 85 *NJ* 235, 426 *A.* 2d 467 (1981).

68 (1985) 19 *DLR* (4th) 255, at p. 285.

69 A fact considered 'obvious' by Gillon, 13 *J. Med. Ethics* 59, 1987 at p. 60, although this is seldom recognized by commentators less astute than he. The existence or otherwise of such a right is thoughtfully discussed by Kluge, 'Sterilization of the Mentally Severely Handicapped' in Bromham *et. al.* (eds), *Ethical Problems in Reproductive Medicine*, NAFPD, London, 1989 at pp. 12–15. See also Liu, *Reproductive Rights and Artificial Reproduction*, Dartmouth, Aldershot, 1991.

70 See Chapter 5.

71 And duty: cf. Thomas, 'For Her Own Good: A Reply', 84 *Law Soc. Gaz.* 1196, 1987.
72 Cf. McLean and Campbell, 'Sterilization' in McLean (ed.), *Legal Issues in Medicine* Gower, Aldershot, 1981 at p. 179.
73 [1989] 2 *All ER* 545.
74 [1976] 1 *All ER* at p. 335.
75 [1987] 2 *WLR* at p. 1218.
76 [1989] 2 *All ER* at pp. 569–70.
77 Ibid. at p. 562.
78 'Sterilisation of Mentally Handicapped Children', 1988 *SLT* (News) 1, at pp. 3 and 4.
79 Ibid. at p. 4.
80 85 *NJ* 235, 426 *A.* 2d 467 (1981).
81 *Re K. and Public Trustee* (1985) 19 *DLR* (4th) 255 at p. 270.
82 *Couture Jacquet v. Montreal Children's Hospital* (1986) 28 *DLR* (4th) 22, in which it was held that it had not been shown that a mother, who refused consent to continued chemotherapy treatment for her three year old child, who was dying of cancer, had not acted in the best interests of the child.
83 *Re K. & Public Trustee*, (see note 81 above) at p. 280.
84 Ibid. at p. 278. See also the similar remarks of Large J. when *Re Eve* was in the Supreme Court of Prince Edward Island (1981) 115 *DLR* (3d) 286 at pp. 293–4.
85 Discussed by Ward, 1987 *SLT* (News) 69.
86 [1989] 2 *All ER* at p. 552.
87 Ibid. at p. 561.
88 Ibid. at p. 568.
89 Dickens, 'Retardation and Sterilization', 5 *Int. J. Law Psy* 295, 1982 at p. 316.
90 As Stephens J. said in another context in a separate concurring opinion in *Bellotti v. Baird* 443 *US* 662 at p. 656, 61 *L. Ed.* 2d 797 at p. 821 (1979), the best interests test on its own 'provides little real guidance to the judge, and his decision must necessarily reflect personal and societal values and mores . . .'.
91 For a useful discussion of the relevant factors, see Dickens, 'Reproduction Law and Medical Consent', 35 *U. Tor. LJ* 255, 1985 at pp. 270–1.
92 [1976] 1 *All ER* 326.
93 85 *NJ* 235, 426 *A.* 2d 467 (1981).
94 In *Re K. and Public Trustee* (1985) 19 *DLR* (4th) 255 at p. 280–281.
95 See further Giesen, op. cit., note 54 above at pp. 449–55, who is unwilling to recognize the validity of any non-consensual sterilization because of this danger. For comments in a similar vein, see also Lee and Morgan, 'Sterilization and Incapacity to Consent' in Bromham *et. al.* (eds), *Ethical Problems in Reproductive Medicine*, NAFPD, London, 1989 at pp. 50–2.
96 (1986) 31 *DLR* (4th) 1.
97 [1989] 2 *All ER* at p. 571.
98 325 *NE* 2d 501, 74 *ALR* (3d) 1220 (1975).

8 Civil Liability in Family Planning Practice

Introduction

A family planner, just like any other health care worker, can be liable in damages for the injuries she or he causes if services are provided negligently. Negligence in law is the unintentional failure to take that care which the ordinary reasonable person in similar circumstances would have taken, and liability in damages flows from any loss, injury or damage caused by that negligence. Family planning practice does not, in itself, give rise to any speciality in the law of negligence as far as actionability, standard of care and causation are concerned, and they will receive no special attention in this book.[1] However, family planning practice is very different from all other forms of medical treatment in relation to the losses that can arise as a result of negligence. For negligence in family planning practice does have one unique consequence: it can lead directly to the birth of a child. This chapter will therefore concentrate on the nature of that consequence and whether, and for whom, the law will regard that consequence as a loss compensable in damages.

There are various different circumstances in which a family planner can be so negligent that a child is born that would not have been born but for that negligence. The simplest example is when the treatment itself fails, due to negligence. A negligently performed abortion, for example, could result in the woman remaining pregnant;[2] a negligently performed sterilization could result in the woman[3] or the man[4] remaining fertile. Similarly, the negligent fitting of an IUD may render that device ineffective.[5] Apart from negligence in treatment, the family planner may be negligent in the advice given to the patient. A failure to warn that the treatment might not be successful could lead to the birth of a child if the partners, believing themselves to be absolutely protected from conception, do not recognize the signs of pregnancy until it is too late for a termination.[6] A similar type of situation is when it is claimed that the patient was not given a proper choice of the most suitable form of birth control.[7] Alternatively, a genetic counsellor may give negligent advice as a result of which a couple become parents when they would have tried to avoid this had proper advice been given (for example, concerning the likelihood of genetic defects).[8] Or a counsellor may negligently inform a pregnant woman that the disease she is suffering from will not harm the child she is carrying, with the result that she fails to undergo the abortion she would otherwise have had. Or a woman who would otherwise have been able to have her pregnancy terminated is denied that opportunity due to a negligent failure to diagnose the pregnancy. Other circumstances in which negligence can result in the birth of a child are when the post-vasectomy tests on a man's sperm are carried out carelessly, with the result that he is told that he is sterile when in fact he is not; or when a pharmacist provides sleeping pills rather than contraceptive pills because he read a prescription form wrongly.[9]

The Actionability of Birth

Before a claim for damages can be made, it must be shown that the birth of a child is a legally recognized loss. If a child is born as a result of a family planner's negligence, who, if anyone, suffers? A number of people are certainly affected, but in order to obtain damages they must show that they have suffered a loss of a legally recognized nature.

Actionability by the Child

There are a number of cases in which the resultant child itself has sued, claiming that its very life is a 'loss' that attracts damages. These claims may be called actions for 'wrongful life', and they have generally been raised by children suffering from physical or mental defects, which render their lives more painful or more disadvantaged than normal.[10] Although the vast majority of these claims have been rejected in the US courts, there are a few cases that indicate a hesitant acceptance that a disabled child has a cause of action against the doctor without whose negligence it would not have been born. So in *Park v. Chessin*,[11] for example, the New York Court of Appeals awarded damages to a child born disabled on the ground that people have the 'right to be born whole or not at all'. Although these cases still form a tiny minority in the USA and many American jurisdictions legislatively deny the child a cause of action,[12] the movement towards recognizing actionability based on 'diminished life' rather than 'wrongful life' is gaining ground.[13]

In England only one such claim has been made, and in *McKay v. Essex Area Health Authority*[14] the Court of Appeal unanimously rejected it on the grounds that a doctor is under no legal duty to a foetus to terminate its existence, and that in any event the court would not be able to evaluate any damages, even had there been a duty which could be breached, because the court knew nothing of non-existence. The Congenital Disabilities (Civil Liability) Act 1976, s. 4(5) will prevent such an action again being raised in England. Although the statute does not apply to Scotland, it is highly unlikely that the Scottish court would come to a different conclusion from the English Court of Appeal in *McKay*.[15]

Actionability by the Parents

In contrast to their approach when faced with actions by children claiming they had suffered through the negligence of family planners, courts have been much more willing to accept that parents who bear unwanted children have a cause of action. These claims may be termed actions for 'wrongful birth'.[16] Defendants have, however, put forward a number of policy reasons in order to persuade the courts that childbirth ought not to be considered an actionable loss. In a previous age it is certain that the birth of a child, even when unwanted, would not have been regarded as a loss in law, but more as a blessing from heaven. However, as Lord Donaldson MR put it, 'the common law . . . adapts to sea-changes in the attitudes of reasonable people',[17] and it is probably true to say that childbirth is no longer (if it ever was) self-evidently good.

Many American courts have accepted policy arguments for denying liability for the birth of a child, or at least particular heads of liability, and they have done this more readily than the English courts: it is now probably easier to sue for wrongful birth in England than it is in the USA – a very unusual situation in the law of civil liability.

The earliest view expressed in the USA was that there was simply no loss suffered by parents when a healthy child was born, because society does not regard the birth of a child as an injury. So in *Shaheen v. Knight*[18] the court said:

> We are of the opinion that to allow damages for the birth of a normal child is foreign to the universal public sentiment of the people.

This argument has, however, lost much of its strength today, and may be countered by pointing out that many millions of individuals take very great care and effort to avoid childbirth and that the law reflects this by allowing for the provision of contraception and even abortion. Once family planning is accepted as a good, its failure can logically be regarded as a bad.

Rather than adopting the patent fiction that no loss at all flows from the birth of a child, some courts argue that, while some losses are caused by that event, they are, as a matter of law, always outweighed by the benefits that parenthood brings. In particular, it has been argued that the costs of bringing up a child cannot be compensated for because the benefits of parenthood outweigh these costs. The most eloquently expressed (and most frequently quoted) judicial expression of this inflexible approach is that of the court in *Terrell v. Garcia*:

> The satisfaction, joy, and companionship which normal parents have in rearing a child make such economic loss worthwhile. These intangible benefits, while impossible to value in dollars and cents, are undoubtedly the things that make life worthwhile. Who can place a pricetag on a child's smile or on the parental pride in a child's achievement? . . . Rather than attempt to value these intangible benefits, our courts have simply determined that public sentiment recognizes that these benefits to the parents outweigh their economic loss in rearing and educating a healthy, normal child.[19]

Although this has been worded in the form of balancing the legal loss with the legal benefit, it should be recognized that the approach reflects a policy judgement of the court rather than the legal principle of offsetting benefits and losses.[20] The judgement has been made that a certain event, childbirth, ought always to be regarded as a greater benefit than all the tangible losses it causes. But that judgement is inconsistent with other policies now accepted by the law. The law today allows individuals to avoid childbirth by a variety of different means, and thus allows these individuals to decide that for them the balance of benefit and loss levels out with more losses than benefits. And illogically, the argument tends to be restricted to damages for the costs of upkeep of the child, while other losses are often allowed, such as for the pain and suffering of pregnancy and childbirth. This approach clearly reflects social *mores* that are, it is suggested, no longer accepted. Robertson dismisses *Terrell* and cases like it on the ground that they 'were clearly influenced by anti-contraception/abortion sentiment and by the feeling that the wrongful birth claim in some way undermined the sanctity of the family'.[21] Cases such as these were also based 'on the ground that the purpose of the marital union *is* to have children'.[22] It is suggested that this view of marriage is repugnantly out-of-date. One of the *consequences* of a happy loving heterosexual relationship may be the procreation of children, but to regard that as the very *purpose* of such a relationship is to reduce sexual love to a bestial and sterile level. It is the principle upon which much of this book is based that men and women should be allowed, by using birth control, to express their love and even their physical attraction for each other in a sexual way, *good in itself,* without fear of the consequences.

A slightly different argument to the above was put forward in the case of *Gleitman v. Cosgrove,*[23] for there it was argued not that the losses were outweighed by the benefits of childbirth and parenthood, but rather that any such losses were, of their nature, too indeterminate to give rise to any claim for damages. This argument was accepted by the court, although as Robertson points out, this argument is just as illogical as that based on the overwhelming joys and blessings of childbirth:

> It is manifest that, in the wrongful birth situation, assessment of damages is a formidable task; however it is doubtful that such a task is so onerous as to be impossible. Is the evaluation of the intangible benefits of parenthood any more difficult than the computation of damages under such nebulous headings as 'pain and suffering' and 'emotional distress'? Courts find such computations difficult, but not impossible.[24]

Another tactic was adopted by the Supreme Court of Wisconsin in *Rieck v. Medical Protective Co,*[25] where the Court held damages irrecoverable on the ground that the damages that would follow from the birth of a child born as a result of a doctor's negligence would be out of all proportion to the culpability of the negligence of the defendant.[26] Now, certainly, lack of proportionality is one reason why the fault-based system of damages has come in for increasing criticism in recent years, but that is a consequence that applies throughout the law of damages, and it would be illogical to use this criticism to deny damages only in this particular situation. Again, it is little more than an excuse to deny damages when it is felt that they are undeserved but there is no real argument of legal principle enabling the court to do so. Certainly, in the common law systems, it is regarded as fundamental that the level of delictual or tortious damages depends on fair compensation, not fair retribution, and any change must come through legislation rather than through piecemeal judicial decision.

Apart from the judicial reluctance to award damages when healthy children are born, some US jurisdictions have legislated to disallow wrongful birth actions being raised.[27]

The Canadian courts have tended to resist the absolutist arguments that deny liability completely, or deny it for particular heads of damages, but have rather accepted in principle that damages can be recoverable, so long as a suitable deduction is made from the damages to take account of the benefits the child brings. At first, there was a judicial reluctance in Canada to award any damages in wrongful birth cases. For example, in *Doiron v. Orr*[28] the judge avoided having to decide the issue of public policy argued before him since he found that there was no negligence established; but he went on to record his distaste at the action having been brought in the first place:

> Personally, I find this approach to a matter of this kind which deals with human life, the happiness of the child, the effect upon its thinking, upon its mind when it realizes that there has been a case of this kind, that it is an unwanted mistake, and that its rearing is being paid for by someone other than its parents, is just simply grotesque.[29]

However, these comments were *obiter*, and in the first Canadian case to award damages for wrongful birth, policy considerations were held not capable of denying the plaintiffs damages altogether. In the case of *Cataford v. Moreau*[30] the Quebec Superior Court, after an historical examination of public attitudes, asked:

> Is it still contrary to public order to grant damages following the birth of a healthy child, on the ground that the event constitutes a blessing intended by the natural order of things?

It then gave the following answer:

> The Court does not believe itself justified in concluding that the undesired birth of a healthy child, especially in a poor family consisting of 10 living children, constitutes such a happy and normal event that it would be offensive to the public order to have attached thereto a pecuniary compensation in an appropriate case.[31]

Consequently, damages were awarded under a number of heads, including 'the inherent suffering of confinement', the inconvenience of pregnancy, anxiety, and interruption of sexual relations. However, no damages were awarded to the plaintiffs for the child's upkeep, but only because *in this particular case* the benefits it brought to the plaintiffs outweighed these losses. Policy arguments have not figured in the later Canadian cases.[32]

Similarly, in New Zealand it was held in *Accident Compensation Commission v. Auckland Hospital Board*[33] that the normal process of conception following a failed sterilization operation could amount to 'personal injury by accident' for the purposes of that country's accident compensation scheme. No policy objection was raised, although the decision was restricted to failure of a sterilization caused by some operational or mechanical failure in the procedure, and it was made clear that a failure through natural means such as recanalization would not be covered by the scheme.[34]

It is suggested that the policy reasons for denying or limiting damages suggested in many of the American cases are, for the reasons given above, not persuasive. English defendants have tended to rely upon other arguments of policy, but these too are not convincing, and English law has now clearly rejected them conclusively.

In *Udale v. Bloomsbury Area Health Authority*,[35] a child had been born after the admittedly negligent performance of a sterilization operation upon the plaintiff and she was awarded damages for her pain, suffering, and anxiety connected with the operation and pregnancy, and loss of earnings. Jupp J. however rejected the plaintiff's claim for the cost of rearing the child until he was 16, and the cost of extending the family home to make room for him. He said that, on grounds of public policy, insofar as the claim was based on the life of the child coming into being, it should not be allowed. He then listed four policy reasons that convinced him to deny the contentious claims flowing from the birth of the child. Each of these reasons was analysed and rejected by Pain J. in the later case of *Thake v. Maurice*,[36] which involved a failed vasectomy operation.

Jupp J.'s first reason for holding that damages based on the life of a child coming into being should not be allowed was that it would be highly undesirable for any child to learn that a court had publicly declared his or her birth a disaster or a mistake: such claims would disrupt families which are the structure of our society. The Ontario High Court in *Doiron v. Orr*[37] appears to have accepted that such an argument had some validity, for, in that case, the court felt obliged to have the child examined in order to determine whether the discovery of its origins had had an emotionally adverse impact on it (no harm was found). But Pain J. in *Thake v. Maurice* did not consider this argument a valid ground for denying liability. He said that he did not think an award of damages would lead to the child feeling rejected:

> What matters to a child is how it is received when it enters life. It

> so often happens that parents reconcile themselves to an unwelcome conception and accept the child with joy.[38]

Any potential harm to the child would be purely speculative, and that ought not to be regarded as sufficient to deny liability.[39]

Jupp J.'s second point was based on the premise that the benefits brought by the birth must be deducted from the damages awardable. He saw these benefits as primarily emotional, and considered them to be dependent upon the parents' own efforts. So the parents who seek and find joy in parenthood would be penalized, and the mother who 'nurtures bitterness in her heart' would be entitled to large damages since there would be no joy to set off against the economic losses:

> In short virtue would go unrewarded: unnatural rejection of womanhood and motherhood would be generously compensated. This, in my judgement, cannot be right.[40]

Pain J., on the other hand, found Jupp J.'s approach illogical and considered that it would itself lead to virtue going unrewarded. He accepted that the joy the parents acquire will largely be of their own making, but regarded this as a reason for *not* applying the set-off in such circumstances.[41] It should also be pointed out that later courts have adopted a different and, it is suggested, preferable approach to the issue of setting off benefits against losses (see below).

The third argument of public policy that Jupp J. found persuasive was the fear that doctors would be under subconscious pressure to encourage abortions in order to avoid claims for medical negligence which could arise if the child were allowed to be born. Pain J. did not find this a realistic fear:

> In view of the divisions within the medical professions, I think it has little force. The decision whether to abort or not will usually rest with an obstetrician, who may well be quite independent of the medical man who faces a possible charge of negligence.[42]

The argument had, in fact, been taken from the judgement of Ackner L.J. in *McKay v. Essex Area Health Authority*[43] (who had himself taken it from the (English) Law Commission's Report on Injuries to Unborn Children).[44] But *McKay* was a case not of wrongful birth but of wrongful life,[45] and the Law Commission was not concerned with injuries to the parents but with injuries to the child. The action for wrongful life postulates a duty to perform an abortion, and the existence of *that* duty might very well encourage doctors to carry out abortions. But actions for wrongful birth do not concern the duty to perform an abortion, but rather the duty to act carefully to avoid injury to the parents. As this latter duty is something quite different from that with which Ackner L.J. and the Law Commission were concerned, this too is not a persuasive argument for denying damages in a case of wrongful birth.[46]

On their own, or even taken all together, the above arguments are not strong grounds for denying liability. But Jupp J. probably saw them as little more than precursors to his main policy objection to awarding damages to compensate for the costs of the child's upkeep, which he set out in the following memorable sentence:

> It has been the assumption of our culture from time immemorial that a child coming into the world, even if, as some say, 'the world is a vale of tears', is a blessing and an occasion for rejoicing.[47]

This is the 'joys and blessings' argument, familiar in the USA and accepted in a number of jurisdictions there. Pain J. took particular care in answering this part of Jupp J.'s case.

Pain J. disagreed with Jupp J. because he did not accept that the policy of the law is inevitably to regard childbirth as a blessing and an occasion for rejoicing. He pointed out that family planning is a type of medicine commonly practised and legislatively recognized, and he continued:

> The policy of the state, as I see it, is to provide the widest freedom of choice. It makes available to the public the means of planning their families or planning to have no family. If plans go awry, it provides for the possibility of abortion. But there is no pressure on couples either to have children or not to have children or to have only a limited number of children.[48]

He concluded:

> I do not accept that it is part of our culture that the birth of a healthy child is always a blessing. It may have been the assumption in the past. I feel quite satisfied that it is not the assumption today.[49]

It is submitted that Pain J.'s reasoning is much to be preferred over that of Jupp J. It has been pointed out that, if childbirth were always a blessing, 'society would in fact owe a debt of gratitude to every rapist or seducer whose efforts produced a child'.[50] There are clearly other circumstances in which childbirth is not an occasion for rejoicing. Certainly the birth of a disabled child cannot always be regarded as a joy and a blessing: it would be presumption indeed for the law to tell the parents of such a child that they must joyfully accept its birth as such. But even the birth of a perfectly healthy child could constitute a disaster for the parents. Huge numbers of people decide that, for them, the disadvantages outweigh the advantages in having children at any particular time, and the existence – and legislative or constitutional countenance[51] – of family planning allows them the opportunity to put that decision into practice. It is suggested that the policy of the law in providing for individual choice is vastly more important to a free society than a policy based upon the patent fiction that everyone would rejoice at the blessing of becoming a parent. Also, it would be illogical for the law to allow for that free choice and yet hold contrary to public policy the exercise of the choice in one particular way.

For all these reasons, it is suggested that the reasoning of Pain J. is more appropriate to today's society than the reasoning of Jupp J.; and the English Court of Appeal followed that line in *Emeh v. Kensington, Chelsea and Westminster Area Health Authority*.[52]

In this case, a woman underwent a combined abortion and sterilization operation. The abortion was successful, the sterilization not so (a clip having been placed on a nearby ligament rather than on the fallopian tube). Subsequently, 14 months later, the patient gave birth to a child with congenital abnormalities, and then underwent a second sterilization operation. The defendants admitted negligence in the performance of the first operation, and the plaintiff claimed damages for pain and suffering, lost wages, and, for the first time in England, the costs of bringing up the child (the issue that has proved most contentious in North America). Although public policy was not discussed at first instance, it was fully examined by the Court of Appeal, which overruled the trial judge and awarded damages. Waller L. J. accepted the arguments of Pain J., and suggested that the courts were not necessarily the best forum to decide matters of social policy. He quoted Lord Scarman's statement in *McLoughlin v. O'Brien*[53] to the effect that 'if principle leads to results which are thought to be socially unacceptable Parliament can legislate to draw a line or map out a new path', and he concluded:

> In my judgement the court should not be too ready to lay down lines of public policy; and I would reject the argument in this case that public policy requires that damages should be confined in the way in which it has been submitted.[54]

A year later *Thake v. Maurice* itself reached the Court of Appeal,[55] and although part of Pain J.'s judgement was reversed, his reasoning on the issue of public policy was left undisturbed. In subsequent cases the public policy issue has been dropped. Although there are still occasional expressions of judicial qualm about awarding damages for the birth of a healthy child,[56] it will now need legislation or a ruling of the House of Lords to stop such awards in England in the future. For the reasons given above, it is to be hoped that no such legislation or ruling is forthcoming.

In Scots law, an award of damages after the birth of a child is by no means completely novel. The action for seduction has long existed in Scotland, and there are cases in which the seduced pursuer became pregnant: in such circumstances the pursuer has been held entitled to conjoin an action for aliment, and also claim 'inlying expenses' connected with the birth.[57] Now, while pregnancy and birth are not of the essence of the action for seduction in the way they are of an action for wrongful birth, seduction is nevertheless a long-established example of Scots law awarding damages to reflect the loss caused by childbirth. In discussing the elements of damages claimable in the action for seduction, Walker says, 'heavier damages are due if [the pursuer] has been made pregnant'.[58] Scots law therefore recognizes, and has long recognized, that pregnancy and childbirth can be losses that attract damages. Possibly for this reason, policy was simply not an issue in the first (and so far only) wrongful birth case to reach the Court of Session.[59]

The Causes of Action

Once it is established that childbirth and its consequences are legally recognized losses, there must be established a legal wrong on the part of the family planning practitioner that leads to these hurts. The wrong will be constituted by negligence, and this may take one of two forms.

First, there may be negligence in the actual treatment given by the family planner to the patient (such as the incorrect fitting of an IUD, or the negligent performance of a sterilization operation); and if that negligence is the direct cause of the failure of the treatment, then the family planner will be liable for the consequences. The standard of care in treatment required of a family planner is determined in the same way as the standard of care required of any professional person, and is discussed more fully in the following chapter.

Secondly, there may be negligence in the advice or information given by the family planner to the patient, and the majority of the English cases have in fact been raised on this basis.[60] As will be seen in the next chapter, the House of Lords has unequivocally recognized that there exists on the part of health care workers a duty to advise and inform their patients of the nature of the treatment they are proposing, as well as the risks and the consequences that the treatment involves.[61] With family planning treatment, one of the risks inherent in all methods is the risk of failure; and the negligent omission to give a warning of this risk could result in a child being born since the parents, not knowing of the risk, may not recognize the symptoms of pregnancy until it is too late to terminate that pregnancy. As a result, a wrongful birth case could be raised on the basis of a negligent failure to inform, or negligence in disclosure, because that negligence, like negligence in treatment, has led directly to the birth of a child.

An omission to disclose the existence of the risk of the treatment failing is not to be taken as a guarantee of success, for the reasonable family planner would never give such a guarantee. This has been accepted by the English Court of Appeal in two cases, *Thake v. Maurice*,[62] a vasectomy case, where the trial judge was overruled for holding that a contractual guarantee of success could be implied from the doctor's omission to warn of the risk of failure, and in *Eyre v. Measday*,[63] in which it was held further that a surgeon who emphasized the irreversible nature of a female sterilization could not, by so doing, be taken to have guaranteed that it would achieve its purpose. This has also been accepted by the Scottish court.[64]

While not a guarantee of success, an omission to warn of the possibility of failure might amount to negligence in the sense of being a failure in the duty of disclosure, but only if it is an omission such as no doctor acting with ordinary skill would be guilty of. This sort of case is simply an example of the general principle of negligence in disclosure to be discussed in the following chapter.[65] It follows that no special rules are applied to such cases except those otherwise applicable to ordinary actions for medical negligence. This was recognized in the South Australian case of *F. v. R.*[66] Here, a woman underwent a tubal ligation which failed through the natural process of recanalization. The Supreme Court of South Australia analysed the case as one of negligence in disclosure and concluded that, on the facts of the present case, the plaintiff had failed to establish that the defendant had not given the information that the reasonably competent practitioner would have given. The judges were, however, careful to point out that, on other facts, such a case might be successful. In particular, Bollen J. postulated that had procedures alternative to tubal ligation been available, a reasonable practitioner would have given statistical information about the differing rates of success. A successful case based on this ground of action is the English decision of *Thake v. Maurice* which concerned a vasectomy operation which failed through the process of recanalization, and it was found on the facts that the ordinary competent medical practitioner would have mentioned the possibility of failure to the patient: consequently, since the defendant had not, his failure amounted to negligence and damages were awarded. Since this and other cases in England have been well publicized and have led to changes in informational practices among health care workers, it is likely that doctors there will be less able to claim that it is an accepted practice to omit any warning about the risk of failure of sterilization. The risks of contraceptive methods failing are less commonly warned against, but the courts may well hold that the reasonable family planner will discuss failure rates of *all* proposed methods. As genetic counselling comes more into the forefront of reproductive decision-making than it has been hitherto, it is likely that this will become the major source of actions on the basis of negligent giving of advice and information.[67]

Causation in Wrongful Birth Cases

The claimant in an action for wrongful birth cannot obtain damages unless it is proved that the negligence actually caused, or at least materially contributed to, the harm complained of – that is, the birth of the child. It must be shown that the losses sued for would not have occurred but for the negligence of the defender. The negligence, in other words, must alter the course of events. Because the nature of the wrong in a negligent treatment case is different from the nature of the wrong in a negligent disclosure case, so the causal link to the losses suffered will be established differently.

Causation in Treatment Cases

Generally speaking, if the negligence is referable to treatment there will be little difficulty in proving causation. All medical family planning procedures have a failure rate, but this is normally low and, in the vast majority of cases, the treatment is successful. If the claimant can show that the failure to carry out the procedure in a proper fashion increases, to a material extent, the likelihood of the procedure failing, and it does fail, then this will be sufficient to establish on the balance of probabilities a causal link between the wrongful act and the failure of the family planning procedure.

However, it must also be shown by the claimant that the losses suffered would not have occurred in any case. It may be that some of the losses, though directly referable to the birth, would in fact have been suffered, whether or not there was negligence, and such losses therefore could not be said to have been *caused* by the negligence. This can be illustrated from the facts of the Canadian case of *Fredette v. Wiebe*.[68] Here, a 17 year-old girl became pregnant and underwent an abortion. Due (partly) to the doctor's negligence it was not discovered that this operation had failed until it was unreasonable to expect the mother to undergo a further abortion. She eventually gave birth to twins. She was awarded damages for her pain and suffering, anxiety, loss of amenities and loss of enjoyment of life; but *not* for the costs of upkeep of the children because the court found that she would eventually have had children anyway and be subject to these costs: in other words, whether there was negligence or not, these costs would still ultimately be incurred by the plaintiff. As Taylor J. put it:

> This is not, like most of the reported 'wrongful birth' cases, a case of a married woman who has had to bear one child too many. It is the case of an unmarried teenager who had to bear two children too soon.[69]

Likewise, it has to be shown that the losses were not caused by the claimant's own actions. In the early American case of *Christensen v. Thornby*[70] a claim against a doctor who performed a vasectomy operation negligently was dismissed, partly on the ground that the significant cause of the birth of the child was the parents' act of intercourse rather than the doctor's negligence. This was disapproved in the first successful wrongful birth case in the USA, *Custodio v. Bauer*,[71] on the ground that the law does not require that a defendant's negligence be the sole cause of the injury complained of: rather all that is required is that it be a proximate cause of the injury. This must be correct. If an operation is undertaken specifically to allow an act (unprotected intercourse) to take place without injury (the birth of a child), the doctor who is negligent in the performance of the operation ought not to be heard to say that the cause of the injury is the taking place of that act.

An argument against claimants that is rather more difficult to refute is that the birth of a child is, in reality, caused by the pregnant woman's decision not to abort the foetus once she realizes that she is pregnant. It may be claimed that this supersedes or overwhelms the initial negligence and takes over as the effective cause of the loss. This argument was accepted at first instance in the English case of *Emeh v. Kensington, Chelsea and Westminster Area Health Authority*,[72] concerning a woman who had already had three children and who became pregnant and underwent an induced abortion and simultaneous sterilization. Fourteen months later she discovered that she was pregnant once more and refused to undergo another abortion. The child was born with congenital abnormalities, and the woman sued for her losses flowing from the pregnancy and birth. The trial judge was not impressed by the plaintiff, finding her unreliable and untruthful as a witness, and he accepted the contention put forward by the defendant that her decision to continue with the pregnancy once it had been discovered was so unreasonable that it eclipsed the defendant's admitted wrongdoing. Her reasons for not seeking an abortion he described as 'unacceptable'. She had claimed that she was frightened of doctors, that she had already had one abortion and could not face another, and that she believed that her life would be in danger in undergoing an abortion at such a late stage: the judge held that she had no grounds for believing such things. Consequently, he restricted the damages he awarded to those accruing before the date on which the plaintiff discovered herself to be pregnant. The losses suffered after that date he held to have been caused by the plaintiff's own unreasonable actions rather than by the defendant's negligence.

The Court of Appeal overruled this disturbing decision, and expressed 'profound disagreement' with it. Waller L.J. found that the judge had misinterpreted the evidence and that, on a true analysis, Mrs Emeh's decision could not be described as 'utterly unreasonable', which was the test for determining whether a plaintiff's actions had superseded a defendant's negligence. Slade L.J. went further and said:

> Save in the most exceptional circumstances, I cannot think it right that the court should ever declare it unreasonable for a woman to decline to have an abortion, in a case where there is no evidence that there were any medical or psychiatric grounds for terminating the particular pregnancy.[73]

The third judge, Purchas L.J., went even further, laying down as an absolute rule that since the choice of whether to accept an abortion or not had been forced on to the plaintiff by the defendant's negligence, the defendant could never criticize the way in which the choice was made.[74] Effectively, he was holding the defendant estopped, or personally barred, from raising this as a defence.

The reasoning of Purchas L.J. is particularly persuasive. Just because a plaintiff reacts 'unreasonably' to a situation created by a defendant does not, in itself, mean that the defendant's negligence is not the cause of the reaction, if the situation ought not to have been created in the first place. A negligent defendant must take his victim as he finds him, and if that victim has emotional or moral objections to abortion, then the defendant cannot complain. And, in principle, it would be wrong for the courts ever to be put in a position of threatening financial retribution upon a woman who refuses to undergo an abortion. That decision is not one that the courts should ever attempt to influence one way or the other.

The same arguments can be used against the suggestion that claimants, who have a duty to minimize their own losses, ought to do so by putting the resultant child up for adoption and thereby avoiding the losses caused by the obligation to maintain the child. This issue was raised and discussed in the Canadian case of *Fredette v. Wiebe*. The defendant claimed that the mother ought to have put the twins she bore up for adoption, and that she ought not to be able to claim damages since, in reality, she had simply changed her mind about not wanting children. Taylor J. said this:

> I have concluded that the advance of pregnancy may be expected to be accompanied by progressive development in the expectant mother of a need to bear the child – the need to have, to know and to raise the child – which may not necessarily have been felt at all earlier in the pregnancy . . . I find that her change in attitude was foreseeable, was not inconsistent and was, in essence, a reasonable response to her changing state of pregnancy.[75]

It is to be hoped that this sensible approach is followed by the courts in other jurisdictions.

Causation in Disclosure Cases

In the normal (that is, non-family planning) disclosure case, causation from the wrong to the loss will be established by the claimant showing that had proper information been given, consent to the treatment would have been withheld.[76] However, in the family planning situation this will almost certainly never be the case, and few people would be able truthfully to claim that, had they been warned of a risk of the birth control procedure failing, they would have withheld consent. Rather, if a patient is told of a risk of failure with a particular family planning treatment, she or he will normally accept that risk, and simply hope for the best.

Exceptionally, it can be argued and proved that consent would have been withheld. This was accepted at first instance in *Gold v. Haringey Health Authority*.[77] Here, a woman who had given birth some time after a laparoscopic sterilization claimed that had she been told of the lower failure rate for vasectomies, about which she claimed she had a right to be told, then her husband would have undergone that operation and she would have refused consent to the laparoscopy. It was held by the trial judge that there had been negligence in failing to inform the couple of that vital fact, and it was also held that the plaintiff had established the necessary causal link, because she had proved that her husband would have undergone a vasectomy if they had been advised of this possibility. On the other hand, it was held that this causal link was not established in the Canadian case of *Grey v. Webster*,[78] in which a woman who had undergone a tubal ligation which failed alleged that had she been told of the risk of failure she would have refused consent to that operation and chosen another, more certain, form of sterilization. The court, on being given evidence that the only form of female sterilization that is virtually 100 per cent effective was a radical hysterectomy, held that the woman would not have chosen that other form of treatment. The evidence showed that after her first operation had failed she had undergone another operation of exactly the same nature. Consequently, although there had been a breach of duty in failing to warn of the risk of failure, that was held not to be causative of the plaintiff's loss, for fulfilment of the duty would have led to the same result: in other words, the breach did not alter the course of events. The same result was reached by the Supreme Court of South Australia in *F. v. R.*,[79] where the plaintiff had argued that she would have refused consent to the type of sterilization she underwent had she known of the greater success rates of another type of sterilization. The court held that, in the circumstances, there was no medically acceptable alternative to the operation that had been performed, and that causation was therefore not established.

Because of this major difficulty of proof, a causal link has evolved for family planning disclosure cases that is somewhat different from that used in other disclosure cases. When the negligence consists in an omission to warn of the risk of failure, this can be held to have led directly to the birth of a child if the woman, through that negligence, fails to recognize her own pregnancy and is consequently denied the chance to terminate the pregnancy, which she could *and* would otherwise have taken. In this way, the course of events would have been altered by the negligence.

This can be illustrated by the facts of *Thake v. Maurice*, for there the negligence consisted in the failure to warn that a vasectomy, although initially successful, could exceptionally reverse itself by the natural process of recanalization. This negligence resulted in the failure of Mrs Thake to recognize that she was pregnant (because the couple believed themselves incapable of conceiving together) until it was too late for her to obtain an abortion. The injury, in other words, is not the conception but the denial of the opportunity of abortion.

It follows that, with this type of negligence, it must be shown that an abortion would have been undergone; and a woman who refuses that operation must therefore be denied damages. This is not – as it might appear at first sight – inconsistent with *Emeh v. Kensington, Chelsea and Westminster Area Health Authority*, because the initial injury in that case was the conception, while in *Thake* it was the lost opportunity for abortion. The difference is not so much in the nature of the causal link, but more fundamentally in the nature of the loss itself. If the loss is admittedly a lost opportunity for abortion, the claimant must accept – indeed must aver and prove – that the opportunity would have been taken had it not been denied, otherwise there is no loss suffered, and the negligence has created no change in the course of events.[80]

As part of the proof that the opportunity for abortion has been denied, it must be shown that the pregnant woman failed to recognize the symptoms of pregnancy until it was too late for abortion. 'Too late' must mean too late in fact as well as in law. Many of the English cases contain special circumstances that have allowed the courts to accept that the symptoms of pregnancy were not recognized. In *Thake* the female plaintiff put down the symptoms of her pregnancy to an early onset of the menopause, her mother having experienced an early menopause. In *Jones v. Berkshire Area Health Authority*[81] the plaintiff had a past history of irregular and missing periods, which she assumed was recurring. However, these extra elements ought not always to be required, and a couple who believe themselves wholly protected from pregnancy ought not usually to be penalized for failing to recognize a pregnancy that they believed (through the defendant's negligence) was impossible.

Quantification of Damages

The purpose of an award of damages in an action founded on negligence is to put the injured person in the position she or he would have been had the injury not been suffered – so far as this is possible – by the payment of money. In actions for wrongful birth the position in which the claimants would have been but for the negligence is that they would not be the parents of a child. Becoming parents is the cause of many losses, of a financial, emotional and even physical nature. But it also brings many benefits. It follows that in order to put the claimant in the position she or he would have been in but for the negligence (and but for the birth), two separate processes must be undertaken. First, the losses of a legally cognizable nature that flow from the negligence must be identified and converted into monetary terms; and, secondly, the benefits that flow from the negligence and accrue to the claimant as a consequence thereof must also be identified, and set off against the relevant losses.

If a child is born that would not have been born but for the negligence of a health care worker in undertaking some family planning procedure, that negligence can be said to cause losses of various different kinds, and the claims made in the reported cases reflect that variety.

Personal Injuries

Conception and childbirth will always result in some physical injury to the pregnant woman, and in most wrongful birth cases this will be a significant head of damages. So too will the birth process, which will almost invariably be a painful and unpleasant experience. The person whose negligence led directly to that pain and suffering is rightly held liable to compensate for it.

Whenever a woman becomes pregnant, any complication arising from that pregnancy will not be regarded as being unforeseeable or too remote to attract damages.[82] In the English case of *Jones v. Berkshire Area Health Authority* it was held that the extra pain and suffering undergone during the birth because that birth required a caesarian section would increase (though only slightly) the damages which could be awarded under this head. Any long-term scarring that followed such an operation would also be claimable. If the pregnant woman decides to terminate her pregnancy, then damages for the pain and suffering for that operation will be payable: in the Canadian case of *Dendaas v. Yackel*[83] damages were awarded for the physical injury of being subjected to an undesired abortion.

The particular patient's circumstances may lead to other types of physical loss. So a negligently performed sterilization operation may have to be repeated, and damages will be available to cover the second operation which ought not to have been necessary. If the mother dies as a consequence of the pregnancy or childbirth, then, because giving birth is not so safe today that maternal death is utterly unforeseeable, damages for that death will be payable to those dependents entitled to claim.[84]

Damages for any emotional injury may also be claimed for. In most common law legal systems, emotional hurt is only compensable when it is tied in parasitically with some physical hurt, unless it is so severe as to amount to some form of psychotic illness. As pregnancy and childbirth will themselves amount to physical hurts, then in actions for wrongful birth even minor emotional injuries will be compensable as separate heads of damage.

A number of the English cases illustrate special emotional aspects peculiar to their own facts which led the courts to increase damages (but which might not have been sufficient on their own to found an independent claim for damages). In *Emeh v. Kensington, Chelsea & Westminster Area Health Authority*, where the child was born handicapped, the mother's distress at this fact was held relevant to the quantification of the damages she could claim. In *Udale v. Bloomsbury Area Health Authority* the mother had taken drugs to combat the symptoms of pregnancy (before she discovered the true cause of these symptoms) and her worry at the damage this might have done to the child was held to be a factor that increased the amount of damages awarded under this head. Similarly, in *Jones v. Berkshire Area Health Authority* the mother thought her symptoms of pregnancy were really symptoms of cancer, and her damages were increased to take account of the emotional distress this naturally caused. In a number of English cases, damages were awarded to reflect the distress the plaintiffs suffered on the realization that their plans for the future had been disrupted.[85] And in the Canadian case of *Dendaas v. Yackel*, in which the pregnancy had been terminated by abortion, damages were awarded to the woman for the guilt and depression that this had caused her.

Economic Loss

There are various different types of economic losses that can be claimed for.[86] If the pregnancy and birth cause the mother to give up her work, and thus lose earnings, then this will be a relevant claim. Also, the medical expenses of carrying and bearing the child would be recoverable if they were incurred. Another expense that has been claimed in some of the English cases[87] is the 'layette' – that is the provision of clothes and equipment necessary for the care of a newborn child.

It is, however, the issue of the maintenance of the child that has been the most contentious of the economic losses. As pointed out above, the English and Canadian courts have concluded, unlike the courts in most US jurisdictions, that there is no policy objection to allowing such a claim. This is now usually the most significant element of the economic losses that will be claimed in jurisdictions that allow recovery. Being economic, the loss can be quantified much more precisely than with the other forms of injury, but problems can arise in relation to future costs of upkeep. There is a dispute as to whether the costs of upkeep of the child are to be assessed taking account of the standard of living of the family into which it was actually born, or the standard of living of the average normal family. Robertson suggests[88] that, while strict theory would demand the subjective approach, the objective approach is preferable as being more equitable. But it is suggested that it would be more logical and more consonant with accepted principles of assessment of damages to adopt a wholly subjective approach for quantification of economic losses. This for the following reason.

Damages is the conversion of loss into monetary terms. With losses that cannot realistically be so converted, such as physical and emotional injuries, there is room for an objective approach, and the court must make its estimates based on past practice and currently accepted ideas of worth. But economic loss is loss of a monetary nature and no estimation and conversion is required. The purpose of an award of damages is to compensate the *actual* claimant for the *actual* loss, not to compensate for the losses that a reasonable or average claimant would normally suffer. That in itself would be inequitable. It would follow that the expenses actually incurred and to be incurred in raising the particular child should determine the level of damages awardable. An analogy with a claim for lost earnings is apt. The claimant is compensated for the earnings she or he actually loses, and if these earnings are less than the average, then the damages awarded will reflect that fact. Similarly, if the earnings are substantially above average then the defender must pay proportionately more damages. The English courts clearly adopt this approach. In *Thake v. Maurice* the trial judge pointed out that the child had been born into a 'humble household':

> The plaintiffs have claimed for [costs of upkeep] on a moderate basis. They have made their calculations on the basis of the supplementary benefit scales. This is right.[89]

In total, under this head, he awarded £6,677 for the costs of the child's upbringing until its seventeenth birthday. That figure was not disturbed by the Court of Appeal. This case may be compared with that of *Jones v. Berkshire Area Health Authority*.[90] Little detail about the family circumstances comes from the judgement, but a figure of £30,213.58 was agreed between the parties to cover the expense of raising the child. This is far in excess of the amounts awarded in the previous English cases, and the fact that it was agreed before the case reached the court to determine the issue of liability suggests that the family Jones was rather better off than the Thakes, and that it was accepted that this would necessarily increase the amount to be awarded.

The issue was sharply raised in the case of *Benarr v. Kettering Health Authority*.[91] Here, liability for the negligent performance of a vasectomy was accepted by the defendants, and the only argument concerned whether the costs of upkeep of the resultant child should include a figure for the school fees that would be incurred. The family was described as an 'upper middle class family' by the judge, who held that since the plaintiff would, in any event, have paid for the education of the child, this would be an actual expense that had to be compensated for. It followed that 'in the circumstances of that family [the school fees] could properly be called a necessary'.

Although this results in compensation levels being determined to a large extent by the claimant's economic position, this is no different from any other claim for compensation. Throughout the law of damages, different people receive different levels of awards for essentially the same hurts, because their actual suffering consequent upon these hurts is different. It would be anomalous for the courts to adopt a different approach in wrongful birth cases, and if the principle is inappropriate, or particularly inequitable in wrongful birth cases, then the legislature should step in to change the rule.

Other Losses

Various other losses have been, or can be, claimed by the parents of a child born as a result of a family planning doctor's negligence. In *Sciuriaga v. Powell*[92] the plaintiff, who became a mother after a negligently performed abortion failed to terminate her pregnancy, was awarded, *inter alia*, £3,000 for the impairment of her marital prospects. Loss of enjoyment of sex could also be a head of damage. If pregnancy and birth of an unplanned child have such an effect, even on a short-term basis, then damages ought to be awarded to reflect such loss. In *Cataford v. Moreau*[93] damages were awarded to both parents for the loss of enjoyment of life caused by the interruption of sexual relations for a period of four months.

An analogous claim, loss of amenities of life, was made successfully in *Emeh v. Kensington, Chelsea & Westminster Area Health Authority*, where the child had been born handicapped. And in *Jones v. Berkshire Area Health Authority* a similar claim was successful where the child was not handicapped.

In both Scots and English law loss of potential future earning capacity is a valid head of damages.[94] A claimant seeking damages under this head in a wrongful birth case would probably have to prove that the chosen career was made impossible by the birth, rather than simply more difficult or less convenient to follow. That might be difficult today, and more likely is a claim that the mother's earning capacity is simply reduced rather than destroyed.

A further loss that has been held claimable in England and which could also follow on from an unplanned pregnancy and birth is the break-up of the parents' marriage. In *Jones v. Jones*[95] the Court of Appeal awarded damages to a plaintiff for the losses caused by the break-up of his marriage, and this principle could be applied against a defendant whose negligence resulted in the birth of a child. It is easy to imagine a situation in which a married couple are not told of the risk of a sterilization operation failing or reversing itself and a vasectomized man believing that his wife has been unfaithful if she becomes pregnant some months after a sperm count has shown him to be azoospermatic. Or, alternatively, the extra strain that the unplanned child causes may be sufficient to bring the marriage to an end. In order to succeed the claimant would have to establish that the break-up of the marriage was not unforeseeable or unreasonable as a result of the negligence, and that the marriage would not have broken up in any case.

Deductions from the Damages

If the purpose of an award of damages is to put the claimant as near as is possible to the position in which she or he would have been had the negligence not occurred, it follows that any benefit that accrues to the claimant which would not have accrued but for the negligence of the defender must be used to reduce the amount of damages awarded. Various benefits will accrue to the parents of an unplanned child. The most obvious financial benefit is any entitlement to child allowances provided by the state. These will be deducted from the costs of upkeep. But a child also brings companionship, provides services, and, at a later date, may contribute substantially to the family exchequer. And, of course, parenthood usually involves an emotional advantage: pleasure at a child's growth and achievement will be normal; enjoyment of life, and its very quality, will be enhanced. Although incapable of exact conversion into monetary terms, these things are real and fundamentally important, indeed almost definitional of parenthood, and must be taken into account in determining the true extent of the pursuer's loss.

In Anglo-American jurisprudence the 'same interest' rule requires that benefits be set off only against losses of the same nature. Applying this to actions for wrongful birth would mean, for example, that the costs of the child's upkeep could not be reduced by the emotional advantages the child brings, but only by the extra income the child generates. However, in wrongful birth cases, the losses and benefits are often dependent upon, or indistinguishable from, each other. As Kelley points out:

> It is at once a fact and a mystery that the pain and the joy of parenthood are inextricably bound together. We worry about our children and grieve at their suffering and their failures because we love them. That love is the source of the joy and the sorrow of parenthood. Most parents would find it odd to be asked to count up the joys on one side of parenthood and the sorrows on the other, as if the one did not in some fundamental sense depend on the other.[96]

The truth of this insight means that it is difficult to separate out all the different types of losses and types of benefits; and this has been used as an excuse by a number of American courts to avoid applying the 'same interest' rule: consequently they have been able to deny damages totally on the ground that the emotional benefits outweigh *all* the other losses suffered. So, in *Troppi v. Scarf*,[97] it was held that all the different losses flowing from pregnancy and birth were so interrelated and tied together that the court did not

> . . . think it would be sound to attempt to separate [the emotional] segments of damage from the economic costs of an unplanned child in applying the 'same interest' rule. Accordingly, the benefits of the unplanned child may be weighed against all the elements of claimed damages.

This is not the approach that has been accepted in the English cases. English law and, it is submitted, Scots law also, certainly accepts that benefits flowing from negligence can only reduce damages by being set off against losses of a like nature.[98]

The way the set-off will operate has been discussed in a number of the English cases. In *Udale v. Bloomsbury Area Health Authority*, Jupp J., although disallowing damages to cover the cost of extending the family home in order to accommodate the new baby, pointed out that, had he done so, the parents would ultimately own a much more valuable house and that this should be taken into account in assessing damages. A similar matter was taken into account in *Benarr v. Kettering Health Authority*,[99] where the family had moved to a larger house, which was later sold 'at a substantial profit'. This profit did not flow from the original negligence, and so was not used to offset the other economic losses of a like nature (in this case removal expenses, for which £1,000 was awarded). Likewise, in *Gold v. Haringey Health Authority*, Schiemann J., at first instance,[100] in assessing damages referable to the plaintiff's future loss of earnings, said that he specifically bore in mind the possibility of Mrs Gold being re-employed in the future, as well as the fact that the Golds now had two sons who might in due course be of some financial benefit to them and help look after them.

However, it is the issue of emotional benefit that has caused most problems for the courts. Such benefits are, of course, difficult to quantify, but this is no more difficult than quantifying the emotional losses of the same nature. The major problem is, rather, what to set these benefits off against. The issue was first raised in England in *Emeh v. Kensington, Chelsea and Westminster Area Health Authority*. Here, Purchas L.J. quoted from the American decision of *Sherlock v. Stillwater Clinic*,[101] in which the Supreme Court of Minnesota had said:

> Additionally, parents may recover the reasonable costs of rearing the unplanned child subject to offsetting the value of the child's age comfort and society during the parents' life expectancy.

He pointed out, however, that in the present case such a set-off would be inappropriate as the child involved, having been born with congenital abnormalities, would provide little in the way of aid, comfort, and society.[102]

Notwithstanding that, however, the court felt constrained to point out that the mother did receive a great deal of emotional pleasure from the existence of her handicapped child, but nevertheless refused to make any off-set to diminish the damages for that reason. The joy was clearly of the mother's own making, and it would be wrong to penalize the mother for that reason.

The issue of how emotional benefit is to be regarded in the assessment of damages received its fullest consideration in relation to English law in the case of *Thake v. Maurice*. At first instance, Pain J. pointed out that the plaintiffs had suffered great distress on learning of Mrs Thake's pregnancy. Also, Mrs Thake underwent pain and discomfort in the course of labour. He held that the joy of having a healthy child should be set off against both the prenatal distress and the labour pains so that both these items were cancelled out, but that the joy cancelled nothing else out and could not be used to diminish such economic losses as costs of upkeep. The Court of Appeal agreed that the emotional blessings flowing from the negligence could not be set off against the economic losses, but went further than Pain J., and accepted the plaintiffs' submission that the joy should be set off only against the inconvenience and trouble of bringing up the child, but not against the prenatal distress, pain and suffering. In other words, the joys and blessings flowing from parenthood are relevant to set off only against the post-natal emotional distress that being a parent causes, but not the prenatal emotional distress that the discovery of an unwanted pregnancy causes. The prenatal emotional injuries, according to Kerr L.J.,

> . . . stand on a separate footing, and I think that it would be wrong to apply this set off to this head of claim as well, in effect twice over, bearing in mind that the claim for pain and suffering was otherwise unchallenged. One can perhaps take the analogy of a defendant who sustains some injury and suffers distress because of the risk that he may become paralysed. If he then fortunately and happily makes a full recovery, his ultimate well-being will of course be reflected in a low award of damages. But his relief and joy at the outcome cannot properly be used as a basis for reducing, let alone extinguishing, an appropriate award for his initial pain and suffering.[103]

It is to be noted that Kerr L.J. specifically restricted his remarks to a 'healthy' child, which suggests that his conclusion would apply *a fortiori* if, in the particular circumstances (for example if the child is not 'healthy'), there is no or a greatly reduced benefit. There are many other situations in which parenthood attracts little or no advantages, such as, for example, because the parents consider themselves too old (or indeed too young) to give the child a proper upbringing. Doubtless, however, if the parents deliberately 'harden their hearts' to the child and refuse to find any joy in its birth specifically in order to avoid a reduction in their damages, the court will recognize this and reflect it in the damages awarded. The opposite situation is illustrated in *Emeh v. Kensington, Chelsea and Westminster Area Health Authority*, in which the Court of Appeal refused to penalize a mother by reducing her damages because of the emotional advantages of parenthood, when she had deliberately made an effort, against hard odds, to find some benefit from that state.

Notes

1 On the issue of civil liability in medical practice generally, one could do no better than refer to Giesen, *International Medical Malpractice Law*, Martinus Nijhoff, Dortrecht, 1988.
2 *Sciuriaga v. Powell*, (1979) 123 *SJ* 406, aff. 24 July 1980.
3 *Udale v. Bloomsbury Area Health Authority* [1983] 1 *WLR* 1098; *Emeh v. Kensington, Chelsea, and Westminster Area Health Authority* [1985] *QB* 1012.
4 *Pattison v. Hobbes* 5 November 1985; *Benarr v. Kettering Health Authority* (1988) 138 *New LJ* 179.
5 See the judgement of the *Landesgerichtshof*, Berlin (W.) 17 January 1985, 38 *Neue Juristische Wochenschrift* 2200.
6 *Thake v. Maurice* [1986] *QB* 644; *Eyre v. Measday* [1986] 1 *All ER* 488; *Gold v. Haringey Health Authority* [1987] 3 *WLR* 649.
7 *Gold*, (note 6 above); *Grey v. Webster* (1984) 14 *DLR* (4th) 706, *F. v. R.* (1983) 33 *SASR* 189.
8 *Rance v. Mid-Downs Health Authority & Anor.*, 5 February 1990.
9 *Troppi v. Scarf* 187 *NW* (2d) 511 (1971). On the issue of the manufacturer's liability for the failure of a contraceptive pill, see Bordicks, 'Unwanted Pregnancy and the Pill' 41 *Cinc. LR* 335, 1972.
10 The first few cases made on this basis in the USA were founded on the fact that the children had been born merely socially disadvantaged, for example through illegitimacy. The courts had no difficulty in dismissing these claims: see *Zepeda v. Zepeda* 41 *Ill. App.* 2d 240 (1963), and *Williams v. New York* 223 *NE* 2d 849 (1963). Both these cases are discussed in a Note in 66 *Colum. LR* 127, 1966.
11 400 *NYS* (2d) 110 (1977). See also *Turpin v. Sortini* 31 *Cal.* 3d 220, 182 *Cal. Rptr.* 337 (1982); *Curlender v. Bio-Science Laboratories* 165 *Cal. Rptr.* 477 (1980); *Procanik v. Cillo* 478 *A.* 2d 755 (1984).
12 Such a statute was upheld by the Minnesota Supreme Court in *Hickman v. Group Health Plan Inc.* 396 *NW* 2d 10 (1986).
13 According to Mason & McCall Smith, *Medico-Legal Encyclopaedia*, Butterworth, London, 1987 at pp. 591–2.
14 [1982] *QB* 1166.
15 The action is not without academic support, and strong voices argue in its favour: see, for example, Teff, 'The Action for "Wrongful Life" in England and the United States,' 34 *ICLQ* 423 1985; Dickens, 'Wrongful Birth and Life, Wrongful Death Before Birth and Wrongful Law', in McLean (ed), *Legal Issues in Human Reproduction*, Dartmouth, Aldershot, 1989. Both Teff and Dickens try to fit the action into normal tort doctrine. It is submitted that this cannot be done successfully, certainly not in relation to Scots law.
16 Dickens, op. cit., note 15 above, points out that the settled terminology in the *US* literature is to restrict the term 'wrongful birth' to situations in which the child is born defective, while 'wrongful pregnancy' would cover the case of the child born healthy. Other categories include 'wrongful conception' and 'wrongful life'. Apart from wrongful life, these other categories are only factually different, and give rise to the same problems in law. Consequently, the term 'wrongful birth' will be used throughout the present chapter to refer compendiously to all claims by parents based on the failure of a family planning procedure.
17 *F v. West Berkshire Health Authority* [1989] *New LJ* 183.
18 11 *Pa. D. & C.* 2d 41 (1957).
19 496 *SW* 2d 124 (1973).

20 A fact pointed out by Robertson in 'Civil Liability Arising from "Wrongful Birth" Following an Unsuccessful Sterilization Operation', 4 *Am. J. L. Med.* 131, 1978 at p. 150.
21 Robertson, 'Damages for the Birth of a Child – Some Possible Policy Barriers', 23 *Med. Sci. Law* 2, 1983 at p. 4.
22 Symmons, 'Policy Factors in Actions for Wrongful Birth', 50 *Mod. LR* 269, 1987 at p. 280. This argument was raised, but rejected in the South African case of *Edouard v. Administrator of Natal* 1989 (2) SALR 368, per Thirion J.; and in the Appeallate Division of the Supreme Court of South Africa, 30 May 1990.
23 49 *NJ* 22, 227 A. 2d 689 (1967).
24 Robertson, 4 *Am. J. L. Med.* 1978 at pp. 148–9.
25 219 *NW* 2d 242 (1974).
26 For other cases approving this line of reasoning, see Symmons, op. cit., note 22 above, at pp. 296–9.
27 Dickens, op. cit., note 15 above, at p. 91.
28 (1978) 86 *DLR* (3d) 719.
29 Ibid. at pp. 722–3.
30 (1978) 114 *DLR* (3d) 585.
31 Ibid. at p. 595.
32 Such as *Dendaas v. Yackel* (1980) 109 *DLR* (3d) 455 and *Grey v. Webster* (1984) 14 *DLR* (4th) 706. They were mentioned only to be dismissed in *Fredette v. Wiebe* (1986) 29 *DLR* (4th) 534.
33 [1980] 2 *NZLR* 748.
34 See further *Re Priestley: Decision No. 14/84* [1984] *NZACR* 787.
35 [1983] 1 *WLR* 1098.
36 [1985] 2 *WLR* 215.
37 (1978) 86 *DLR* (3d) 719.
38 [1985] 2 *WLR* at p. 231.
39 Dickens points out, op. cit., note 15 above, at p. 88, 'whether a child will in fact suffer rejection as a result of learning that it was the unwanted result of, for instance, negligent sterilization of a parent, may be doubted if it knows that its parents refused the option of abortion or adoption'.
40 [1983] 1 *WLR* at p. 1109.
41 [1985] 2 *WLR* at p. 231.
42 Ibid. at p. 232.
43 [1982] *QB* 1166 at p. 1187.
44 (1974) *Law Com. No.* 60, Cmnd. 5709, para 89.
45 And Griffiths L.J. in *McKay* pointed out at p. 1192 that the argument is not very strong even in relation to wrongful life cases, because the decision whether to have an abortion or not is always at the end of the day for the mother.
46 See further Dickens, op. cit., note 15 above, the whole thrust of whose argument is to show that 'attempts to refashion tort law judicially or by statute so that it may serve as a weapon in the abortion conflict will lead to distortion and corruption of the law, and should be resisted' (at p. 108).
47 [1983] 1 *WLR* at p. 1109.
48 [1985] 2 *WLR* at p. 230.
49 Ibid at p. 232.
50 Kouri, 'The Legality of Purely Contraceptive Sterilization', 7 *RDUS* 1, 1976 at p. 47.
51 See Chapters 2 and 3.
52 [1985] *QB* 1012.
53 [1983] 1 *AC* 410 at p. 430.

54 [1985] *QB* at p. 1022.
55 [1986] *QB* 644.
56 In *Jones v. Berkshire Area Health Authority* 2 July 1986 Ognall J said this:

> Speaking purely personally, it remains a matter of surprise to me that the law acknowledges an entitlement in a matter to claim damages for the blessing of a healthy child. Certain it is that those who are afflicted with a handicapped child, or who long desperately to have a child at all and are denied that good fortune would regard an award for this sort of contingency with a measure of astonishment. But there it is: that is the law.

57 See, for example, *Brown v. Harvey* 1907 *SC* 588; *MacLeod v. MacAskill* 1920 *SC* 72. In England the action for seduction lay at the instance of the girl's father for his 'loss of services', and the issue would not arise.
58 Walker on *Delict* Green, Edinburgh, 2nd edn. 1981 at p. 702.
59 *Jones v. Lanarkshire Health Board* 1990 *SLT* 19.
60 And is the basis for the only Scottish case that has so far been subject to judicial consideration: see *Jones*, supra..
61 *Sidaway v. Bethlem Royal Hospital* [1985] *AC* 871.
62 [1986] *QB* 644.
63 [1986] 1 *All ER* 488.
64 *Jones*, op. cit., note 59 above.
65 As was affirmed by the English Court of Appeal in *Gold v. Haringey Health Authority* [1987] 3 *WLR* 649.
66 (1983) 33 *SASR* 189.
67 On counselling in family planning, see Allen, *Counselling Services for Sterilisation, Vasectomy and Termination of Pregnancy*, Policy Studies Institute, London, 1985.
68 (1986) 29 *DLR* (4th) 534.
69 Ibid at p. 541.
70 192 *Minn.* 133, 93 *ALR* 570 (1934).
71 251 *Cal. App.* 2d 303, 27 *ALR* (3d) 884 (1967).
72 21 December 1982, overruled at [1985] *QB* 1012.
73 [1985] *QB* at p. 1024.
74 For North American and German decisions adopting similar reasoning, see Giesen op. cit., note 1 above, at p. 247.
75 (1986) 29 *DLR* (4th) at pp. 540–1. The suggestion was also rejected by Thirion J. in the South African case of *Edouard v. Administrator of Natal*, note 22 above, on the ground that 'that would run counter to our accepted community values regarding the inviolability of the family': 1989 (2) SALR 368 at p. 384.
76 McLean, *A Patient's Right to Know: Information Disclosure, the Doctor, and the Law* Dartmouth, Aldershot, 1989.
77 16 June 1986 (overruled on another point in the Court of Appeal: [1987] 3 *WLR* 649).
78 (1984) 14 *DLR* (4th) 706.
79 (1983) 33 *SASR* 189.
80 The interplay between *Emeh* and *Thake* is discussed more fully by the author in 'Liability for Failed Sterilisation', 1986 *SLT* (News) 145.
81 2 July 1986.
82 In *Emeh* Waller L.J. said [1985] *QB* at p. 1019,

> . . . in my view it is trite to say that if a woman becomes pregnant, it is certainly foreseeable that she will have a baby, but in my judgment,

having regard to the fact that in a proportion of all births . . . congenital abnormalities might arise, makes the risk clearly one that is foreseeable, as the law of negligence understands it. There are many cases where even more remote risks have been taken to be foreseeable.

83 (1980) 109 *DLR* (3d) 455.
84 In Scots and English law this is covered by the Administration of Justice Act 1982.
85 *Sciuriaga v. Powell* (1979) 123 *SJ* 406, aff. 24 July 1980, *Udale v. Bloomsbury Area Health Authority* [1983] 1 *WLR* 1098, and *Thake v. Maurice* [1986] *QB* 644.
86 Although the English, and possibly the Scottish, courts tend to be loath to award damages for economic loss unless this is a consequence of physical loss, this should cause few if any difficulties with the action for wrongful birth, because there will invariably be some physical loss involved.
87 *Udale v. Bloomsbury Area Health Authority* note 85 above, and *Emeh v. Kensington, Chelsea & Westminster Area Health Authority* note 52 above.
88 Robertson, op. cit., note 20 above at p. 152.
89 [1985] 2 *WLR* at p. 232.
90 2 July 1986.
91 (1988) 138 *New LJ* 179.
92 (1979) 123 *SJ* 406, aff. 24 July 1980.
93 (1978) 114 *DLR* (3d) 585.
94 *Joyce v. Yeomans* [1981] 1 *WLR* 549; *Drummond v. Foulis* 1972 *SLT* (Notes) 11.
95 [1985] *QB* 704. See also *Pritchard v. J.H. Cobden Ltd* [1987] 2 *WLR* 627, in which the Court of Appeal refused to follow *Jones* insofar as the earlier case had allowed damages for the financial consequences of the divorce other than the obligation to maintain.
96 Kelley, 'Wrongful Life, Wrongful Birth and Justice in Tort Law', *Wash ULQ* 919, 1979 at p. 947.
97 187 *NW* 2d 511 (1971).
98 See *Parry v. Cleaver* [1970] *AC* 1.
99 (1988) 138 *New LJ* 179.
100 16th June 1986.
101 260 *NW* 2d 169 (1977).
102 [1985] *QB* at p. 1028.
103 [1986] *QB* at p. 682.

9 Consent to Family Planning Procedures

Introduction

There is no doubt that one of the most significant political consequences of the increased availability of family planning has been the liberalization of people's freedom of choice in their lifestyles. The acceptance that pleasure is as valid a reason for having sex as reproduction has coincided with an increased medical ability to allow people to exercise that choice. Freedom of choice in family planning, as in other things, is an aspect of the important legal principle of autonomy, or the right to do with one's own body as one pleases.

In all forms of medical and paramedical practice, the principle of autonomy is protected by the important rule that a health care worker may not provide any medical treatment, nor perform any medical examination or procedure, without first having obtained the legally efficacious consent of the patient to that treatment, examination, or procedure.[1] This rule is of fundamental importance to the patient's freedom of choice, for not only does it protect the patient from unwanted bodily interference, but it also ensures that it is the patient rather than the doctor who makes the decision about whether to accept a medical interference, and, if so, what type. For this reason, the requirement for consent ought more properly to be termed the 'right to choose'.

It is of fundamental importance to remember that the right of decision necessarily involves not only the right to consent but also the right to decide to withhold consent, or the 'right of dissent',[2] whether or not that dissent is irrational (in the doctor's view) and whether or not it furthers the patient's best interests (as perceived by the doctor). The right of choice is the right to determine where one's own best interests lie, and to decide whether or not to further them. This follows from a proper understanding of what autonomy is all about: 'since autonomy is the right to make decisions, it includes the choice to exercise judgment unwisely, and to have to bear the consequences'.[3] A relatively early judicial recognition of this comes from the New Zealand Court of Appeal, where, in *Smith v. Auckland Hospital Board* Gresson J. said this:

> An individual patient must, in my view, always retain the right to decline operative investigation or treatment however unreasonable or foolish this may appear in the eyes of his medical advisers.[4]

Protection of the patient's right of choice (including the right to choose unwisely) is important for all forms of medical treatment, but it is all the more important in relation to family planning practice, for two reasons. First, the decision to accept the family planning treatment (in distinction from the decision of what form of treatment to accept) is one that is normally made for other than medical reasons. People seek birth control for social, economic or emotional reasons far more than for the medical benefits it brings them. Much more than with other forms of medical treatment, the decision to accept treatment may be based on personal, non-medical, considerations – factors that the doctor need not know about and is seldom competent to judge. Secondly, possibly more than in any other area of medical practice, there is a large number of very different options available to achieve the desired end result: some choice is inevitable even after the decision to accept the medical interference has been made, and it is for the patient to make that choice, taking into account any advice that the family planner gives.

The Causes of Action

A patient's right of choice will be breached if a health care worker provides any medical treatment or performs any medical examination or procedure without the consent of the patient. In all the major legal systems it is recognized as a first principle of medical law that treatment without consent amounts *prima facie* to a civil, or even a criminal, *assault*.

But it is further recognized that the doctor-patient relationship is seldom a relationship of equals, and that the patient relies upon the doctor not only to give proper treatment but also to show proper respect for the patient's right of choice. It follows from this that the doctor must give the patient proper advice and information concerning the nature and effect of the proposed treatment, so that the choice the patient ultimately makes is meaningful and based on a sufficient understanding of the options available.

The doctor is thus under a duty of disclosure, the unintentional breach of which can lead to civil liability in *negligence*.

These two legal wrongs will be examined separately, for they have different juridical bases, different consequences and different methods of proof.[5] Assault, or trespass to the person, is generally an intentionally committed wrong, and, once committed, there is no need to prove loss, injury or damage apart from the bodily interference itself. Negligence, on the other hand, is an unintentional wrong and, once committed, is legally actionable only when some loss, injury or damage results from it. The place of consent is different in the two wrongs: with assault, consent provides a defence and is therefore for the defender to prove;[6] with negligence, consent based on insufficient information is part of the wrong itself and therefore for the claimant to prove.[7] Very different considerations are therefore brought into play with these two distinct legal wrongs.

Assault, or Trespass to the Person

As stated above, any medical treatment, examination, or procedure that involves an interference or invasion of a patient's body, or mere threat thereof, is *prima facie* an assault, or trespass to the person of that patient. Consent is the primary defence to that legal wrong, and if there is no consent, then the health care worker must rely upon some other defence. In relation to adults, the only defence available when consent is absent is emergency – that is, some immediate necessity to act before consent can be obtained.[8] It should be emphasized that consent and emergency are not alternative defences: if the patient refuses consent then it is no defence that an emergency exists, for a patient is entitled to choose even his own death. Rather, emergency can only come into operation when consent cannot be obtained for some reason. The requirement for consent applies to all types of family planning procedure.

So, for example, to force contraceptive treatment, either hormonal or mechanical, upon a patient without consent would undoubtedly amount to an assault. It is difficult to imagine any medical practitioner giving contraceptive treatment to a woman against her wishes; but the principle applies equally if the patient consents to the procedure in the belief that it is something wholly different from its true nature. Thus, if a doctor prescribed contraceptive pills but deliberately told the patient that they were something else, the patient's consent to taking the pills would be meaningless, and the doctor would be guilty of assault. Or if a family planner inserts an IUD into a woman without telling her what it is, or falsely telling her it was a proper medical treatment for some condition she suffers from, there would be a clear assault. In *R. v. Case*[9] a doctor was convicted of assault after having sexual intercourse with a 14 year-old patient. She had consented to the act of intercourse, having been told by the doctor that this was proper medical treatment (to cure her of fits!). The English Court of Criminal Appeal upheld the conviction on the ground that 'what she consented to was something wholly different from that which was done, and, therefore, that which was done, was done without her consent'.[10]

Apart from the situation of the mentally disabled (discussed in Chapter 7), it is difficult to envisage a situation in which non-consensual contraceptive treatment could be justified by emergency.

The same principles apply also to termination of pregnancy: it would clearly be a very grave assault upon a woman to perform such a medical procedure without her consent. The secondary defence of emergency will seldom be appropriate with abortion. Emergency normally requires some immediacy as well as necessity (again with a potential exception for the mentally disabled). Even when abortion is necessary to preserve the life or health of the pregnant woman, the operation will seldom be so immediately required that there is no time to seek the woman's consent. Again, this principle protects the patient's right of choice, for it is always open to a woman to refuse to undergo an abortion even if her refusal threatens her life or health. And it is by no means inconceivable that some women would prefer to accept that risk than to accept an abortion.

Likewise, these principles apply with sterilization. The removal of a person's reproductive capacity is a serious step, with far-reaching emotional, financial, as well as physical, consequences. It is, as Macfarlane J. put it in *Murray v McMurchy*[11] 'to deprive [the plaintiff] of the possible fulfilment of one of the great powers and privileges of her life'. It is also, for all intents and purposes, irreversible. For these reasons, it is all the more important that the patient her or himself actually makes the decision. There is, however, rather more scope for the defence of emergency with sterilization. Again, the primary defence to the assault that a sterilization operation undoubtedly constitutes will be consent; but because surgical procedures can give rise to or reveal unexpected situations, emergency may sometimes justify an assault when there has been no consent.

A case illustrating this point is that of *Murray v. McMurchy*, a decision of the Supreme Court of British Columbia. Here, fibroid tumours were discovered in a woman's uterus while she was undergoing a caesarian section. The surgeon concluded, in good faith, that it would be dangerous for the woman to become pregnant again, and that it would be in her best interests to be sterilized. He therefore immediately carried out that procedure. The patient sued for trespass to the person. There was clearly no consent and the real dispute before the court was whether there had existed sufficient emergency to justify the surgeon acting as he had done.

The court held that the fact that the sterilization was in the woman's best interests was not sufficient to constitute an emergency demanding *immediate* action. The operation could have been postponed without danger, for the risk was not certain to eventuate. Treatment without consent, the court held, could be justified only where the treatment is 'necessary, as opposed to being convenient'.[12] The court further held that the conclusion reached was not affected by the evidence presented to the court that most women would have wanted this operation done at the same time as the caesarian section. That was not the point: the patient had been denied the chance to make up her own mind, and the doctor had therefore infringed her right to decide for herself whether the risk of another pregnancy outweighed any desire she had for further children. The court quoted the earlier case of *Bennan v. Parsonnet*[13] in which Garrison J. had said, 'No amount of professional skill can justify the substitution of the will of the surgeon for that of his patient'.

An earlier case, also from Canada, illustrates the sort of circumstance in which an emergency can validly be used to justify a non-consensual operation. In *Marshall v. Curry*[14] a surgeon performing a hernia operation discovered that the patient had a grossly diseased testicle and decided to remove it, believing in good faith that if it were not removed immediately gangrene could set in, to the severe detriment of the patient. An action for trespass failed on the ground that such an operation was in these circumstances 'necessary'.

It is clear from cases such as these that a sterilization performed without consent will, in the absence of emergency, be regarded by the law as a serious assault. However, as will be seen shortly, the action for negligence, which is based on a quite different wrong, is becoming of much more significance than assault as the legal remedy for breach of a patient's right of choice. But there is still room in the law for assault, if the facts justify it. Increasingly, however, courts are showing a reluctance to rely upon assault rather than negligence, even in the clearest cases of intentional non-consensual interferences with the bodies of others. Assault implies a deliberate intent to injure and it seems to be felt that this is not a proper way to describe a doctor's actions when she or he is motivated solely by the best interests of the patient. But the point is that it is not for the doctor to determine where the best interests of an adult competent patient lie; and indeed, patients have the right, if desired, to act against their own interests. If that right is deliberately denied by the doctor, then it is perfectly proper that, whatever the motivation, she or he be charged with assault.

The court's reluctance to use assault as a means of protecting the patient's right of choice can be seen in an unreported decision of the English Court of Appeal, *Devi v. West Midlands Regional Health Authority*.[15] Here, a woman underwent an operation to correct a puncture made during the clearing of her uterus after the birth of her fourth child. During this operation, the surgeon decided that it would be in the woman's best interests to be sterilized, so, without asking her, he occluded her fallopian tubes. There was clearly no consent whatsoever, for the possibility of sterilization had not been discussed, nor even contemplated, before hand. There was no suggestion of emergency: the surgeon had merely decided that, the woman's abdomen being open anyway, it would be convenient to perform, there and then, an operation that was (in his view) very much in her best interests.

This case was raised in assault, and on that basis damages were awarded and affirmed on appeal. However, the Court of Appeal was obviously not happy with this approach, and Ormrod L.J. (who, unusually, has both medical and legal qualifications) said this:

> Whether this is, in these days, the right way to deal with it, rather than to deal with it on the basis of failure to give proper advice, is neither here nor there as far as this case is concerned, although it might not be desirable for this case to be treated as authority on the assault point because it has not been discussed at all. I merely say that to reserve it.[16]

Similarly, Fox L.J. talked of 'the assault, if that is the proper description of it'. This case involved a woman who had consented to one operation and who had been subjected to another operation of a fundamentally different character and of much more far-reaching consequences. It was not a case of unintentional failure to give proper advice, but rather of an intentional act committed upon the body of a patient wholly without that patient's consent. The case therefore is clearly one of assault and it is difficult to understand the Court of Appeal's hesitation in regarding it as such. The point of obtaining consent is to allow dissent. Fox L. J.

pointed out that the risk of future pregnancy was one which the woman and her husband had the right to decide whether to take. The surgeon had denied her that right and imposed upon her his own views. Assault was therefore a perfectly proper – indeed the only proper – ground of action in that case. The correct position is described by Wood J. in *T. v. T. & Anor.*:

> The incision made by the surgeon's scalpel need not be and probably is most unlikely to be hostile, but unless a defence or justification is established it must in my judgment fall within the definition of a trespass to the person.[17]

Sterilization and abortion, being surgical, will normally be performed only after a consent form has been signed. This, of course, is good evidence of the existence of consent, but it is never conclusive. Other forms of family planning treatment will not usually be based upon consent forms and, indeed, express consent is seldom given to any treatment provided in a surgery or clinic. Implied consent is, however, just as efficacious and will probably be the norm. A patient who seeks family planning treatment, and accepts that which is given, may be taken to have impliedly consented, through that acceptance, to the treatment provided, if it is of the nature she or he sought.

When consent is given to one form of treatment it cannot be implied from that that consent is also given to another form of treatment, even though both have the same aims. A consent to radiotherapy for breast cancer does not amount to consent to breast removal. Consent to a laparoscopy does not imply consent to a radical hysterectomy.[18] Consent to a progesterone-only contraceptive pill does not imply consent to a combined progesterone-oestrogen pill. On the other hand, consent to one form of treatment may imply consent to another form if, in their essentials, the two treatments are of the same nature. So, for example, consent to the implanting of one type of IUD (say, the Lippes loop) may be taken to imply consent to the implanting of another type (say, the Copper T), unless the patient makes clear that she will accept only one type, or if one type carries significantly more risks than the other.

Negligence

Negligence is an unintentional failure to satisfy a duty of care, and the courts are much more willing to use this ground of action to protect the patient's right of choice in medical treatment. One of the duties that health care workers owe to their patients is the duty of disclosure – that is, the duty to explain the nature and consequences of proposed treatment and to give advice about it: a failure in that duty can give rise to an action for negligence. The basis of the duty of disclosure (which has been recognized by the House of Lords to be part of the doctor's general duty of care)[19] is the need to give such advice and information to the patient as will allow the patient to make a meaningful choice. It is therefore much more subtle than the duty simply to obtain consent, because it is designed not so much to ensure that the patient chooses, but rather to ensure that the choice the patient makes is based on proper advice and information about the nature of the proposed treatment, its consequences and risks, and its alternatives.

If the patient consents to treatment, then the treatment is not an assault, as shown above; but if that consent is based on insufficient advice and information, then the consent itself is not valid – and therefore will remain a valid defence to assault – but the insufficiency itself may amount to a negligent breach of the doctor's duty of care. So, if the complaint is based on insufficiency of advice, the case ought to be raised in negligence. In other words, consent is not vitiated by lack of advice and information, unless that lack is so significant that the patient believes the treatment to be something wholly different in kind from what it actually is, or unless the consent is obtained by fraud or misrepresentation.[20]

That an action for negligence based on insufficient advice may be available even when the consent itself is legally valid can be illustrated from the facts of the unreported English case of *Wells v. Surrey Area Health Authority*.[21] Here, a woman was offered a sterilization during the caesarian delivery of her third child. The possibility of sterilization had not been discussed during the antenatal period, and was mentioned for the first time only after labour had commenced. The woman consented, but later bitterly regretted it. She sued in both assault and negligence. The claim in assault was dismissed because, although in a state of exhaustion when she gave her consent, it was held that she had nevertheless understood the nature of the operation and its implications. However, her claim in negligence, based on failure to give proper advice, succeeded, and she was awarded £3,000 for the loss of her reproductive capacity to which she had consented. The period of labour is clearly not a suitable time to discuss a highly significant matter like sterilization, and to hold such a discussion at that particular time breaches a woman's right to be given sufficient opportunity to make a considered choice based on sufficient advice. The approach in *Wells* was followed in the later and more influential English decision of *Chatterton v. Gerson*,[22] in which Bristow J. said this:

> In my judgment once the patient is informed in broad terms of the nature of the procedure which is intended, and gives her consent, that consent is real and the cause of action on which to base a claim for failure to go into risks and implications is negligence, not trespass.[23]

In negligence, therefore, the essence of the wrong is not treatment without consent (as in assault) but failure to provide sufficient advice and information. This failure amounts to a legal wrong because it denies the patient's right to make a meaningful and informed choice.

The duty of advice is not limited to surgical operations like sterilization, and will apply to all forms of medical family planning. So, a number of cases have been raised based on failure to disclose the risks inherent in contraceptive pill usage. For example, in the Scottish case of *Ingram v. Ritchie*[24] a woman suffered a stroke after a week of taking a daily Logynon contraceptive pill prescribed for her by her GP. She sued on the basis that the defender had failed to advise of the material risk to her health with taking these pills. She argued that, because of her age (35) and the fact that she was a heavy smoker, she fell into an 'at-risk' category in using oral contraceptives, and she alleged that had she been given information about the danger and the fact that she was in an at-risk category, she would have refused consent for these pills and would have adopted another birth control method. Her claim was, in essence, that she had been denied the right to decide for herself whether the risk to her health was significant enough for her to seek other contraceptive methods. The claim was rejected by the Court of Session, primarily because it had not been established that the taking of the pills had actually caused the type of stroke suffered by the pursuer, but also because the advice and information given by the defender did not breach the standard of disclosure required by the law (discussed in the next section).

A similar, though this time successful, case is that of *Buchan v. Ortho Pharmaceutical (Canada) Ltd.*,[25] in which a 23 year-old woman suffered a stroke shortly after beginning to take the oral contraceptive pill Depo-provera. She sued the manufacturers on the ground that they had failed to warn both her and her medical advisers that there was an inherent unavoidable risk to particularly susceptible users, of which the plaintiff was one. Damages were awarded in this case because it was held proven that the taking of the pills had caused, or at least materially contributed to, the suffering of the stroke, and that, because the risk of suffering a stroke was well known to the manufacturers, the defendants were duty-bound to warn both users and prescribers of this risk. If such risks are well known to those who prescribe the pills, then they too will be under a duty to warn the susceptible patient. And the doctor is of course duty-bound to take reasonable care in determining the patient's susceptibility to the risks of treatment.[26]

The duty of advice is a continuing one, and this is especially relevant for continuing treatment, as contraceptive treatment tends to be. As new treatments become established, risks and side-effects may become more widely known, and a duty may be imposed to inform patients of these risks, even though no such duty existed when the treatment was first prescribed. In the US case of *Tresemer v. Barke*[27] a woman was given the IUD known as the Dalkon Shield, at a time when its dangers were not generally recognized. However, even after many cases of injury had been reported in the medical press, the doctor failed to inform the patient of this, and it was held that this failure to warn founded a relevant cause of action as the duty of advice was a continuing one for continuing treatment. Doctors do, of course, have a legal and ethical duty to keep up-to-date with developments in their own fields of practice.

The Level of Disclosure Required

The requirement to obtain the patient's consent protects the patient's right of choice, and the duty to provide the patient with information protects the patient's right to make that choice on the basis of proper advice. The latter duty is variously known as the duty of disclosure, or the duty of advice, or the duty to obtain informed consent. However it is described, the important legal issue is to determine the level of disclosure that the law requires the health care worker to make to the patient. On this difficult problem probably more has been written than any other issue of medical law, and the problems are fully discussed by, for example, McLean.[28] Only a brief summary of the issues will be given here.

In the fields of diagnosis and treatment, the test for the standard of care adopted by England, Scotland and many other common law jurisdictions, is a medically-oriented test. English law adopts what it calls the *Bolam* test, that is:

> A doctor is not guilty of negligence if he has acted in accordance with a practice accepted as proper by a responsible body of medical men skilled in that particular art.[29]

In Scots law the same test is expressed by the words of Lord President Clyde in *Hunter v. Hanley*, which were quoted with approval in *Bolam*:

> The true test for establishing negligence . . . on the part of the doctor is whether he has been proved to be guilty of such failure as no doctor of ordinary skill would be guilty of if acting with ordinary care.[30]

This medically-oriented test has been criticized in relation to the duty to disclose information on the ground that in effect it leaves it to the medical profession to determine its own levels of acceptable disclosure. A number of Commonwealth courts believe that the English courts place too much emphasis on medical evidence in determining the standard of care. So, for example, in the Supreme Court of South Australia Bollen J. said, 'I respectfully think that some of the cases in England have concentrated rather too heavily on the practice of the medical profession',[31] and Zelling J. in the same court in a later case said, 'I do not agree with the English decisions on the decisive weight to be accorded to medical opinion'.[32] The fear that motivates such comments was identified by Laskin C.J.C. in the Supreme Court of Canada as follows:

> To allow expert medical evidence to determine what risks are material and, hence, should be disclosed and, correlatively, what risks are not material is to hand over to the medical profession the entire question of the scope of the duty of disclosure, including the question whether there has been a breach of that duty.[33]

However, these criticisms were based on older English authorities. More recent judicial pronouncements have recognized that the court, and not the medical profession, is the body to determine the standard of care in all areas of medicine, including the level of advice and information to be given to patients. As Hirst J. pointed out in *Hills v. Potter*,[34] the *Bolam* test provides that the court will exculpate a defendant who has achieved a standard accepted by the medical profession only if that standard is upheld by a substantial body of medical opinion *and* if 'this body of medical opinion is both respectable and responsible'. It is for the court to determine whether that body of opinion is respectable and responsible. Lord Goff in *F. v. West Berkshire Health Authority* said that 'for a court automatically to accept an expert opinion, simply because it is concurred in by another appropriate expert, would be a denial of the function of the court'.[35]

That a true construction of the *Bolam* test allows the court to disagree with medical opinion of acceptable practices is clear from the House of Lords decision in *Sidaway v. Bethlem Royal Hospital*,[36] where Lord Bridge made it plain that to apply the standard of the reasonable doctor does not hand over to the medical profession the entire question of the scope of the duty of disclosure. He held that just because no doctor would condemn the level of disclosure made does not prevent the court from condemning it, if the court considers it to be unreasonable. He agreed with Lord Diplock in holding that this was the case for all aspects of the doctor's duty of care, and that the *Bolam* test applied in the same way to cases based on negligent disclosure as to cases based on negligent treatment. It has since been held that the *Bolam* test applies not only to advice about therapeutic treatment but also to advice concerning elective treatment such as family planning.[37]

Some US jurisdictions have moved more categorically away from any test that pays regard to medical practice, and have decided instead that the level of disclosures required by the law is to be determined by what the court decides the 'prudent patient' would want to know about the proposed treatment.[38] By concentrating on the 'prudent' patient, this test seems to diminish the very rationale for giving patients information, which is to allow them to make their own choices, prudent or otherwise.[39] This test was categorically rejected by a majority in the House of Lords in *Sidaway v. Bethlem Royal Hospital*. Nor has it found favour in Commonwealth courts.[40]

Factors Affecting the Standard of Disclosure

However the standard is determined in any particular legal system, it is clear that the level of disclosure legally required to satisfy that standard will vary depending upon the existence of a number of different factors.[41] In determining the weight to be given to each, the purpose of the duty of disclosure ought always to be borne in mind: which is to ensure that the patient's consent to the medical procedure is based upon proper advice and information. It is *not* designed to ensure the 'correct' or the 'reasonable' decision. In relation to family planning practice, it is possible to identify a number of different factors affecting the standard of disclosure.

The Nature of the Treatment

Medical treatment varies in its nature in a number of different ways, and certain characteristics in treatment can be identified which either increase or diminish the amount of advice and information required to satisfy the legal standard of disclosure.

For example, the more bodily invasive a particular medical procedure is, the more in the way of advice and information will the law require the patient to be given. King C.J. put it thus in the South Australian case of *F. v. R.*:

> The more drastic the proposed intervention in the patient's physical makeup the more necessary it is to keep him fully informed as to the risks and likely consequences of the intervention. Major surgery calls for special care in this regard.[42]

This is because, generally speaking, the more invasive a treatment is the more risks there will be, and the more serious will be the consequences: thus the more the patient must be made aware of in order to come to a proper decision. So a patient donating a kidney will require much more information than will a patient donating blood. The different birth control methods span the whole gamut, from the highly invasive, such as a radical hysterectomy (although that is seldom carried out for purely family planning reasons), to the minimally invasive, such as the using of a condom. A family planner would have to spend more time explaining the nature and consequences of the operation to a patient for whom a hysterectomy was proposed than to one for whom a laparoscopy was proposed. The patient fitted with an IUD would require rather less time than either. Abortion is generally highly invasive, the more so the more advanced the pregnancy is, and although this will be less so with methods that can be utilized early in pregnancy, such as with anti-progesterones, a high degree of counselling will always be required, because of the potential psychological consequences.[43]

Another relevant characteristic in treatment is its permanence, and, as a general rule, a medical procedure with permanent effects will require more in the way of advice and information than one with merely temporary effects. Abortion cannot be reversed. Sterilization is normally designed to be permanent. Caps, condoms and coils, however, can be removed, so restoring the fertility they are designed to inhibit. The patient must be made aware of the fact that a permanent effect cannot be reversed, and the family planner will therefore be bound to ensure that the patient understands the irreversible nature of the procedure, and the consequences of that irreversibility. It may be assumed that patients will be aware that abortion cannot be reversed, but they should also be informed that sterilization, because of the high failure rates for reversal attempts, in both males and females, ought to be considered for all intents and purposes irreversible.

Similarly, treatment may be either therapeutic – that is, designed for the treatment or prevention of disease or the maintenance of health – or alternatively non-therapeutic – that is, designed for other purposes. Medical birth control for family planning reasons is an elective, non-therapeutic, procedure. While proper birth spacing is clearly advantageous to a woman's health, the primary motive of most women seeking contraception is to limit the size of their families for economic reasons and to give them the freedom that fertility control provides: their own health is (as it always has been in reproduction), generally, a secondary consideration.[44] Elective treatment requires more in the way of advice and information than does therapeutic treatment because, by definition, there is a greater element of choice, and it is the right of choice that is being protected. In *Gold v. Haringey Health Authority*,[45] the English Court of Appeal overturned the trial judge for suggesting that there was a different test to be applied in determining the standard of care in relation to disclosures between therapeutic advice and contraceptive advice. Certainly, the test is the same – the *Bolam* test, as discussed above – but it does not follow that the same level of disclosure is required for every medical procedure, no matter its nature: the test may be the same for all, but whether it has been satisfied will depend upon the circumstances of each particular case.

Another characteristic that some medical procedures possess is the requirement for continuing action by the patient. The more the treatment requires action by the patient, the more care must the doctor take to ensure that the patient understands what has to be done. For their proper efficacy, most contraceptive methods depend on the patient's comprehension and co-operation. The fitting of caps and diaphragms, for example, will normally be done by the woman herself, but on at least the first visit to the medical practitioner she must be given good and clear instructions as to how these devices are fitted, and how they work. Potts and Diggory give this sensible warning: 'Careful teaching about the use and care of a cap or diaphragm is as important as correct fitting.'[46] It follows that, if the family planner fails to ensure that the woman is fully able properly to fit her own cap or diaphragm then she or he will have failed in the duty of disclosure, and may be subject to an action for damages if that failure causes harm (for example, a physical injury through improper use or care, or an unwanted pregnancy through not having used the device properly). 'Unambiguous instructions are essential and the user's comprehension should be checked'.[47] Any method of contraception that requires a high level of patient co-operation would therefore be inappropriate if the actual patient does not, or cannot, understand what is involved. The family planner will have to ensure that the patient understands not only how to use the method, but also (at least in general terms) how it works. So a patient being given, for example, a cap will have to be told how to fit it, how it works, and also such fundamental matters as how long sperm remain capable of fertilizing her eggs.

The Availability of Options

Another factor that will affect the level of disclosure required will be the number of options available for the achieving of the desired end result. The more options there are, the more they will have to be spelt out to the patient and advised upon. Family planning has one major aim – to restrict fertility – and a large number of very diverse ways of achieving that aim. For this reason, much time will have to be spent ensuring not only that the particular method selected is suitable for the patient but also that it is actually chosen by the patient, on the basis of proper advice. That this is a legally enforceable obligation can be illustrated by the first-instance judgement in *Gold v. Haringey Health Authority*[48] (although the decision itself was overturned for the reason given above). Here, a woman underwent a sterilization operation, which failed, and Schiemann J. held the defendants to be in breach of their duty of advice for failing to inform the woman that her husband could have undergone a vasectomy instead, and that this procedure would have had a better chance of success than her own sterilization. Schiemann J. described the family planner's duty to counsel patients in the following terms:

> It may consist of setting before the patient the various options and describing the pros and cons of each. It may go further and give advice as to what course should be followed.

The failure to inform about the availability of that other option meant that the patient could not make a proper choice: her right to choose had thus been infringed. This was also recognized in the South Australian case of *F. v. R.*,[49] where Bollen J. suggested that had alternative methods of sterilization to the one at issue in that case been available, the defendants would have been under a duty to offer more advice and information than they had actually given.

The Nature of the Risk

A large part of the information to be given to the patient will concern the risks involved in the treatment. The nature of these risks will influence the level of disclosure legally required. In accordance with general delictual principles, both the likelihood and the severity of the risk will be important. As Linden J. put it in the Canadian case of *White v. Turner:*

> In considering whether a risk is material or immaterial, one must balance the severity of the potential result and the likelihood of its occurring. Even if there is only a small chance of serious injury or death, the risk may be considered material. On the other hand if there is a significant chance of slight injury this too may be held to be material.[50]

It is sometimes suggested that there is no need to warn a patient of what are described as ordinary everyday risks that attach to any particular treatment, on the ground that the doctor is entitled to assume that the patient will be aware of them. In the Canadian case of *Kenny v. Lockwood,*[51] for example, Hodgkinson J. A. suggested that a doctor has no need to warn his patients of any danger 'incident to or inherent in, any operation'. And, in England, Browne-Wilkinson V. C. in the Court of Appeal in *Sidaway v. Bethlem Royal Hospital* said:

> It is of course obvious that the doctor is not under a duty to give information as to the ordinary risks normally attendant upon any operation.[52]

However, the House of Lords in that case was not prepared to go so far. Lord Diplock said:

> It may be that most patients, though not necessarily all, have a vague knowledge that there may be some risk in every form of medical treatment: but it is flying in the face of reality to assume that all patients from the highest to the lowest standard of education or intelligence are aware of the extent and nature of the risks which, notwithstanding the exercise of skill and care in carrying out the treatment, are inevitably involved in medical treatment of whatever kind it be but particularly surgical.[53]

There are nevertheless certain inevitable risks and consequences inherent in medical treatment about which it would not be unreasonable for a health care worker to assume that her or his patient knows. But this 'ordinary risk' exception to disclosure ought not to be taken much further than as described by Linden J. in *White v. Turner:*

> There are some common everyday risks that exist in all surgery, which everyone is expected to know about. Doctors need not warn about them, since they are obvious to everyone. Consequently, just as one need not warn that a match will burn or that a knife will cut, because that would be redundant, one need not warn that, if an incision is made, there will normally be some bleeding, some pain and a scar will remain when the cut has healed. So too, everyone is expected to know that there is a chance of infection in any surgical procedure.[54]

With contraceptive treatment, it really cannot be assumed that every patient will know any of the side-effects of the treatment, and therefore there should be a warning about any side-effect that is likely to affect the particular patient's decision. Likewise, the risk of failure, which is clearly a material risk when the procedure is undergone in the hope and expectation of success, cannot always be assumed to be known by patients. Most people know that some methods are not certain. It is common knowledge that condoms can burst, or that the 'safe period' is not 100 per cent safe, or that *coitus interruptus* may not have quite the desired effect: it is probably permissible for the family planner to assume that the patient knows these things. If, however, the patient indicates a belief that such a method will give absolute protection from pregnancy, then they ought certainly to be disabused of that belief. On the other hand, other methods, such as hormonal contraception, or sterilization, tend to have the reputation of being utterly reliable, when of course, for a number of reasons, they cannot absolutely guarantee success. The doctor cannot assume that the patient is aware of the small risk of these methods failing. Few lay people are aware that even a successful sterilization operation may later naturally reverse itself by the process of recanalization. Proper advice requires that the patient be made aware of these possibilities.[55] A number of cases have been successfully raised against doctors who failed to warn of the risk of failure in a family planning procedure.[56]

The sort of common everyday risks associated with contraception that fall within the limited category delineated by Linden J. will be few indeed. One case illustrating such a risk, however, is the unreported English case of *Venner v. North East Essex Health Authority*,[57] in which a woman had been taking oral contraceptives for a number of years. Whenever she came off the pill she became pregnant. After the birth of her third child she decided, with her husband, that she ought to be sterilized, and the defendant recommended that she stop taking the pill one month before the operation (this in order to minimize the risk of venus thrombosis). During that month she became pregnant once more and she sued the defendant on the ground that he had failed to warn her that she might become pregnant if she continued to have sexual intercourse while not taking the pill. Tucker J. dismissed the action on the ground, that, even if she had not been so warned (which on the evidence he found she had been),

> . . . it must have been obvious to the plaintiff that while she continued to take the pill she would not conceive but that she would be almost certain to do so if she ceased to take the pill and continued to have sexual intercourse.

Such a risk was not therefore one about which the surgeon was legally required to warn her. It is doubtful whether the 'ordinary risks' exception can be taken much further than this in the context of family planning treatment.

The Circumstances of the Patient

'Doctors . . . treat patients and not diseases', said Dunn L.J. when *Sidaway v. Bethlem Royal Hospital* was in the Court of Appeal.[58] A family planner is not attempting to prevent conception in the abstract: she or he is attempting to control an actual person's fertility. It follows that the actual patient's own particular circumstances ought to be taken into account in determining the level of advice and information to be given. This naturally includes warning the patient of risks particularly relevant to them due to their own physical condition;[59] but it goes further than this, and the family planner will be bound to assess the patient's intelligence and capacity for understanding, and will also be bound to tailor the advice and information given accordingly. Giesen reports a decision of the Federal Supreme Court of West Germany in which a graduate architect sued on the ground that he had not been given sufficient medical information, and the court 'observed that the degree of information required on possible undesirable consequences is in the first place to be governed by the intelligence and education of the patient and particularly his experience, as found in his medical history'.[60] Giesen also points out that if the health care worker is aware that the patient has some medical knowledge her or himself, then it may be permissible to disclose less information than would otherwise be required. This is probably based on the view that it can be assumed that the patient is aware of certain things. However, Giesen does warn that 'if in doubt about what the patient really knows, the physician must ascertain what the patient really understands'.[61]

A person's religious or cultural background can have a profound effect on how she or he would regard particular forms of treatment, and if such background is, or ought reasonably to be, known to the family planner, this too must be brought into the equation. This can be of particular significance in relation to family planning treatment, about which different cultures have widely differing, and often opposing, views. A case illustrating this is the English decision of *Devi v. West Midlands Regional Health Authority*.[62] Here, a 29 year-old woman underwent an abdominal operation after the birth of her fourth child. The surgeon, acting in what he believed to be her best interests, but without her consent, also performed a sterilization. The woman involved was a Sikh, and, in awarding damages, the Court of Appeal made clear that this fact rendered the duty to explain the procedure of even more significance to that particular patient, given both the Sikh religious and cultural objection to sterilization and the fact that Sikh women would normally expect to produce six children. The Court suggested that a procedure like sterilization can be of greater or lesser significance to different people depending upon the actual patient's outlook. Ormrod L. J. pointed out:

> There would be some people who are sterilized either without their consent or inadvertently perhaps, who would welcome it; others would be quite neutral about it; others who would feel the loss of the ability to have children is a very grave matter.

So, the more significant a procedure is for a particular patient, for whatever reason, the more it behoves the family planner who is, or ought to be, aware of this to ensure full understanding of the nature and consequences of the treatment proposed. And, as is clear from *Devi*, if the duty is breached, this is a matter that will also affect the assessment of damages.

The Therapeutic Privilege

However the duty to advise and inform is defined, most jurisdictions that recognize such a duty also recognize an exception thereto, known as the therapeutic privilege, whereby the doctor may deliberately withhold information that she or he would otherwise be obliged to give, if giving that information would be to the positive detriment of the patient. The existence of the principle has been expressly recognized by, *inter alia*, the US Court of Appeals in *Canterbury v. Spence*, the House of Lords in *Sidaway*, the Supreme

Court of Canada in *Reibl v. Hughes*, and the Supreme Court of South Australia in *Battersby*. 'Its true analysis is that it is a defence available to the doctor which, if he invokes it, he must prove'.[63]

The principle carries with it certain dangers, for it involves a substitution of the patient's right to decide with the doctor's determination as to what is in the patient's best interests. It denies that very right which the legal requirement to give information and advice is designed to protect, and, if widely drawn, this privilege could 'prove to be the exception which erodes the rule'.[64]

Clearly, certain situations exist in which there is no room for the application of the therapeutic privilege. Purely experimental medical procedures will, for example, require full information to be given to the subject and it has been held in Canada that the doctor cannot rely upon a therapeutic privilege to withhold information from research volunteers.[65] Similarly, if the person being informed and advised is not actually the person being treated (such as when parents are consenting to treatment of a child), the therapeutic privilege cannot apply. To this list, it is submitted, there ought to be added elective treatment such as all family planning procedures. There is no room for the therapeutic privilege in situations where the procedure is being undergone for other than therapeutic reasons. The reason for choosing a family planning procedure is to ensure that one does not again become a parent, and therefore it is necessary to be fully aware of the risk that the treatment might not succeed. That need cannot be affected by a therapeutic privilege in a non-therapeutic situation.

Questions from the Patient

A final matter that will increase the level of advice and information to be given will be whether the patient actually asks questions about the proposed treatment. In normal medical practice patients seldom do ask questions, and most rely upon the doctor to make the first approach in relation to advice and information. But doctors ought to remember that they are duty-bound actually to make that approach, and to give patients the opportunity to pose questions.

In many types of medical practice, questions from patients are often no more than requests for reassurance: 'I will be alright, doctor, won't I?' is not an enquiry about the possible risks and side-effects of the treatment. But, in family planning practice, questions from patients will normally be genuine requests for information and ought to be treated as such.

The extent to which doctors are obliged by law to answer questions is a matter of great doubt. In principle, the asking of a question ought to indicate that the patient considers the answer material to her or his decision, and the doctor ought therefore to answer both truthfully and fully. There is much to be said for the view[66] that questions from the patient deny the doctor the option of silence. However, the courts have been somewhat equivocal in imposing an obligation of absolute truthfulness in the face of questions.

The matter was discussed by the New Zealand Court of Appeal in *Smith v. Auckland Hospital Board*,[67] and there the court decided the issue by applying the principles laid down in *Hedley Byrne & Co. Ltd. v. Hellar & Partners Ltd.*[68] It was held that the doctor is bound to give 'due care' in answering questions posed by the patient, and that a 'reasonably adequate answer' had to be given.[69] The Court of Appeal did *not* hold that a full and true answer must be given to every question, although normally an answer, to be reasonable, would have to be true.

Other courts have gone further. In the Supreme Court of Canada in *Hopp v. Lepp* Laskin C.J.C. said that 'questions must be answered';[70] and in the Supreme Court of South Australia in a case of failed sterilization Bollen J. said 'A specific request to be told if there are risks demands a completely accurate answer'.[71] Likewise, in the House of Lords in *Sidaway, v. Bethlem Royal Hospital* Lord Bridge said that, when asked questions, 'the doctor's duty must . . . be to answer both truthfully and as fully as the questioner requires'.[72]

However, the English Court of Appeal has drawn back somewhat from the obligation as described by Lord Bridge. In the case of *Blyth v. Bloomsbury Area Health Authority*[73] a patient had asked about the side-effects of the contraceptive pill Depo-provera. The Court of Appeal held that she should have been given only the information that she would have been given if she had not asked questions: accordingly the 'trivial' and 'remote' side-effects which had in fact materialized did not require a warning in response to a general question about side-effects. Neill L.J. said that Lord Bridge and Lord Diplock in *Sidaway* were not intending to lay down any rule of law that when asked questions the doctor is under a duty to put the patient in possession of all the information to which the doctor has access. Kerr L.J. said this:

> The question of what a plaintiff should be told in answer to a *general* enquiry cannot be divorced from the *Bolam* test, any more than when no such enquiry is made. In both cases the answer must depend upon the circumstances, the nature of the enquiry, the nature of the information which is available, its reliability, relevance, the nature of the patient, and so forth.[74]

It may be that this dictum is restricted to questions of a general nature. If a patient asks about the likelihood of a specific risk (say, the likelihood of suffering a stroke through high dosage oral contraceptive pill usage) then, whether or not the doctor was obliged to mention this before the question was asked, a specific and truthful answer ought to be given. The very asking suggests that the subject of the question is a matter material to the patient's decision, and the only way properly to protect the patient's right of choice is therefore to give a true and full answer. Consequently, it is suggested that Lord Bridge's comments in *Sidaway* have rather more substance to them than the Court of Appeal in *Blyth* was willing to recognize.

Notes

1 This principle is recognized in the common law jurisdictions, and is also of fundamental importance in civil law systems, where it is often bolstered as a constitutional protection: see for example, Shaw, 'Informed Consent: A German Lesson' *ICLQ* 864, 1986; Giesen, *International Medical Malpractice Law*, Martinus Nijhoff, Dortrecht, 1988.
2 In Dickens' words: 'Reproduction Law and Medical Consent', 35 *U Tor. LJ*, 255 1985 at p. 259.
3 Cook & Dickens, *Issues in Reproductive Health Law in the Commonwealth*, The Commonwealth Secretariat, London, 1986 at p. 38.
4 [1965] *NZLR* 191 at p. 219.
5 See generally Feng, 'Failure of Medical Advice: Trespass or Negligence?', 7 *Leg. Stud.* 149, 1987.
6 See La Forest J. in *Re Eve* (1986) 31 *DLR* (4th) 1 at p. 37.
7 See Norrie, 'Medical Malpractice: The Scope of Informed Consent in Negligence', 32 *ICLQ* 229, 1983.
8 *F. v. West Berkshire Health Authority* [1989] 2 *All ER* 545, per Lord Bridge at p. 548, and per Lord Goff at p. 564.
9 (1850) 4 *Cox. CC* 220.
10 Ibid. at p. 223.
11 (1949) 2 *DLR* 442 at p. 445.
12 Ibid. at p. 443. In *Brushett v. Cowan* (1987) 40 *DLR* (4th) 488 a patient signed a consent form consenting to a particular procedure and 'such further or alternative measures as may be found necessary'. It was held that this was no consent to a procedure that was advisable but which did not require immediate action. The defendant who had performed the procedure on the basis of this consent form was held liable in battery.
13 83 *NJLR* 20 (1912) at p. 26.
14 (1933) 3 *DLR* 260.
15 9 December 1981.
16 LEXIS transcript, p. 4.
17 [1988] 2 *WLR* 189 at p. 203.
18 In *Devi v. West Midlands Regional Health Authority* consent to a surgical operation to the womb was held not to include consent to an operation of sterilization.
19 *Sidaway v. Bethlem Royal Hospital* [1985] *AC* 871.

20 Per Sir John Donaldson M. R. in the Court of Appeal in *Sidaway v. Bethlem Royal Hospital* [1984] *QB* 493 at p. 511. Cf. his remarks to identical effect in *Freeman v. Home Office* [1984] *QB* 524 at p. 556, and those of Laskin C.J.C. in *Reibl v. Hughes* (1980) 114 *DLR* (3d) 1 at p. 11.
21 *The Times*, 29 July 1978.
22 [1981] *QB* 432.
23 Ibid. at p. 443. Cf. the similar remarks made by Morden J. in the Canadian case of *Kelly v. Hazlett* (1976) 75 *DLR* (3d) 536 at pp. 558–9 and the approval of *Chatterton* in the South Australian case of *F. v. R.* [1983] 33 *SASR* 189.
24 28 July 1989, Court of Session, Outer House.
25 (1984) 8 *DLR* (4th) 373, aff. (1986) 54 *DLR* (4th) 92.
26 See also *Blyth v. Bloomsbury Health Authority, The Times* 11 February 1987, which concerned an allegation of failure to warn of the risks associated with the progesterone-only pill Depo-provera (the Court of Appeal dismissed the action). For a similar US case in which liability was upheld, see *Klink v. G. D. Searle & Co.* 26 *Wash. App.* 951, 9 *ALR* 4th 364 (1980) (although in that case there was a much more significant failure in communication than in *Blyth*).
27 86 *Cal. App.* 3d 656, 12 *ALR* 4th 27 (1978).
28 McLean, *A Patient's Right to Know: Information Disclosure, The Doctor and the Law*, Dartmouth, Aldershot, 1989. See also, as representative of the numerous other works on this issue, the significant articles by Meisel, 'The Expansion of Liability for Medical Accidents: From Negligence to Strict Liability by Way of Informed Consent', 56 *Neb. LR* 51, 1977; Robertson, 'Informed Consent to Medical Treatment' 97 *LQR*, 102 1982; and Teff, 'Consent to Medical Procedures: Paternalism, Self-determination or Therapeutic Alliance?', 101 *LQR* 432, 1985.
29 Per McNair J. in *Bolam v. Friern Hospital Management Committee* [1957] 2 *All ER* 118 at p. 122.
30 1955 *SC* 200 at p. 205. These two tests were approved and equiperated by the House of Lords in *Whitehouse v. Jordan* [1981] 1 *WLR* 246, and *Maynard v. West Midlands Regional Health Authority* [1984] 1 *WLR* 634.
31 *F. v. R.* (1983) 33 *SASR* 189 at p. 205.
32 *Battersby v. Tottman* (1985) 37 *SASR* 524 at p. 537.
33 *Reibl v. Hughes* (1980) 114 *DLR* (3d) 1 at p. 13.
34 [1983] 3 *All ER* 716 at p. 728.
35 [1989] 2 *All ER* 545 at p. 569.
36 [1985] *AC* 871, a case searchingly analyzed by McLean, op cit., note 28 above, at pp. 109–22, though her conclusions concerning the case differ in certain important respects from those reached in the present text.
37 *Gold v. Haringey Health Authority* [1987] 3 *WLR* 649.
38 See, in particular, *Canterbury v. Spence* 464 F. 2d 772 (1972).
39 McLean and Maher, *Medicine Morals and the Law*, Gower, Aldershot, 1983 identify the very essence of the issue when they point out that while the prudent patient test is consistent with the doctor's philosophical and professional commitment to healing and curing, 'it does ignore the possible claim that there is a right to remain or become ill rather than accept treatment or prevent ill-health' (p. 92).
40 See *Battersby v. Tottman*, note 32 above. *Reibl v. Hughes*, note 33 above, is often interpreted as if it adopted a prudent patient test, but this is so only in relation to causation, *not* the issue of liability. Picard, 'Consent to Medical Treatment in Canada', 19 *Os. H. LJ* 140, 1981 is one of the few commentators to recognize that this important distinction was being made.
41 There is a very useful discussion of the different factors that will affect the

level of disclosure required in the judgement of King C. J. in the case of *F. v. R.* (1983) 33 *SASR* 189 at pp. 192–4.

42 (1983) 33 *SASR* at p. 192.

43 See Dickens, 'Reproduction Law and Medical Consent' 35 *U. Tor. LJ* 255, 1985 at pp. 272–3, who points out that abortion counselling must be non-judgemental and should not be designed either to induce a particular decision on the woman's part or to induce guilt in her. In England the Department of Health and Social Security issued a circular to Area Health Authorities (HC (77) 26, July 1977) in which it was stressed that 'counselling should be both non-judgemental and non-directional.'

44 See Christopher, 'Abortion in the 1980s', 15 *BJ Fam. Plan.* 21, 1989.

45 [1987] 3 *WLR* 649.

46 Potts & Diggory, *Textbook of Contraceptive Practice* 2nd edn, Cambridge University Press, Cambridge, 1983 at p. 128.

47 Ibid. at p. 129. They relate an amusing tale, which, whether apocryphal or not, does make the same point in graphic terms: 'A Wyoming woman instructed to use a diaphragm and jelly produced a purple discoloured device when she returned pregnant and was found to have been using grape confiture from the breakfast table as her jelly.'

48 16 June 1986.

49 (1983) 33 *SASR* 189 at p. 207.

50 (1981) 120 *DLR* (3d) 269 at pp. 284–5, aff. (1985) 12 *DLR* (4th) 319. See also King C. J. to similar effect in *F. v. R.* (1983) 33 *SASR* at p. 192.

51 (1932) 1 *DLR* 507.

52 [1984] *QB* 493 at p. 522. The US Court of Appeals in *Canterbury v. Spence* said that there was no need to warn of such dangers as persons of average sophistication would be aware of, such as infection.

53 [1985] *AC* 871 at p. 894.

54 (1981) 120 *DLR* (3d) 269 at p. 285.

55 Cf. Linden J. in *White v. Turner* at p. 289: 'Because of the well-known public misconception that plastic surgery is scarless surgery [information concerning scarring] was specially necessary.'

56 See Chapter 8.

57 *The Times*, 21 February, 1987.

58 [1984] *QB* 493 at p. 516.

59 See *Buchan v. Ortho Pharmaceutical (Canada) Ltd.* (1984) 8 *DLR* (4th) 373, aff. (1986) 54 *OR* (2d) 92.

60 Giesen, *Arzthaftungsrecht: Medical Malpractice Law*, Giesking, Bielefeld, 1981 at p. 128.

61 Giesen, *International Medical Malpractice Law*, Martinus Nijhoff, Dortrecht, 1988 at p. 313. See also Woodhouse J. in *Smith v. Auckland Hospital Board* [1964] *NZLR* 241 at p. 250 (overruled for other reasons [1965] *NZLR* 191).

62 9 December 1981.

63 Per Lord Scarman in *Sidaway v. Bethlem Royal Hospital* [1985] *AC* 871 at p. 889.

64 Robertson, op. cit., note 28 above, at p. 118.

65 *Halushka v. University of Saskatchewan* [1965] 53 *DLR* (2d) 436 per Hall J. A. at p. 444.

66 Expressed, for example, by Robertson, op. cit., note 28 above, at p. 119.

67 [1965] *NZLR* 191.

68 [1964] *AC* 465.

69 [1965] *NZLR* at p. 206, per Turner J.

70 (1980) 112 *DLR* (3d) 67 at p. 77.

71 *F. v. R.* (1983) 33 *SASR* 189 at p. 206. See also Legoe J. at p. 199, and King C. J. at p. 196.
72 [1985] *AC* 871 at p. 898. See also Lord Diplock at p. 895.
73 *The Times*, 11 February 1987.
74 Emphasis added.

10 Conclusions

It is quite clear that, in Western cultures, both the medical profession and society as a whole today regard family planning as a proper and acceptable form of medical treatment. From society's point of view it is seen as perfectly proper for an individual to choose to adopt a family planning method: this is an exercise of the right of personal autonomy in choosing one's own lifestyle. Indeed, increasingly, as people become more aware of the dangers of world overpopulation, the utilization of birth control is being seen as a socially responsible reaction to a problem that potentially threatens the very existence of the human race. And from the medical profession's point of view, with the increasing recognition that proper birth spacing is essential to women's health, medical birth control is no longer perceived as the not quite respectable side of medicine that it once was. Indeed most forms of birth control – including all those with acceptable rates of reliability – are now effectively within the control of the medical profession. It has been persuasively argued by Keown that in relation to abortion at least this has always been the case.[1] It is not the purpose of this book to examine that thesis: suffice it to say that it is accepted here.

The issue of the legality of family planning has, for the most part, been resolved. As society and the law have recognized that sex and reproduction can be separated one from the other, so family planning methods have been accepted as legal ends to give practical effect to that recognition. In the legal systems considered in this book, there is no doubt that, in principle, contraception and sterilization are legal forms of medical treatment. Abortion is also legal, although the criteria for its legality are a good deal stricter, and the law does place much control on the availability of this operation. Today's problems for the law in relation to the legality of family planning concern not so much the acceptability of, but rather the boundaries between, the different forms.

Because abortion is subject to a very different legal regime from contraception, it becomes essential to know how to differentiate between the two. Before our knowledge of the reproduction process was as advanced as it is now, a strict differentiation was in practical terms neither possible nor necessary. The law would punish, or limit the availability of, abortion only when it could be established (beyond reasonable doubt, since abortion is a criminal charge) either that the woman was pregnant or was believed to be pregnant:[2] Because proof was not available at the boundaries between contraception and abortion, no charges were ever brought. This was nothing unusual, for the courts in any legal system can provide remedies or prescribe punishment only when the facts upon which the action is founded can be and are proved. Now, however, medical science has made it possible to identify the factual boundary between contraception and abortion, although the law still lags behind as it is unable to agree a definition for these very different acts (though neither should it be forgotten that the medical profession too is not in agreement as to acceptable definitions). The problems here will remain as medical science becomes even more sophisticated, and the law falls even further behind mankind's knowledge and capabilities.

Apart from the problem of definitions, the legality of family planning is not the real issue today. After examining the legality of the various forms of family planning, this book considered a number of other problems that have arisen in family planning practice. These included the rights of the sexual partner, the rights of children and the mentally disabled, and the issue of civil liability. While, for practical reasons, all these issues were dealt with separately, there is nevertheless a common thread that runs through them all – namely the problem of consent. The use or non-use of family planning, possibly more than any other medical treatment, can have profound effects on people other than the family planner's patient. So the sexual partner of the patient may, or may not, become a parent, depending upon the patient's acceptance of family planning. Becoming a parent is an event of awesome significance in an individual's life: ought sexual partners therefore to be able to take part in the decision-making process, even be asked for consent? The patient's parents may also be seriously affected, more particularly the younger the patient is: the family structure is affected and potentially threatened. Does this give the parents a right of consent, or a right of veto, in order to protect the integrity of their own family? The major problem with the mentally disabled is also consent, although it arises in a slightly different fashion: who, if anyone, can consent on their behalf, or can consent be dispensed with? And the issue of civil liability also often resolves itself in large part on the validity and nature of consent.

At the end of the day, spousal or parental consent, or proxy consent for the mentally disabled, have all been discussed in relation to family planning in the way that the courts deal with these issues in connection with other forms of medical treatment. The issues may be raised in their sharpest form with family planning, particularly with abortion, but the courts in the systems examined have not laid down significantly different rules and principles to deal with them in a family planning context. This is as it should be. Family planning at one time was significant primarily because of its affect on the sexual relationship, which had a peculiar place in Christian and moral philosophy. Sex today is demythologized, and family planning can now be regarded as a normal part of a person's general health care.

However, the fact that medical family planning constitutes a significant invasion into the bodily integrity of patients does render the issue of consent of particular importance. Treatment without any consent amounts, of course, to an assault; and a failure to provide sufficient information upon which the patient can base a proper consent can constitute the legal wrong of negligence. The factors discussed in Chapter 9 affect to a greater or lesser degree the level of information and advice required. The consequences of a failure to achieve that level are discussed in Chapter 8. But here too we see the importance of consent.

Consent has therefore become the great and significant issue, whether dealing with the competent or with children or with the mentally disabled. And logically this is not surprising. The availability and acceptability of family planning in our culture reflects the fact that autonomy of the individual has become the predominant ethic in medical law. This may not yet be the predominant ethic in medical practice, but there is evidence that attitudes are changing, and that the Tannochbrae[3] philosophy in medicine is coming to the end of its useful life.

Most people are born with a capacity to reproduce, and acquire in late childhood a desire to indulge in sexual activity. Reproduction will usually have much more significant effects on a person's lifestyle than mere sexual activity. Family planning allows a person to indulge in the one without running the risk of the other. It recognizes that sexual pleasure is justified for its emotional and loving aspects and not just because of its potential reproductive consequences. The point is choice. One can now choose to have sex without risking becoming a parent, and the law allows, indeed protects, that choice. Proper choice is based on consent, and consent should be based on knowledge: through the duty to provide advice and information the law protects the right to knowledge. In so doing, the law recognizes and protects an individual's right to be an individual. That is what family planning is all about. And, at the end of the day, that is what democracy as we understand the term is all about.

Notes

1 Keown, *Abortion, Doctors and the Law*, Cambridge University Press, Cambridge, 1988.
2 See Chapter 3.
3 The thought is that of Cameron, *Medical Negligence: An Introduction*, Law Society of Scotland, Edinburgh, 1983.

Index